Impossible Images

New Perspectives on Jewish Studies

A Series of the Philip and Muriel Berman Center for Jewish Studies
Lehigh University, Bethlehem, Pennsylvania

General Editor: Laurence J. Silberstein

Impossible Images

Contemporary Art after the Holocaust

Edited by
**Shelley Hornstein, Laura Levitt, and
Laurence J. Silberstein**

NEW YORK UNIVERSITY PRESS
New York & London

NEW YORK UNIVERSITY PRESS
New York and London
www.nyupress.org

Library of Congress Cataloging-in-Publication Data
Impossible images : contemporary art after the holocaust / edited by
Shelley Hornstein, Laura Levitt, and Laurence J. Silberstein.
   p.   cm. — (New perspectives on Jewish studies)
ISBN 0-8147-9825-X (cloth : alk. paper)
ISBN 0-8147-9826-8 (pbk. : alk. paper)
1. Holocaust, Jewish (1939–1945), and art. 2. Art, Modern—20th
century.   I. Hornstein, Shelley. II. Levitt, Laura, 1960– III. Silberstein,
Laurence J. (Laurence Jay), 1936– IV. Series.
NX163.I46 2004
700'.458—dc21   2003006563

New York University Press books are printed on acid-free paper,
and their binding materials are chosen for strength and durability.

10 9 8 7 6 5 4 3 2 1

To Muriel M. Berman, whose vision, continuing support, and generosity made possible the publication of this volume.

To all those who will continue imagining the past toward a different future.

Contents

Acknowledgments

The editors wish to express their gratitude to Muriel M. Berman and the Philip and Muriel Berman Foundation for their generous support in making possible the publication of this volume. We are grateful to the Lucius N. Littauer Foundation, which also provided a grant to assist in its publication.

The editors and contributors thank Shirley Ratushny for her diligence and meticulous care in supervising the editorial process and preparing the manuscript for publication. We also thank Carolyn Hudacek for her ongoing assistance and for her contribution to the preparation of the manuscript and Inbar Gilboa for her help in imagining what the cover of this book might look like. Our special thanks to Yvonne Singer, who graciously allowed us to use her work *The Veiled Room* on the cover of this volume.

The cooperation of the following publishers is gratefully acknowledged:

Indiana University Press for permission to reprint "Racism and Ethics: Constructing Alternative History," by Sidra DeKoven Ezrahi, which first appeared in *Humanity at the Limit: The Impact of the Holocaust Experience on Jews and Christians,* edited by Michael Signer (Bloomington and Indianapolis: Indiana University Press, 2000).

The Jewish Museum and Rutgers University Press for allowing us to reprint Ernst van Alphen's essay "Playing the Holocaust" and an earlier version of Norman Kleeblatt's essay "The Nazi Occupation of the White Cube." These essays were first published in *Mirroring Evil: Nazi Imagery/Recent Art* (exhibition catalog), edited by Norman L. Kleeblatt (New York: The Jewish Museum; New Brunswick: Rutgers University Press, 2001).

Tikkun for permission to reprint Adi Ophir's "On Sanctifying the

Holocaust: An Anti-Theological Treatise," *Tikkun* 2, no. 1 (January/
February 1987), 61–66.

The University of California Press for permission to quote "Written in Pencil in the Sealed Railway Car," by Dan Pagis, which appeared in *The Selected Poetry of Dan Pagis*, edited and translated by Stephen Mitchell, © 1996 The Regents of the University of California.

Introduction

Framing the Holocaust: Contemporary Visions

Shelley Hornstein, Laura Levitt, and Laurence J. Silberstein

This collection of articles, like previous volumes in the New Perspectives on Jewish Studies series, explores the boundaries of current Jewish studies scholarship. Rather than trying to determine what are sometimes posited as true, legitimate, or authentic meanings, this volume, like the previous ones, asks: What are the mechanisms, techniques, and discursive practices through which these meanings have been made and what specific forms of identification do they foster or exclude? A recurring concern is how cultural representations and the meanings attached to them are produced and disseminated.

Building on scholarly work on representation and the Holocaust, this volume seeks, like many of those earlier works, to contribute to the emerging field of Jewish cultural studies. In contrast to the majority of discussions concerning the representation of the Holocaust, which focus on literary and historical representation, this book focuses on the visual. The cross-disciplinary structure of the volume was intended to encourage our contributors to reflect on some of the basic assumptions of the various fields in which they were trained. In dialogue with one another, artists, architects, art and architectural historians, curators, cultural critics, literary scholars, and religious studies specialists challenge one another to highlight issues often rendered invisible by the disciplinary assumptions of their respective fields. Furthermore, an objective of this book is to situate these cross-disciplinary discussions on the visual representation of the Holocaust within the context of Jewish studies.

Informed by contemporary critical perspectives, the book directs a series of questions widely discussed in cultural studies to the visual representation of the Holocaust: What are the processes by which the past is remembered and represented in the present? What is the relationship between memory, history, and visual culture? How does the representational work of art resemble or differ from that which is performed by and in literary or historical texts? To what extent and in what ways do these representational processes challenge some of the normative assumptions about the Holocaust within Jewish studies or notions of the aesthetic in the field of visual culture? What difference do the physical or geographical locations where works are displayed make in terms of how they are seen or understood? How do particular kinds of spatial arrangements, forms, and sites of representation position the viewer so as to encourage or discourage, include or exclude specific interpretations? To what extent do these works challenge prevailing notions of Jewish history and Jewish identity?

Impossible Images: Contemporary Art after the Holocaust evolved out of "Representing the Holocaust: Practices, Products, Projections," a conference held at Lehigh University on May 21–23, 2000. The conference brought together Jewish studies scholars, historians, art historians, and scholars of literature as well as artists and curators. A primary goal was to open up a critical space for the kinds of interdisciplinary conversations about the visual arts and the Holocaust that are now at the heart of this collection. Like the volume, the original conference invitation asked participants to consider a similar set of questions and how they informed their work.[1]

It was at this conference that the editors first met, and it was here that most of the contributors presented early versions of their essays. This unusual multidisciplinary gathering in a Jewish studies context highlighted the conveners' concern that Jewish studies scholars critically engage with works of visual culture and the representational problems that this entails. We have included a selection of works by those artists who presented at the conference at the end of this volume.[2]

Dialogue and cross-fertilization also inform the work of the editors, coming as we do from different fields of inquiry and crossing academic and disciplinary as well as geographical boundaries. Shelley Hornstein comes to Holocaust and Jewish studies from her work in theories of visual culture and the disciplines of art history and architecture. Laura Levitt and Larry Silberstein come to visual culture and the Holocaust through their work with Jewish religious, literary, and philosophical texts. Laura's approach is an outgrowth of, among other things, her extensive work on gender and American Jewish identity. In contrast, Larry's engagement with representational practices and their effects is informed by his extensive reading in French poststructuralist philosophy and British cultural studies, an approach that he has recently applied in his study of postzionism in Israeli culture. In her most recent work Shelley is concerned with issues relating to how architecture and place capture memory and the theoretical issues that relate to aesthetics, architecture, and place.

As we have already indicated, *Impossible Images: Contemporary Art after the Holocaust* builds on scholarly work on the Holocaust and representation.[3] These Jewish studies discussions have often focused on the problematic of representing what many consider to be the unrepresentable. Recognizing that there already exists a growing legacy of creative works that engage the Shoah, we undertake to probe the processes by means of which these works have come into being and how they function in particular contexts. The authors, focusing on specific works of visual art, and in one instance a musical composition, pose a number of important questions about representation that, while often raised in discussions of culture, are less frequently asked in Jewish studies discussions. These questions include: What is made visible, what is concealed, and what is obscured by specific kinds of artistic production? How and in what ways do these artistic works continue to unravel some of our assumptions about the role of the Holocaust in the present? What effects do geographical and cultural contexts have on the ways in which visual works are viewed, how they are shown, and the kinds of exhibition spaces that are used? How do responses to works differ according to the audience? What is the relation of memory and visual representations of the Holocaust to the formation of contemporary Jewish identity?

A highlight of the conference out of which this volume grew was Art Spiegelman's powerful keynote presentation. Spiegelman held forth on the context, conditions, and creative processes that resulted in his now-classic *Maus*. This work was one of the first to open up a new space that shattered boundaries between language and visual culture in relation to the Holocaust. As his comments that evening, like his work, make clear, all representations of the past are already acts of the present.[4]

Unravelings, Contexts, Locations

Several of these essays may be viewed as thought experiments, bridging disciplines and fields in an effort to grapple with what it means to represent the Holocaust or its resonances in and for the present. Several authors question some of the operative assumptions in the field of Jewish studies in order to better address these questions. They are particularly concerned about the ways in which the conceptual and representational frameworks we deploy directly shape the kinds of knowledge we produce. Taking it as a given that all knowledge is culturally constructed, *Impossible Images: Contemporary Art after the Holocaust* draws our attention to assumptions that are commonly taken for granted in Holocaust scholarship. Of particular concern is the notion that memory and history can be anything but partial and constructed in the present. The collected essays also make explicit the ways in which context matters. They thus seek to make explicit how and in what ways the places where an artist works shape what he or she produces; how and in what ways the space or place in which a work of art is exhibited and how it is identified or named influence what is seen or not seen; how and in what ways calling attention to certain details in a visual work, a gesture, a color, an icon, can change the meaning assigned to the work as a whole.

For example, seeing a monument at Yad Vashem is different from seeing and reading about it on a web site (Stier), or hearing Hitler's taped voice appear to speak Hebrew in Jerusalem before an audience of Israelis at the Israel Museum differs from hearing Hitler's same taped and manipulated voice at the Jewish Museum in New York (Azoulay). Other issues addressed in the volume include: What does it mean for someone in a place and time far removed from the site and time of the events being represented to remember and represent these events? How, and in what ways, does the physical structure of a museum exhibition shape or encourage particular understandings of history while discouraging or precluding others? Who controls the space in which a memorial is situated (Bonder)?

At stake in all these discussions is the difficulty of approaching the legacy of the Holocaust visually. At a 2002 exhibition at the Jewish Museum in New York, *Mirroring Evil,* curated by Norman Kleeblatt, the floodgates opened to an enormous controversy.[5] The controversy demonstrated the specter of morality and propriety that is raised when the unwritten codes relating to visual images of the Holocaust are transgressed. Who gets to own these images or who has the right to construct or display images that invoke this past? What are the boundaries of what can be represented, and who has the right to display or to play with these evocative images?

As many of these essays explain, works of visual culture relating to the Holocaust are often the site where issues of obscenity, and propriety, and aesthetics are tested. Is it obscene to ask viewers to identify with Nazi imagery, to be invited to play with images of the Holocaust, to color in coloring books, or to play with Legos (van Alphen)? Who is the viewer as he or she goes through an exhibit at the Israel Museum (Azoulay)? Can one imagine being Eva Braun reflecting on the final days of her life with her lover Adolf Hitler, as Roee Rosen asks us to do in his piece *Live and Die as Eva Braun*? Is it morally or aesthetically legitimate in a play about the Holocaust and contemporary Israeli life to position Israeli actors as perpetrators and Palestinian actors as victims (Katz-Freiman)?

Impossible Images: Contemporary Art after the Holocaust also raises questions about Israeli national identity and the Holocaust. It explores the ways in which the Holocaust informs contemporary Jewish identity in the United States (Friedman), in Canada (Hornstein), and in Western Europe, and the complex issues that the Holocaust poses for non-Jews.

Specific Organization

There are any number of ways of reading these essays. As we have already suggested, the issues they raise overlap and intersect at various points. One may read them in relation to pedagogy and the role of museums in telling the story of the Holocaust. Here Susan Derwin's essay may be read together with those of Ernst van Alphen and Ariella Azoulay. One might also reflect on the haunting memory of the Holocaust discussed by Michelle Friedman in relation to Oren Stier's reading of icons. Additionally, one might connect the taboos of identification raised by Norman Kleeblatt in conjunction with the dramatic production discussed by Tami Katz-Freiman. The model of groupings we propose is only one of many different possible pathways through this material. Although we cluster the essays in a particular order, we encourage readers to experiment by reading them in other configurations, using any of the various broad themes we have suggested or others of their own choosing.

I. Geographies of the Heart: Places/Spaces of Remembrance

All the essays in this section address issues of Holocaust memory in places far removed from where and when those events took place. These essays include Shelley Hornstein's "Archiving an Architecture of the Heart" and Michelle Friedman's "Haunted by Memory: American Jewish Transformations." Both these essays explore how certain architecture, while seeking to anchor in a physical place memories that have no place of their own, actually subvert permanence and objecthood. It concludes with Julian Bonder's "A House for Uninhabitable Memory," an essay about his own attempt to build a place for this kind of memory at Clark University and the controversy that this entailed.

II. Israel and the Politics of Memory

While Israel is clearly another place far removed from the site of the events of the Holocaust, the founding of the state was imbricated in most Jewish discourse relating to the Holocaust shortly after the end of the war. Ariella Azoulay, in "The Return of the Repressed," explores the recent "return" of a powerful subject that has been "repressed" in Israeli imagination: the engagement with Nazi culture.

She does this by examining works by Israeli artists that incorporate images and likenesses of Hitler in a culture where his name and image have been virtually absent. In "Racism and Ethics: Constructing Alternative History," Sidra Ezrahi explores the ways in which Israelis' understanding of the Holocaust continues to shape the ways in which Israelis view the Israeli-Palestinian conflict and the effects of these ways of seeing on contemporary Israeli politics.[6] In "'Don't Touch My Holocaust'—Analyzing the Barometer of Responses: Israeli Artists Challenge the Holocaust Taboo," Tami Katz-Freiman explores the controversy over who has the right to "touch," that is, artistically engage, the Holocaust in contemporary Israel.

III. Transgressing Taboos

In this section, Ernst van Alphen, in "Holocaust Toys: Pedagogy of Remembrance through Play," explores the sacralizing of the Holocaust, also discussed by Tami Katz-Freiman and Adi Ophir. What does it mean, van Alphen asks, for artists to invite viewers to "play" with the Holocaust? In his essay, "The Nazi Occupation of the 'White Cube': Piotr Uklański's *The Nazis* and Rudolf Herz's *Zugzwang*," Norman Kleeblatt, like van Alphen, explores the discomfort that is produced in viewers of popular cultural representations of the Holocaust. Looking carefully at Piotr Uklański's *The Nazis*, Kleeblatt asks us to reflect on the ways in which the Nazis have been glorified in popular culture and raises the provocative possibility that the legacies of avant-garde and fascist aesthetics may be more closely related than we might want to believe.

We end this section with a now-classic essay by Adi Ophir. Although not focusing on questions of visual culture, "On Sanctifying the Holocaust: An Anti-Theological Treatise" serves to make clear some of the dangers that result from sacralizing the Holocaust and its visual representations. Drawing our attention to the importance of engaging imaginatively and critically with the legacy of the Holocaust, the chapter challenges the reader to render visible in his or her own social contexts those political and cultural processes that help to make possible fascistic forms of life in the present.

IV. Curating Memory

"Holocaust Icons: The Media of Memory," by Oren Stier, and "Sense and/or Sensation: The Role of the Body in Holocaust Pedagogy," by Susan Derwin, pointedly raise the question of how museums authorize certain ways of seeing while inhibiting others. How are the images we see in museum settings constructed? What images or objects are selected for us to see, and in what order are we asked to view them? These chapters make explicit the ways in which mechanisms of control operate to create ways of seeing and not seeing. More specifically, they analyze how, in Holocaust museums, these operations close off certain discussions about the Holocaust while authorizing others.

NOTES

1. These included some of the following questions: How are memory and awareness of the Holocaust being transmitted and produced through representational practices? What are the diverse visual genres being used and to what effect? What are the distinct problems confronting artists who seek to represent the Holocaust? What are the visual strategies being used by contemporary Holocaust museums and memorials to convey something about this past? And what are the intended audiences for these works?
2. Larry Silberstein thanks Oren Stier and Stephen Feinstein for their valuable assistance in conceptualizing and structuring the conference. Speakers who contributed to the conference but whose work is not represented here include Art Spiegelman, Peter Novick, Stephen Feinstein, Michael Berenbaum, Barbie Zelizer, Edward Lucie-Smith, and Andrea Liss. We gratefully acknowledge the contributions of all those who both attended and presented at the conference in shaping these discussions. Echoes of Peter Novick's important book, *The Holocaust in American Life*, are also evident in some of the articles in this book. Novick, too, made a major contribution to the conference, providing a broader cultural context within which to situate the proliferation of visual representations of the Holocaust, particularly in the United States.
3. This scholarship has raised crucial questions about the limits of representation, using literary and critical theory. It has challenged the limits of historical discourse and the importance of memory. Some important works in this growing field include: Sidra Ezrahi, *By Words Alone: The*

Holocaust in Literature (Chicago: University of Chicago Press, 1980); James Young, *Writing and Rewriting the Holocaust: Narrative and the Consequences of Interpretation* (Bloomington: Indiana University Press, 1988); Saul Friedlander, ed., *Probing the Limits of Representation: Nazism and the "Final Solution"* (Cambridge: Harvard University Press, 1992); and the ongoing discussions in the interdisciplinary journal *History and Memory.* Also important to this volume is the work of James Young on Holocaust monuments and memorials. This work helped open up Jewish studies to discussions about the work of visual culture more generally. See, for example, James Young, *The Texture of Memory: Holocaust Memorials and Meaning* (New Haven: Yale University Press, 1993); James Young, ed., *The Art of Memory: Holocaust Memorials in History* (New York: The Jewish Museum, and Munich: Prestel-Verlag, 1994); James Young, *At Memory's Edge: After-Images of the Holocaust in Contemporary Art and Architecture* (New Haven: Yale University Press, 2000).

4. Art Spiegelman's address was entitled "*Maus*: Packing Memory into Little Boxes." Norman Kleeblatt's original presentation for the conference was entitled "Art after *Maus*: Contemporary Art and the Imaging of Nazism." This title came from Kleeblatt's working title for the exhibition that he was then in the process of putting together, which became *Mirroring Evil.*

5. We have included Ernst van Alphen's essay on Holocaust toys that he delivered at Lehigh University at the "Representing the Holocaust" conference. This essay has since been published in a somewhat different form in *Mirroring Evil: Nazi Imagery/Recent Art*, ed. Norman Kleeblatt (New York: The Jewish Museum, and New Brunswick: Rutgers University Press, 2002), the catalog for the *Mirroring Evil* exhibit at the Jewish Museum, March 17–June 30, 2002. The exhibit included many of the works van Alphen discusses in his essay. We have also included an essay by Norman Kleeblatt that discusses two of the works that he, as curator, included in *Mirroring Evil.*

6. While Sidra Ezrahi chaired a session but did not present a paper at this conference, the editors wish to acknowledge her important contributions to the conference. Although written for another occasion and focusing on literature, her chapter, like Adi Ophir's, offers an incisive statement of the political effects of representational practices. Both these chapters help to highlight the social and political implications of the other essays in this volume.

Part I

GEOGRAPHIES OF THE HEART

Places/Spaces of Remembrance

Chapter 1

Archiving an Architecture of the Heart

Shelley Hornstein

> I would like there to exist places that are stable, unmoving, intangi-
> ble, untouched and almost untouchable, unchanging, deep-rooted;
> places that might be points of reference, of departure, of origin.
> . . . Space melts like sand running through one's fingers. Time bears
> it away and leaves me only shapeless shreds. . . . To write: to try metic-
> ulously to retain something, to cause something to survive; to wrest
> a few precise scraps from the void as it grows, to leave somewhere a
> furrow, a trace, a mark or a few signs.
>
> —Georges Perec[1]

In Canada, a place unlike Europe with no furrows marked or erased
by the history of World War II, how can we begin to think about our
connections to that war other than through almost nothing more
than a second- or third-hand fragment retelling of that history? While
there is documentation that Jews were in Canada as early as the eigh-
teenth century, the strongest waves of new settlement began in the
early years of the twentieth century. For the artists I will discuss, who
reflect on home, national and personal identity, and their connections to the Holocaust, how can Canada be in any way a touchstone
to that past?

Without specific associations to their ancestral sites in Europe—
this is the butcher shop your grandmother frequented; over there is
the house where your great grandfather was born—four Canadian
artists probe the archives of our collective memory and ask, What
shapes our sense of identity? Canadian national identity might be
framed by some as a loose series of crisscrossing lines and multiple

points of contact that can best be described as a picture that, while seemingly one, is anything but monolithic. What makes these four artists' works interesting on the level of national and personal identity is the way in which their works suggest imagined places that exist, in fact, nowhere and everywhere. These disparate places—a transit bar, a veiled room, a temple, and a portrait gallery—function as nomadic spaces, that is, where the idea of home is determined by the place of the now—in the present tense—and that the geography of home is defined by the architecture of the tent, wherever it is pitched.

Keeping this in mind, these artists confront history and open up the vexing question of why it is important—or not—to create an archive of collective memory. It is not unimportant to present the concept proposed by philosopher Walter Benjamin that in order to

> approach . . . [one's] . . . buried past [one] must conduct . . . [oneself] . . . like a man digging. . . . [One] must not be afraid to return again and again to the same matter; to scatter it as one scatters earth, to turn it over as one turns over soil. For the matter itself is only a deposit, a stratum, which yields only to the most meticulous examination what constitutes the real treasure hidden with the earth: the images, severed from all earlier associations, that stand—like precious fragments or torsos in a collector's gallery—in the prosaic rooms of our later understanding.[2]

Vera Frenkel, Melvin Charney, Yvonne Singer, and Raphael Goldchain point to what it means to try to capture places that can no longer be reached or identified. Their works consider displacement and mourn a lost or nonexistent archive. They attempt to construct places that we come to know, and it is through the process of building these temporary or imagined architectures that an archive is constituted. They construct ideas in materials to document places and hint at what might be imagined as permanent tracings of the places that are not but that could be. Perhaps these are political manifestations or fantasy musings, but for each, they are deeply emotional, personal works in newly configured, theoretically resonant, constructed spaces where, ultimately, identities are forged by way of a process of becoming.

From their perspective as Canadians, these artists reconsider the wandering and displacement of Jewish culture and tradition in a sense of newfound significance "after Auschwitz." With no guaranteed pathway to safety and security, they follow the meandering pattern of their forebears as an operative strategy for their work. They set out searching for rootedness, only to find rootlessness. Symptomatic of rhizomatic growth and dispersion, and characterized by Gilles Deleuze and Félix Guattari as "variation, expansion, conquest, capture, offshoots," this diasporic movement is spatial and atemporal. Something quite different from "detachable," as they put it, this growth or movement is "reversible, modifiable . . . [with] . . . multiple entryways and exits and its own lines of flight."[3] Clearly this shifted their move from "arborescent thinking . . . [which] . . . privileges unity over multiplicity [to a Deleuzian] rhizomatic model where mapping privileges multiplicity. . . . Rather than statis and stability being the norm and movement and change having to be explained, becoming is the norm and being has to be explained."[4]

In this essay, I am suggesting the importance of digging and mourning a displaced past in order to enter into a process of remembering—a process of building a more fluid sense of identity, one that moves freely across borders and is not abbreviated by any external constraints. Through the making of art and architecture, the process is a personal and communal act of archive making. We are reminded of Nora's idea that the nature of modern memory is first of all archival and that "the less memory is experienced from within, the greater its need for external props and tangible reminders."[5] So too, while built forms are indeed strong physical reminders of the past, part of architecture's specificity is that theoretical imaginings operate in tandem with the built environment. To imagine a place in the mind (and the heart) is to suggest that we carry with us at all times a semblance of a world in the process of becoming something formed and defined and that the shape of the world as we know it is never finite. In many ways, this world that is becoming something concrete (but never achieves this status) continues its building activity within our imaginations on a regular basis. It is a world that evolves and dissolves, that reconfigures depending upon the suitability or reliability of our memories.

An *architecture of the heart,* I want to suggest, is a theory about an architecture of memory and imagination that is not a physical and functional object in space, fixed in a geographic location. Instead, this is architecture that speaks not so much against the idea that monuments are permanent visual and spatial markers, but to the idea that there is an architectural construction recorded daily by each of us as we imagine the world not before our eyes. Such a construction has the freedom, therefore, to imagine places unbounded by space or time, yet spurred, to be sure, by actual locations. This theoretical and imagined architecture of the heart crystallizes the nature of personal memory and confers meaning on the invisible, that which is imagined, the spaces we shape in our minds every day, the invented and reconfigured places where we locate our thoughts. An architecture of the heart is part of each of us and exists in those junctures of time and place in our imagination where linear measurement and ideas of containment are meaningless. All too often ignored, not even defined, this place of architecture within our memories acts concurrently with our visually perceived world and indeed informs the uses we make of that world. Its intangibility is its essence. It is this intangibility that bridges the gaps of our physical perceptions of space.

Let me return to the buried treasures: to reveal the treasures to which Benjamin refers one begins with the work of digging, as he suggests, of turning inward and introspectively recuperating them by conducting an internal archaeology. This is an act of excavation. As an act of excavation, it is action as such, and an act of mourning; it constitutes thinking about and uncovering what is no more, as loss, as absence. It is work that is archival: the dig is followed by the documentation to create archives of a history not yet recorded. This work is spurred by a soul that aches for a grounding in the past, to redress the absence of collective and personal memory. One way of stirring a soulful awakening is through creative acts that are performative and expressive.

Art is thus a result of the performative *act* for the artist, a performance to remember. The Hebrew term *zachor*, to remember, translates as the *act* of remembering and, as Jewish studies scholar Yosef Yerushalmi suggests, is always performative. Passive listening, he tells us, is not a way to remember; rather, to engage or act through questioning is to participate in an enactment of memory.[6] Surely, the *process* of becoming, the way to build an architecture of the heart ensures, for the artists I will be discussing, an engagement in the process of remembering a history they never experienced, but one that has profound resonance for them nonetheless. This newly imagined place doubles as the place in their hearts and their need to perform its possibility to exist.

In a work entitled *Canada* by French artist Christian Boltanski (1988), over six thousand pieces of second-hand clothing are layered on four double-height walls of a large room in the exhibition gallery. On the floor are dense piles of sorted clothing that appear to be randomly scattered and stacked. Multiple hangings of clothing on the walls seem to thicken the space and muffle all sound. Together with an intense odor exuding from the garments, this creates a stifling aura of claustrophobia. The piece refers to the storehouse at Auschwitz that housed the prisoners' belongings, clothing, suitcases: the euphemistic *Canada,* so named by the inmates, twisted the image of a rich country that could offer paradise. Canada, a landscape bountiful in natural resources and proud defender of a "true north strong and free," as the lyrics of the national anthem recount, has always been seen as cleanly distinct from what *took place* in Europe during World War II.[7]

The piece in the permanent collection of Toronto collector and curator Ydessa Hendeles brings with it a distinctly personal note.[8] Hendeles's mother was a prisoner who sorted clothing in the barrack. Ydessa Hendeles selected Boltanski to create this piece that would subsequently serve to inaugurate the Hendeles Art Foundation she established in Toronto in November of that year, 1988. Later this would become her very first acquisition for the collection. Notwithstanding Boltanski's remarkable career and penetrating work, it is still significant that this piece constitutes the first of her collection, thereby pointing to a quiet, yet powerful, decision on the part of Hendeles to choose this work above all others as her first acquisition. An artwork is meaningful in its own right, of course. But the history of its making and its acquisition, as well as where it finds its home or how it journeys from museum to gallery to collector, is not inconsequential.

It tells a tale, too. Here, the background story of Ydessa Hendeles as collector, and her personal history vis-à-vis the collection she has built in Toronto serves in many ways as a mirror to her life, and the timeliness of certain artists in the visual arts. What any collector assembles reflects his or her values and interests, and for this reason it is impossible to dismiss the very first object to form Hendeles's collection. More than this, Hendeles is also a thoughtful, deeply sensitive curator who keenly measures one work against another. She is guided by a mission to shape the perceived geography of art (both internationally, as her gallery attracts international visitors, and locally, to introduce, educate, and even hope to effect change among the Toronto community). Perhaps we might want to see Hendeles's purchase of the Boltanski installation as a gesture, a memorial tribute by the collector/curator, who, as a child of survivors, takes her own journey of re-memoration, however unwittingly, and by becoming an agent between herself and her parents' past, performs a critical act of remembering.

Vera Frenkel, a multimedia artist, questions what it means to take visual constructions of the mind (or "heart") to the three-dimensional reality of our tangible world. Her constructions develop imaginary narratives and underline the expression of complex identities and the multiplicity of positions from which to think about notions of fixed places, homes, or nations. An architectural space and imagined geography entitled . . . *from the Transit Bar*[9] is built as a bar for visitors (where drinks are actually served). The installation contains six video monitors distributed throughout the space that run fifteen videotaped written and spoken texts in different languages with different narrators. Voices are overdubbed in Yiddish and Polish and subtitled in alternating English, French, and German (thus images and text that are read and seen but not heard). This layering of languages and texts reveals the complexity of the stories told and not told, voices heard and not heard, at once cacophony and silence. Frenkel wanted visitors to experience a sense of dislocation as a result of seeing and reading the fragments of the stories told.

Initially conceived for *documenta IX,* in Kassel, Germany, where Yiddish and Polish are marginalized (as they are in North America), Frenkel privileged the marginal and ensured a constant state of displacement for most viewers. Destinations in this "transit bar" are rendered meaningless, for there is no place to go to; there is an aura of agony and pleasure in this space of the in-between: between places and languages. We are forever in transit and suspended between here and there, beginning or end. There is no specific, geographic place in which we can locate this bar: is this a bus terminal, train station, or airport? This is a manufactured site of rupture and rapture where we

Vera Frenkel, . . . *from the Transit Bar,* 1992. Six-channel videodisk installation/ functional piano bar (partial view; variable dimensions). Built first at the Museum Fridericianum, documenta 9, Kassel (1992); reconstructed in Canada at the Power Plant, Toronto, the National Gallery, Ottawa (1994–96); then as part of an eight-museum Riksutställningar touring exhibition through Scandinavia and Poland, including site-specific versions at the Kungl Konsthögskolan, Stockholm, and the Centre of Contemporary Art, Warsaw (1997–98), among others. Collection of the National Gallery of Canada. Photograph by Dirk Bleicker, Kassel.

are captive in a sequestered space. Situated between documentary and fictional spaces, the visitor yearns for the solid and tangible; the spatial presence is a template for our personal and active engagement with our own memories, our own identities, and what it means to possess and at the same time to be stripped of self.

What adds layer upon layer to this interminable waiting station are the bits and pieces of our parceled selves stuck in the languages that are a mix of haunting voices, condensing the past in the present, holding the deeply etched memories of lost lives. Part of this profound *expulsion* travel that Frenkel creates traces the invisible

contours of identities that have been murdered yet exist in the in-
eluctable snippets of memory. Here, Frenkel constructs a space of
defeat, that is, defeat of permanence. What I mean by this is that she
builds a fantasy waiting station, a place that has the very specificity of
nowhere, not here, and not yet there, but somewhere always in between: the place that keeps us occupied as we wait and promises, in
its capacity of "waiting station," to usher us on to the next place. Yet
this promise is never really fulfilled, because we learn, while we wait
in this space of midzone—at once rapture and rupture, which titil-
lates with libation and confuses by the video with its incomprehensible languages written and spoken—that we are not going anywhere
we imagined, that in fact this place does not take us to the place of
dreams or expectations.

Instead, this place defeats all hopes of placement, of fixity, of
being somewhere and, therefore, defeats any suspicion we might
have that this party continues, that it is permanent. This geographical dystopia is actually anchored to a "geographical plot" that is the
temporary exhibition space. In turn, that space attempts to hold
steady images that avoid permanence. And while this installation trig-
gers an impulse that conflicts the conscience (rupture/rapture), we
are also aware that this is but a place of transit from which we must
depart—and the exhibition continually underlines and perhaps even
undermines our inability to take flight.

In a different yet connected way, Melvin Charney's works operate
as architecture of the heart as well, but also mark physical places and
attempt anchorage—in the face of all contradiction. In a series entitled *Better if they think they are going to a farm . . .* , he superimposes contradictory, even irreconcilable types of architecture: a concentration
camp and a dairy farm, only to play out the ironic absurdity of the
Pan-Germanic "volk" superimposing its symbolic presence in an idealized farm façade to camouflage the main entrance to Auschwitz-
Birkenau. No less biting is his *Visions of the Temple* where he recon-
structs the Temple of Jerusalem (or the Temple of Ezekiel) from a
1631 etching by the German, Hafenreffer, friend of Martin Luther,
and, in an unbridled gesture, overlays it on what reads as the plan of
a concentration camp. Charney's sardonic representation suggests
that Hafenreffer—indeed, all Lutherans—appropriated, usurped the
temple, originally a symbol of hope and Jewish regeneration. "Three

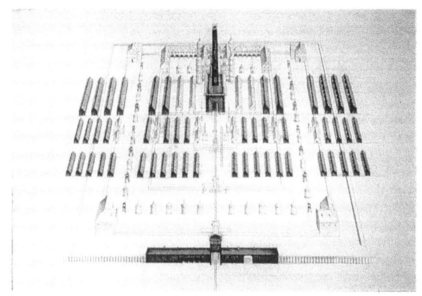

Melvin Charney, *Visions of the Temple (after Matthias Hafenreffer's "Reconstruction of the Temple of Jerusalem," Tübingen, Germany, 1631)*, 1986. Pastel on paper (Arches, 100 percent rag, 640 gsm.), 102.5 x 152.5 cm. Collection of the National Gallery of Canada.

hundred years later, in displacing the image of the Jews from Jerusalem, I found in this reappropriation of the Celestial City, the prefiguration of the City of Death of the 20th century: the forms of the extermination camps built by the German Nazis are clearly modeled on the logic of the same sketch by Hafenreffer."[10] Charney builds a contemporary archive in two dimensions of layered and multiple images that are the inverse of any palimpsestic activity: his are the affirmations through recognizable associations of any work of architectural history and historical precedents. His work refutes the clean slate, instead drawing upon historical references to consider the present moment. These drawings are dynamic evocations and even insistent cues to the past so that the necessary links to models bubble up to provide the footing for (re)constructing memory.

Charney's textures of reenactment and reembodiments at former sites in limited portions or durations insist on the importance of cultural patrimony and architectural legacy—a theme of working against an architecture of permanence that resonates throughout his work. One permanent public example is the Canadian Centre for Architecture Garden (1987–90) in Montreal.[11] On a plot of land that faces the Canadian Centre for Architecture (CCA) and responds to it, Charney records how the shifting and temporary qualities of imagination and experience are underscored by topographies. As such, they are signposts marking from whence we have come. This tract of land seems to hang on the edge of the city as it falls off to the ribbons of expressways below it. Yet for Charney, the project was to introduce classical architectural references and fragments of history that engage the visitor or the passer-by with pertinent and forgotten details of the restored Shaughnessy House it faces (bracketed and enhanced by the rest of the CCA building). For Charney, a Montreal urban garden has the task of recalling its place within the context of gardens and architectural elements within that city. The city is a conjunction of public and personal memories where actions and interactions are constantly at play. The memories he wishes to elicit are deeply embedded in private storehouses; and when he offers architectural fragments or elements, it is with the intention of teasing out the memories in some of our personal or collective archives through these partial hints. These are suggestions in partial architecture, of constructions we may have known or imagined. These are ways for us to recognize that our constructed physical surroundings contain powerhouses of meaning. We rarely take the time to see that in each and every element, every chip of our built environment, lie the treasures to which Benjamin refers.

While never able to take flight, Yvonne Singer's *The Veiled Room* defeats anchorage even as it operates as an architecture of the heart. Singer's work is not fixed to a place but is imagined at all times as becoming, or in process. This evocative installation cues us to the past, but in this case a private past gendered female. Singer works against architecture as we commonly know it: her architecture here is not what is imagined to stand the test of time—an architecture of stone. It displaces the solidity of permanent architecture and instead creates a fragile, cocoonlike diaphanous nest. She proposes material textures of impermanence: curtains of semi-transparent veils wrapping a space marked only by an amorphous and suggestive triangular shape, subject to subtle change as it billows in any given direction. *The Veiled*

Yvonne Singer, *The Veiled Room*, 1998. Silk-screened polyester sheer fabric, video, TV monitor, steel cables and hooks, 14' x 10' x 12'. Conceived and exhibited at the ACC Gallery, Weimar, Germany. Photograph by Isaac Applebaum at the Red Head Gallery, Toronto.

Room, or perhaps in this Veiled Womb, Yvonne Singer grapples with the spatial and linguistic intricacies of concealment (of self, of other, of personal and very public identity as well). Originally designed to be site-specific for Weimar, Germany, and therefore in dialogue, however fractious or cautious, with the history of that place and her own personal reminiscences as a child survivor, the installed *Room* invites us to pull aside the double overlay of curtains to reveal what lies hidden inside, and to acknowledge its transparencies while recognizing its inherent opacities. Is this a safe space of containment and protection, swaddled as we are by the fabric, or is it a place of danger, where the boundaries of what is and what is not are never revealed?

Texts are silk-screened on double-hung curtains that wrap around an inner chamber like billowing veils: on the outside layer are screened texts from Freud's *Standard Edition* in English and German translation, including excerpts from *The Interpretation of Dreams* and *Civilization and Its Discontents*, while the inside layer lists the names of influential politicians, artists, and philosophers predominantly from the Weimar Republic. Each of these is imprinted in *fraktur* font. Singer plays with the history of this font. Designed by Leonhard Wagner at the behest of German Emperor Maximilian (1493–1517), this new typeface was to be purely German. After three centuries, it had fallen out of style after World War I, but the Third Reich embraced it again as expressive of the spirit of the New Germany, even though Hitler had declared it "Un-German" and "of Jewish origin" in 1941. Still, presses had continued to use it and it was closely linked to the Nazi era.

The layering Singer produces with the screened-on names in this font is highly effective. Together with the random associations between names she introduces and prints on the veiled *walls*, we note a sampling of the members of Germany's intellectual elite, artists, scientists: Berthold Brecht, Albert Einstein, Adolph Hitler, Walter Benjamin, Johann W. Goethe, Theodor Adorno, Charlotte Salomon. A silent video monitor dominates the space looping a video that recounts an amorous encounter. This staged love scene is proposed through a female eye. Her back is to us, and the man, who is performing for her, looks at her, at us. The narrative is framed by theories of the gaze, long a standard reference and concept in the visual arts,[12] where issues of power, identity, and construction of self are central concerns. Singer pursues this further by coddling the television monitor with voluptuous drapery folds stamped with the monikers and Freudian lexicon of the Oedipus complex. We are cued to making the link between text and image, walls of impermanence that bulge and flutter and a video monitor that never moves.

This is a semi-autobiographical sojourn for Singer as she links her own uprooted history that began with her birth in Budapest and subsequent flight through Europe with her parents to Germany's past and the consequences of confrontations between Germans and Jews, especially at the site of this installation in Weimar. This is a confrontation between Weimar, site of history and fixity, against the vaporous quality of lives that have sought fixity and history; it is a confrontation between the self and the other, the impossibilities of holding down a physical space, an architecture that questions and challenges permanence in a defeated effort to fix the fleeting images.

In the final piece I want to examine, *Angels and Ghosts,* an installation by Rafael Goldchain, we experience another enactment, this time through doubling and retelling. Here, Goldchain, through generational and gendered layering, wittingly betrays truths through his photographs, while creating new histories and memories. What this means is that in these transparent renderings, Goldchain builds a family tale in scrapbooks and photographs of his family who fled Nazi threats in Poland, going first to Santiago de Chile, then to Mexico City, to Southfield, Michigan, and eventually to Toronto. Goldchain pieces this archival information and disguised self-portraits together photographically. In his title *Angels and Ghosts,* Goldchain alludes to Walter Benjamin's allegory on the Angel of History, and his reference to Paul Klee's painting *Angelus Novus,* which he had purchased. In an epigraph for one of his "theses" on the philosophy of history, Benjamin quotes his friend Gershom Scholem: "My wing is ready for flight, / I would like to turn back. / If I stayed timeless time / I would have little luck."[13] Concurrent with the image of this angel, Goldchain pairs the "messenger" with a ghost or specter. What do these mean in his photographic essay?

He begins with his own portrait as a point of departure where his face serves as the base onto which he will build, with layers of semi-transparent disguises, a new image that he will then photograph. These newly appropriated images of an aunt, a grandfather, or a

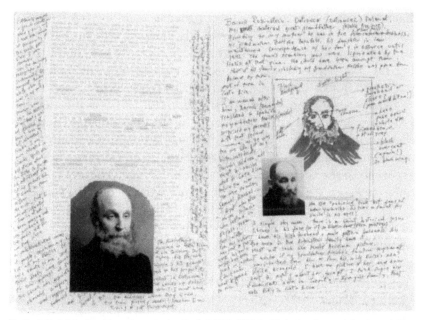

Rafael Goldchain, *Page from Artist Book*, 1999–2000. Gicleé print on Arches, 15" x 22", exhibited with other pages on 24" x 30" x 40" lectern. Reproduced from digital original. First exhibited as part of an exhibition entitled *Angels and Ghosts: Mourning, Remembrance, and the Work of Inheritance* at The Gallery, Faculty of Fine Arts, York University, April 2000. Currently part of an exhibition entitled *Familial Ground*, first shown at the Koffler Gallery, Toronto, September–October 2001. Courtesy of Rafael Goldchain.

great-grandmother always reveal—almost as though the images were in *pentimento*, where the trace of an earlier image is visually present— the image of Rafael Goldchain, recognizable as the central figure throughout this Portrait Gallery. Infusing newly fashioned characters from family photographic archives, he invents a family photographic album (and past in the present), albeit fictional, of some historic-like dream. Goldchain dresses up: with makeup and costume in one photograph, he becomes Chaja Golda Precelman née Ryten; in another, Dona Balbina Baumfeld Szpiegel de Rubinstein; and in yet another, Mojszes Precelman.

Through this feminization of himself through layered enactment Goldchain actually moves forward toward the viewer. Ever meticulous about making himself up to appear as the mythic relative, he is the ghost and the substance of the future memory chain he wishes to establish for his son: his presence is the anchor of a history unknown and a legacy undocumented. *Angels and Ghosts* splices images and truths and builds an archive, a collection of data that is present but mostly absent; this photo album is an architecture of the heart that, by recuperating his personal history through imaginative reenactment, allows him to construct a past he never knew. The Angel of his title is a reminder to us to turn back, as Benjamin's text states imperatively. And through his doubling of his own image, with its referent to history, his personal history, Goldchain personifies history. This action of figuring history (through the Angel or through his portraits) is prosopopoeia or personification, also described with regard to the photograph by Benjamin in his "A Short History of Photography."[14]

In this way, Goldchain puts a literal and familiar (as in "family") face to history, forcing us, as viewers, to confront the archival, and eventually decaying, spectral face in the photograph. It is his own imperative to us and to himself to confront his architecture of the heart, his emblem of history. This performative enactment with time brings that past into the material present, again following the spirit of Benjamin who said, "History is the subject of a structure whose site is not homogeneous, empty time, but time filled by the presence of the now."[15] And again, "Historical articulation of the past does not mean to recognize it 'as it really was.' It means to seize hold of a memory as it flashes up in a moment of danger. It is for historical materialism to arrest that image the way it suddenly seizes, in a moment of danger, the historical subject."[16]

Each of these artists and collectors wrestles with the need to dig and build archival memory that has been buried. Their responses are active ways of telling and therefore remembering. Their work asks questions, researches deep within the archive, and imagines a place from the heart where the construction of a personal identity in a newly configured nation is not always simple and, what is more, is never passive. Self and geography are located by means of heightened engagements the artists perform in their work. Above all, these artists recognize that the archive and the architecture of their hearts are declared in these works in the present tense and that history is not the space between two fixed points but rather the experience of

immersion in a space whose dimensionality is not necessarily determined by the relays between origin and destination, beginning and
end, then and now.

NOTES

1. Georges Perec, *Species of Spaces and Other Pieces* (London: Penguin Books, [1974] 1997), 90–91.
2. Walter Benjamin, "A Berlin Chronicle," in *Reflections*, ed. Peter Demetz (New York: Schocken, 1978), 26.
3. Gilles Deleuze and Félix Guattari, *A Thousand Plateaus: Capitalism and Schizophrenia*, trans. and ed. Brian Massumi (Minneapolis: University of Minnesota Press, 1989).
4. See Laurence J. Silberstein, "Mapping, Not Tracing: Opening Reflec- tion," in *Mapping Jewish Identities*, ed. Laurence J. Silberstein (New York: New York University Press, 2000), 8. This is similar to W. J. T. Mitchell's idea of making landscape into a verb. See W. J. T. Mitchell's "Introduc- tion," in *Landscape and Power*, ed. W. J. T. Mitchell (Chicago: University of Chicago Press, 1994), 1.
5. Pierre Nora, "Between Memory and History," in *Realms of Memory: Re- thinking the French Past*, ed. Pierre Nora and Lawrence Kritzman, trans. Arthur Goldhammer (New York: Columbia University Press, 1996–97), 8.
6. Yosef Yerushalmi, *Zakhor* (Seattle: University of Washington Press, [1982] 1996), 44.
7. The music of the Canadian national anthem was composed by Calix Lavallée and the lyrics (in French) by Judge Adolphe-Basile Routhier. First performed in French on June 24, 1880, in Quebec City, a variety of English versions followed. But it was Robert Stanley Weir's lyrics of 1908 that gained the widest currency:

> O Canada!
> Our home and native land!
> True patriot love in all thy sons command.
>
> With glowing hearts we see thee rise,
> The True North strong and free!
>
> From far and wide,
> O Canada, we stand on guard for thee.

God keep our land glorious and free!
O Canada, we stand on guard for thee.

O Canada, we stand on guard for thee.

See "The Music of Canada," *Canadian Heritage Government of Canada*
<http://canada.gc.ca/> (official web site), 2001.

8. For a photograph of *Canada*, see Lynn Gumpert, *Christian Boltanski*
(Paris: Flammarion, 1994), or Ernst van Alphen, *Caught by History: Holo-
caust Effects in Contemporary Art, Literature, and Theory* (Stanford: Stanford
University Press, 1997), 113.

9. Built initially at *documenta IX*, Kassel (1992), and installed subsequently,
among other European venues, at the Power Plant, Toronto (1994–95);
the Setagaya Museum, Tokyo (1995); the Gesellschaft für Aktuelle Kunst
(GAK), Bremen (1996); the National Gallery of Canada (1996); the
Kungl Konsthögskolan—Royal University College of Fine Arts (KKH),
Stockholm (1997); and the Centre of Contemporary Art, Warsaw
(1997). See the exhibition catalogs . . . *from the Transit Bar/du transit-
bar/aus der Transitbar* (the Power Plant/the National Gallery of Canada,
1994) and *Vera Frenkel, . . . from the Transit Bar, Body Missing and the Body
Missing Website*, Riksutstallningar, Stockholm, 1997–98.

10. Catherine Millet, "Melvin Charney, Explorateur de la mémoire collective," *Art Press* (May 1995): 56–60 (translation mine).

11. For an exceptional series of photographs and a larger discussion of "A
Garden for the Canadian Centre for Architecture," see the catalog *Para-
bles and Other Allegories: The Work of Melvin Charney, 1975–1990* (Montreal:
Centre Canadien d'Architecture/Canadian Centre for Architecture,
distributed by MIT Press, Cambridge, 1991), especially 182–93.

12. See Laura Mulvey's widely cited and anthologized article on this subject,
"Visual Pleasure and Narrative Cinema," *Screen* 16, no. 3 (1975): 6–18.

13. Translation taken from Susan Handelman, "Walter Benjamin and the
Angel of History," *Cross Currents* (fall 1991): 344–52. His "Uber den Be-
griff der Geschichte" was completed in spring 1940 and first published
in *Neue Rundschau* 51, no. 3: 150, and is found in English in *Illuminations:
Walter Benjamin Essays and Reflections*, ed. Hannah Arendt, trans. Harry
Zohn (New York: Schocken Books, 1968), 253–64.

14. See *One Way Street and Other Writings* (London: NLB, 1979). Ian Balfour
describes personification in Benjamin's concept of "aura" as "the imposition of a face and voice on something that has neither, but the prosopopoeia of aura is not set out as if the return of the gaze by the inanimate
object were an imposition by a subject." Later, Balfour reminds us that

the aura in Benjamin's writing "is experienced primarily in the mode of its disappearance. Hence the ghostly or spectral character of the aura, for not only is the inanimate endowed with a kind of life in the fleeting moment of its disappearance, that very moment raises the specter of the subject's own disappearance, the prospect of the subject as thing." See his "Reversal, Quotation (Benjamin's History)," *MLN (Modern Language Notes)* 106, no. 3 (1991): 622–47.

15. Ibid.
16. Ibid.

Chapter 2

Haunted by Memory: American Jewish Transformations

Michelle A. Friedman

The recent proliferation in the United States of Holocaust museums and memorials, of fiction and nonfiction about the Holocaust, and of Holocaust courses being offered in schools and colleges makes it apparent that the history of these events has had an effect on contemporary American cultural consciousness. But what relevance does this European history really have for this place and this time? It makes sense that the Holocaust plays a part in the cultural life of Israel, Germany, or other European countries in which "the parents or grandparents of the present generation directly confronted—resisted, assisted, or in any case witnessed—the crime" (Novick 1999, 2).

In the United States, however, these connections do not exist: the events of this history occurred thousands of miles away and Americans were neither persecutors, victims, nor direct witnesses. For American Holocaust survivors and their children, it is clear that they have no choice but to engage in this project of remembrance. For them, the legacy of the Holocaust, experienced as repetitions and reverberations, can never be "over and done with," as it has been transported here in their bodies and has been sustained in the way they live their lives. But Holocaust survivors and their descendants constitute only a small fraction of American Jewry and an even smaller fraction of the general population and, for those not directly related to survivors, the answers are not so evident.

This essay considers how and why it may be relevant to remember the Holocaust in America, by examining the work of two artists—

Shimon Attie and Steve Reich. Both focus on the geography of memory; in doing so, both make connections between the histories of Europe and America. In his multimedia installations *The Writing on the Wall, Trains,* and *Between Dreams and History,* Attie makes the past visible by reinscribing German and American landscapes with images and memories that have become obscured by time. Meanwhile, Reich layers several different places over one another in his composition *Different Trains,* in order to situate an incomprehensible European history in relation to his familiar American one. In locating their work within particular places in this way, both artists seek to recall what has been seemingly forgotten; their work makes manifest the histories that haunt these various places. But what does it mean for Attie and Reich to do this work as American artists? What does it mean to remember the Holocaust in America and to engage in the present with a European past that they have never known?

To begin to answer these questions, I turn to a passage from Toni Morrison's novel *Beloved,* which considers what it means to remember the past in the present and suggests the power of a place to invoke that past. The themes and images that emerge here resonate with those that Shimon Attie addresses in his artistic installations and reverberate with those evoked by Steve Reich in his music. In this passage, Sethe warns her daughter Denver about how the plantation on which she once was enslaved still poses a threat, though the days of slavery are long over:

> Places, places are still there. If a house burns down, it's gone, but the place—the picture of it—stays, and not just in my rememory, but out there, in the world. . . . I mean, even if I don't think it, even if I die, the picture of what I did, or knew, or saw is still out there. Right in the place where it happened. . . . Someday you be walking down the road and you hear something or see something going on. So clear. And you think it's you thinking it up. A thought picture. But no. It's when you bump into a rememory that belongs to somebody else. Where I was before I came here, that place is real. It's never going away. Even if the whole farm—every tree and grass blade of it dies. The picture is still there and what's more, if you go there—you who never was there—if you go there and stand in the place where it was, it will happen again; it will be there for you, waiting for you. (Morrison 1987, 36–37)

As a former slave, Sethe feels that even though slavery may appear "over and done with," the place where it happened is still not safe, not for her and not for her daughter. Even if Sweet Home—the plantation from which Sethe escaped shortly before Denver was born—is no longer there, even "if every tree and grass blade of it dies," she believes the past will still be there waiting. Preserved by the power of memory, it will continue to exist even if she no longer thinks of this place and even if she herself dies.

Morrison suggests that for Sethe and Denver a return to Sweet Home—a place that was not sweet and was never really home—will result in an uncanny encounter with a past that refuses to die. In Freud's theory of the uncanny, what is *heimlich* becomes *unheimlich*, and what was once homely, intimate, and friendly is no longer that (Freud 1953–74, vol. 17, 220–22). This "sweet home" that was neither is thus dangerous for both Sethe and Denver because it offers a place for the uncanny return of the traumatic past. As Sethe explains, if Denver were to visit this place, it would reawaken dangerous forces; if she goes there, "it will happen again." Morrison implies that, for Sethe and Denver, this history can never be over and the trauma of slavery can never be resolved; what happened at Sweet Home can never be made familiar or known and will "always be there waiting."

Morrison articulates the enduring quality of the past not only with the substance of Sethe's message but with the words she chooses. In the second sentence of the passage above, she uses the word *rememory*. Just as the word *representation* contains within it the idea of repetition, of presenting again, the word rememory does as well. Distinguished from the word *remember*, which appears in the sentence immediately following, rememory implies not that past events are "over and done with" but that they continue into the present and that what happened in memory can happen again. Additionally, since one can "bump into a rememory that belongs to somebody else," a rememory constitutes not only an individual act of remembrance but is linked to what happens "out there, in the world." Its effects can be felt as a tangible, material presence haunting not only a place, but a cultural and social consciousness.

In this concept of rememory, Morrison articulates what it means to encounter places that shelter the memorial residue of a haunting past. Attie and Reich do the same. As neither are survivors, in their work both examine what it means to "bump into a rememory that belongs to somebody else" and to confront places that sustain the memory of the Holocaust. Different as they are in form and content from Morrison's novel about African American slavery, Attie's installations and Reich's composition similarly explore material confrontations with a history that, though hidden from sight, continues to be felt in the present. Like Denver, Attie and Reich must contemplate such encounters with the past from afar, separated as they are in both time and space from the traumatic events themselves. They must negotiate not only the distance that separates them temporally from these events, but the distance that separates them geographically as well. Though performed in very different ways, Attie's art and Reich's music emerge from and are sustained by these movements between past and present and between Europe and America; and in these movements, Attie and Reich reveal what remembering the Holocaust in America entails and illustrate what kind of labor it requires.

Someday You Be Walking Down a Road

Shimon Attie's photographic installations *The Writing on the Wall* (Berlin, 1991–93) and *Trains* (Dresden, 1993) are two of six European projects inspired by the Holocaust that are "part photography, part installation, and part performance. . . . [They] might best be described as 'acts of remembrance'—retaining the resonance of actions, staged acts, actors, and acting out" (Young 1998, 10). Attie uses similar techniques to produce most of these installations. By projecting photographic images onto sites seemingly forgetful of their history, he makes visible a past that, though it may be unseen, unacknowledged, and unnoticed, continues to haunt these places. Projected onto "ordinary" sites, his images appear as ghostly figures who announce that the traumatic history from which they emerge has not been resolved but has merely been covered up and hidden from sight.

The idea for the first of these installations, *The Writing on the Wall,* emerged out of Attie's response to moving to Germany in the summer of 1991. Though Attie grew up in California and is the grandson of Syrian Jews, the Holocaust played a big part in his life and helped

Shimon Attie, *Almstadstrasse 43* (fruhere Grenadierstrasse 7), Berlin, slide projection of Hebrew bookstore (1930) from the series *Writing on the Wall,* 1993. Ektacolor print. Courtesy of Jack Shainman Gallery, New York.

to shape his perspective as an artist. As C. Carr (1998) reports in the *Village Voice,* "Many of [Attie's] parents' friends were survivors, and his father began telling him stories about it when he was very young. By the time he was 10, Attie was going to the library to look for books on the Holocaust." Attie himself reveals that he "learned through these stories . . . that part of being Jewish meant [being] connected to a life and culture that no longer existed. This feeling of having lost something [he had] never had . . . was a powerful thread running through [his] childhood" (Carr 1998). Because of these influences, in that summer of 1991 Attie found himself mentally projecting onto the German landscape images from a past he had not lived, but which had shaped his imagination and his knowledge of the world.

As he wandered through Berlin, for example, he was very aware of the Jewish life and community that no longer existed. Attie explains: "Walking the streets of the city that summer [of 1991], I felt myself asking over and over again, Where are all the missing people? What has become of the Jewish culture and community which had once been at home here? I felt the presence of this lost community very strongly, even though so few visible traces of it remained" (Attie 1994, 9; quoted in Young 1998, 11). Although he felt the presence of this absence, it seemed to him that it went unnoticed among the city's residents and unmarked within the city's geography.

In response to the fact that so few visible traces remained of a past that to him was so alive and so tangible, Attie felt compelled to mark its uncanny presence. He did so by projecting archival photographs of former Jewish residents of the Scheunenviertel district of East Berlin—a neighborhood in which Eastern European Jewish immigrants had lived from the late nineteenth century until World War II —onto the same places where they had been taken originally in the 1920s and 1930s.[1] These images were not the extraordinary ones of the mid-1930s to mid-1940s portraying Jewish persecution and death, but simple, ordinary pictures of Jewish life before the war. Walking around Berlin that summer, he had been carrying these images around in his head. He wanted not just to bring these figures back to life within the city's landscape; he wanted to project them into the minds of others who walked these same streets.

To use Morrison's term, Attie wanted others to bump into his "rememory." As James Young asserts in the introduction to *Sites Unseen* (the catalog of the photographs Attie produced of his six European installations), he "hope[d] that once seen, the images of these projections [would] always haunt these sites by haunting those who [had] seen his projections" (Young 1998, 10). He sought not to re-populate Berlin with long-dead Jews, but to illuminate the haunting presence of their absence. Freud writes that, according to Schelling, "everything is *unheimlich* [uncanny] that ought to have remained secret and hidden but has come to light" (Freud 1953–74, vol. 17, 225). With his photographic projections, Attie literally used light to make manifest a past that, despite an increasing willingness among Germans to confront their painful history, still remained "secret and hidden" within Berlin's forgetful cityscape. By projecting these photographic images back onto the buildings and into the neighborhood from which they originated, Attie returned to these sites—and to those who moved through them—the once-familiar figures that had now become unfamiliar. The projected photographs made visible the now invisible Jews of Germany who continued to haunt not just these particular sites, but the national imagination. His ghostly images thus served as a reminder of historical, social, and political realities that had pushed living Jews literally and figuratively out of the German landscape.

As Attie's photographs of these installations make manifest, his projections not only reveal the traumatic history hidden within these particular places, but make translucent the boundaries between past and present.[2] With their neatly lettered signs, the storefronts projected from the past contrast sharply with the abandoned buildings and graffiti-covered walls that surround them in the present; and the human figures populating these scenes counter the desolation of the littered streets into which they are projected. Yet despite these distinctions between past and present—made even sharper by the contrast between the black and white archival photographs and the "real life" colors of the surfaces on which they appear—the past and present appear intertwined.

It seems, for example, as though Attie has simply peeled back the flaking paint and the chipped exterior walls to reveal a Hebrew bookstore and a window-shopper gazing in at the wares, or a theater and a Torah reading room, and that these are scenes that have always been there, only hidden from sight. What can be considered a kind of temporal transparency becomes most apparent in the images projected into doorways. They appear as ghostly forms that seem not only to step from inside a building to the outside, but to move through the solidity of walls and open up the pre-Holocaust past into a present that has been irrevocably marked by that trauma.[3] In stepping toward the viewers, these ghosts embody the return of this repressed history; and they make visible and nearly tangible what, though seemingly not there, is really a "seething presence" (Gordon 1997, 8).

In Attie's installation entitled *Trains*, he repeated the project of the Berlin installation but produced images that were more confrontational. For two weeks, beginning on November 9, 1993, Attie projected the faces of former Jewish inhabitants of Dresden onto the trains, tracks, and walls of the Dresden train station.[4] This station, unlike Berlin's Scheunenviertel, was not just a place in which Jews once lived, but was the site of deportations from Germany and the first stop on many German Jews' journey toward death. Unlike the figures in the Berlin installation, the faces projected onto the trains do not appear unaware of the viewer's gaze; they seem to stare accusingly and demandingly in return. Attie wanted these ghostly images to haunt the minds and imaginations of German travelers too, making palpable their repressed history and enacting the return of what was thought to be "over and done with." Thus, in his projection of a woman's face onto the tracks, Attie makes the image appear as though it emanates from the tracks themselves. From this perspective, the spectral form seems to have been released by the power of memory and imagination, intent on revealing the unacknowledged and unremembered history of this place.

Returning to America

As Attie discloses in an interview, he went to Berlin to confront the traumatic history of the Holocaust (Carr 1998). While he does this effectively with each of his European installations, examining these projects alone does not shed any light on what it means for Attie to remember the Holocaust in America. With his German projects, the landscape he works in is German, not American, and he prompts only Germans to confront a history that he, an American Jew, has made visible for them. To understand how Attie's work helps explain what it means to remember the Holocaust in America, then, it is necessary to put Attie's European projects in context with his subsequent American ones. Doing so suggests what, after journeying into the European past, he was able to bring back with him into an American present.

Though Attie felt obligated to travel to Germany in order to remember the Holocaust, he subsequently returned to America to confront the ghosts that populate his own home. In the first series he created after coming back to the United States, *Untitled Memory* (1998), Attie literally comes home. In his new work, he projected images from personal photographs of old friends and lovers into his former apartment in San Francisco. Like his European projects, he then reproduced these projections in photographs.[5] In many ways, however, the similarities between these projects end there.

Unlike *The Writing on the Wall* and *Trains*, the images in *Untitled*

Memory occupy domestic spaces and reflect Attie's personal memories. As with his European installations, these projections also blur the distinctions between past and present, but with differing effects. The figures in these images are not eerily unfamiliar, but seem as though they have always been there, simply waiting. One figure (Armand V.), for example, whose intangible plate matches one placed across from him on the table, looks expectantly as though for a reply. Another figure (Thomas P.) appears as though he has turned away only momentarily to select tea for the water currently being boiled in the kettle atop the stove.[6] The figures sitting at the kitchen table or standing beside an open cupboard may be ghostly, but they have names and labels (friend, lover) that attach them directly to the artist, and they appear engaged with and connected to the here and now. The absent presence in these installations, in fact, is the artist himself, signified by the empty chair at the table and the vacant space in front of the sink where the water still runs. Attie absents himself, perhaps, in order to bear witness not to a collective history, but to the particulars of his own past.[7]

This literal homecoming prepared the way for Attie to return metaphorically to America and to create an art of memory situated within a broader American context. After *Untitled Memory*, he embarked on a project entitled *Between Dreams and History*, which appeared in Manhattan's Lower East Side in the autumn of 1998. For this installation, he projected not photographic images, but written text excerpted from recollections of dreams and memories about the neighborhood, elicited from Jewish, Puerto Rican, Dominican, and Chinese residents. As in Berlin, Attie needed to do some research to find material for this project. Rather than searching in archives, however, he interviewed members of various cultural groups: a Yiddish class of Jewish seniors, a choir of Latino seniors, a tai chi class of Chinese seniors, as well as various youth groups (Carr 1998). For several weeks, lasers inscribed these recollections in Yiddish, Spanish, Chinese, and English onto tenement walls and storefronts. Written out in real time, letter by letter, this ghostly writing mirrored the ebb and flow of memory (*Shimon Attie's Between Dreams and History*, 1998, artist's statement).

There are a number of connections between this installation and Attie's European ones, though they are not ones that Attie makes overtly or directly. In Manhattan, as in Berlin and Dresden, Attie intended to make memory visible by unburying a history that had been covered over; he aimed to help viewers see this history as material and present. He again used luminous projections to foreground the idea that he was shedding light on social and historical realities that had become obscured or hidden from sight. In his Berlin installation, *The Writing on the Wall,* Attie wrote on walls symbolically to represent the narratives figuratively etched into, under, and onto the streets of Berlin. In *Between Dreams and History,* Attie configured this metaphorical work more literally; he really did write on walls, inscribing words that recalled the neighborhood's past.

Despite these connections, however, there are also a number of important differences between Attie's Lower East Side project and his earlier ones; and, I contend, understanding these helps explain some of what it means to remember the Holocaust in America. Whereas the connections relate to form, the differences concern intentions. In the earlier installations, Attie sought to uncover a Jewish history that had been occluded and forgotten. In *Between Dreams and History,* on the other hand, he needed not to excavate the neighborhood's Jewish past, but to move it aside in order to bring other histories out of obscurity. Specifically, he wanted to show that, though the history of the Lower East Side often has been viewed as one of Jewish peddlers and pushcarts, the reality is that large numbers of other immigrant groups have also made this place their home.

The reasons why these other histories have been obscured are complicated. They do not, however, have to do with ruptures resulting from a history marked by trauma, but are related to other, more ordinary losses.[8] In the Berlin installation, Attie projected once-familiar images that had become unfamiliar, emphasizing their uncanniness by isolating the figures against a backdrop of deserted, ruined streets. In the Lower East Side project, on the other hand, Attie intended his ghostly writings to represent the ordinary rhythms of memory. No single group of words or memories stood apart; the narratives overlapped and flowed into one another. As Attie remarks, "an 80-year-old Chinese resident's memory would relate to a 15-year-old Dominican's anxiety dream, which related to a Yiddish folk song" (Silberman 1998). In this project, then, Attie sought to balance Jewish narratives with other histories and legacies. He did not, however, attempt to connect the histories of two continents, but only those that belong to America and to a common experience of immigration and assimilation.

The Holocaust is not a history that literally belongs to this country or to this American landscape; and Attie does not try to make it fit. To do so, in fact, could erase the fact that the place of Jews and Jewish history in this country is not the same as it is in Germany. Part of what it means to remember the Holocaust in America, then, means acknowledging these differences. In going to Europe and walking through that haunted landscape, Attie's vision shifted and he learned how to make the forgotten visible; in returning to America, he used this ability to see underneath the surface of things to reveal the complex histories of this place.

In distinguishing between Attie's European and American projects, it becomes clear that with each he made choices about what he wanted his work to accomplish. As Norman Kleeblatt points out, "upon arriving in Berlin, Attie had fallen into the 'German fascination' with the Holocaust and World War II; on returning to America he entered into a world transfixed by questions of identity, where multiculturalism held sway. Without missing a beat, Attie began reflecting these concerns in his work" (Kleeblatt 2000, 102). Kleeblatt's observations suggest that Attie possesses a certain market savvy that comes from his ability to tap into the cultural pulse of a nation. In making these choices, Attie demonstrated an awareness not only of the continents' different histories and legacies, but also of his different audiences and their "fascinations."

He also made decisions about the ways in which he would position himself. In Europe, his identification with the history of the Holocaust helped him lay claim as a Jew to his culture's history. In America, on the other hand, he chose a site and a project that directly reflected his own family's past, as well as a more familiar American past that need not be considered specifically Jewish.[9] Despite these differences, however, the resonances between his installations evocatively point to connections between the histories of Europe and those that belong to America; they imply that the Holocaust has relevance not only for those who "go there and stand in the place where it was" (Morrison 1987, 37) but for those who are here in this place, as well.

Different Trains

The resonances suggestively noticeable in Attie's work are developed more fully and convincingly in Steve Reich's composition for the Kronos Quartet, *Different Trains*. Like Attie, Reich uses the trains of Europe to summon the ghosts of the Holocaust; his music makes audible the spectral figures that Attie's installations make visible. Unlike Attie, however, Reich's music itself moves back and forth between America and Europe, between the histories and legacies of each continent. In this movement, the music not only gestures toward what it means to remember the Holocaust in America but does so more explicitly, resulting in what Avery Gordon has called "transformative recognitions": moments in which ghosts become clearly visible and yield new ways of understanding the histories they signify (Gordon 1997, 8). By making these connections, Reich uncovers not only the ghosts of a European past but also the phantoms that haunt and are native to this American landscape.

Different Trains performs musically in some of the same ways that Shimon Attie's work functions visually. The first movement, "America —Before the war," describes some of the same themes Attie captures in *Between Dreams and History*, communicating a sense of America's expansive possibilities. The second movement, "Europe—During the war," shares a haunting and haunted quality with Attie's European projects; in some ways, it could be argued, this music gives voice to the ghosts that Attie's installations illuminate. The third movement, "After the war," explores the interconnections that Attie's work only begins to imply by fully intertwining the voices of America with those of Europe.

In *Different Trains*, Reich combines the music of a string quartet, train whistles, air raid sirens, and small speech samples in order to weave together different places and moments in history. The speech samples come from interviews with Reich's boyhood governess, Virginia, and a retired Pullman porter, Mr. Lawrence Davis, as well as three child survivors of the Holocaust now living in America—Rachella, Paul, and Rachel—who, as Reich points out, are his contemporaries. The speakers recount their memories of America before the war and of Europe during the war, and the strings imitate the "speech melody" of the speakers. Both words and strings thus conjure up the past. Simultaneously, the train whistles pull the words and music together, evoking the rhythm of trains and the feeling of movement through space and time. Using the hypnotic repetition of words, sounds, music, and rhythm, Reich's music propels listeners in and out of memory, in and out of different places and times. The quite literal repetition of speech and melody thus dramatizes the reverberations of the Holocaust as they become perceptible and audible in the here and now.

In the liner notes, Reich explains the autobiographical motivation for the composition's first movement. From 1939 to 1942, while a young boy, he was shuttled back and forth from New York to Los Angeles, accompanied by Virginia, his governess, in order to travel between parents who had divorced and who had arranged divided custody. As the music suggestively implies, to him these journeys were "exciting and romantic," captivating his imagination and helping to shape his vision of America.

Beginning with a rush of strings that repetitively and compellingly move the piece and the listeners forward, the first movement, "America—Before the war," conveys the excitement of transcontinental rail travel in the late 1930s and early 1940s. After the first rush of strings, the train whistles sound and resound. Then, the first voice enters. Over and over, Virginia repeats "from Chicago to New York." Train whistles underscore the reiteration of that phrase. As the whistles blast again and again, they seem to proclaim the possibilities of this American continent.[10] Virginia's second speech sample, "one of the fastest trains," emphasizes this promise, which then is recapitulated as the porter, Mr. Davis, announces, "the 'crack train' from New York," "from New York to Los Angeles." Once his voice enters, the tone and pace of the music shift, becoming more rhythmic and pulsing, settling into a new era of technology that permits such speed and such far-ranging travels.

With Virginia's next speech sample, "different trains every time," the music starts to alter subtly and then more dramatically, as first Virginia, then Mr. Davis, then Virginia once more, repeat "1939," "1940," and "1941" over and over again. Reich uses the phrase "different trains" to refer not only to the variety of trains he and his governess rode as they traveled across the country, but to forecast where the music is headed next, toward very different trains—ones that resonate not with excitement and adventure, but with fear and horror. The repetition of dates thus slowly begins to propel listeners toward the second movement, Europe, World War II, and the Holocaust. The strings, punctuated by blasts of the train whistles, carry the listeners along. Then, as Mr. Davis declares "1940" again and again, the rhythm becomes faster, more urgent, implying a sense of inevitability. Until, once again, the music slows; the tone changes and becomes darker, more haunting.

The transition to the second movement is almost seamless, even though the contrasts in tone, language, and mood are pronounced: the train whistles are transformed into air raid sirens; Virginia's words, "1941 I guess it must have been," segue into Rachella's "1940"; and the optimistic overtones of the first movement concede entirely to the minor key that has played underneath all along. In "America—Before the war," the dates move forward, from 1939 to 1941, reflecting the time frame of Reich's "exciting and romantic" cross-country journeys. In "Europe—During the war," however, the only date mentioned is 1940. In moving from America to Europe, time that has been racing forward takes a step back; and it stays there. The repetition of dates is replaced by the repeated sounding of an air raid siren. In this way, the second movement disrupts and interrupts the joy and excitement of the earlier one. Instead of these emotions, the music communicates panic, devastation, and destruction.

In the second movement, the strings are muted, as are the voices, eclipsed by the sound of the sirens. Throughout *Different Trains*, the voices can be difficult to understand. In this movement, however, they seem even more so. Without the liner notes, in fact, it would be nearly impossible to decode these speech samples. It is conceivable that these fragments are more difficult to decipher simply because Rachella, Paul, and Rachel speak accented English. Given that the words—abstract and evocative, haunted and haunting—have become more like ghostly evocations of speech than speech itself, however, it is more probable that Reich wanted to underscore the metaphysical impossibility of understanding these survivors' words:

"into those cattle wagons"
"for 4 days and 4 nights"
"and then we went through these strange sounding names"

"Polish names"
"Lots of cattle wagons there"
"They were loaded with people"
"They shaved us"
"They tattooed a number on our arm"
"Flames going up to the sky—it was smoking"

The images conjured by these testimonial phrases have become symbolic of what has come to be seen as the unimaginable, unspeakable, and unrepresentable horror of the Holocaust. Reich emphasizes this point by making these words almost literally incomprehensible. In this way, too, Reich underlines the stark contrasts between the first movement—in which the porter's call is familiar and easily recognizable—and the second.

Unlike the seamless transition between the first movement and the second, the transition from the second to the third is marked by a profound rupture. At the end of the second movement, the music and the words slow down. The final phrase, "flames going up to the sky—it was smoking," is interrupted by repeated train blasts that sound deeper, rougher, and more ominous than those of the train whistles featured in "America—Before the war." The music and words then continue to slow until all that remains finally is the sounding of the sirens, followed by absolute silence.

Across this fissure, the music and voices of the first two movements come together in a new time and place: "After the war," in America. Listeners notice, as an example of this coming together, that Rachella's words echo the phrases of Mr. Davis in the first movement. These words, "to Los Angeles," "to New York," are accompanied by music that is brighter and quicker than that of the second movement. Her words no longer evoke unspeakable images, but speak of vast possibilities and lead directly to those of the porter, whose voice returns with a recognizable refrain from the first movement: "from New York to Los Angeles." Listeners recognize Mr. Davis's words and speech melody as familiar. At the same time, these, as well as those belonging to Virginia—"one of the fastest trains"—are made less familiar because, in this movement, they are reframed and recontextualized by the voices that have recounted the catastrophe in Europe.

This frame and new context are constructed out of Paul's words
—"and the war was over"—which begin the movement, and Rachella's, which on some level belie Paul's, both as they respond to
his opening lines and as they end the composition. Whereas Paul's
speech melody—his words and the music combined—imply optimism and new beginnings, Rachella's are less certain that these are
possible. First, Rachella's words and melody respond questioningly to
Paul's statement that the war is over: "Are you sure?" Her words suggest not only her own disbelief, but seem to question more broadly
whether it is even possible for these events to be over. Her final words
and the music accompanying them reiterate these doubts, by concluding not with optimism, but with an image of what happened in
Europe, during the war: "There was one girl, who had a beautiful
voice"; "and they loved to listen to the singing, the Germans"; "and
when she stopped singing, they said, 'More, more' and they ap-
plauded." While not overdetermined like the words and images expressed in the second movement, these speech melodies leave listeners haunted.

By thus using Paul's and Rachella's voices to frame Mr. Davis's and
Virginia's, Reich dramatizes what it means to remember the Holocaust in America, as well as the relevance of doing so. In this musical
composition, Reich not only represents and remembers a European
tragedy, but he also gestures toward the haunting and haunted voices
that belong to America itself. As I mention above, Rachella's speech
melodies—"to Los Angeles" and "to New York"—echo and are ech-
oed by Mr. Davis's, "from New York to Los Angeles." Similar reverberations emerge when Mr. Davis states, "but today, they're all gone."
With this statement, he refers specifically to the trains that no longer
run. Nevertheless, in this composition, these trains that are "all gone"
evoke thoughts of the Jews who are too. The ghosts of the Holocaust
thus haunt the American tracks and trains that had earlier been remembered with such a tone of excitement and adventure.

At the same time, these European ghosts conjure up other histories that, like the one Shimon Attie illuminates in Dresden, lie within
the railroads and buried beneath the ground on which the tracks
are laid here, in America. Evoking connections between trains and
trauma, Reich's music encourages listeners to recall the history of the
oppressed Chinese laborers who built the American transcontinental

railway and to remember the displacement and genocide of the Native Americans who once occupied the land upon which the railroads were built. In laying the history of Europe next to that of America, Reich also urges us to listen more carefully to Mr. Davis—not only to what he is saying, but to why he is the one saying it. In the call "from New York to Los Angeles," we can also hear the history of American racism and the limited employment opportunities available to African American men during the 1930s and 1940s. Perceiving these connections does not simplify the complexities of any of these histories nor does it erase their differences. Additionally, it still does not mean that the Holocaust literally belongs to this place. Nevertheless, as Reich's music demonstrates, echoes of the Holocaust can reverberate across this American landscape and can set off sympathetic vibrations with this country's own histories.

Different Trains opens up these reverberations and re/percussions as the composition moves metaphorically across space and time from America to Europe and back again. According to Avery Gordon, "being haunted draws us affectively, sometimes against our will and always a bit magically, into the structure of feeling of a reality we come to experience, not as cold knowledge, but as a transformative recognition" (1997, 8). Steve Reich's music suggests that he has been haunted in this way. Beginning with the trains of his own childhood, he makes connections that allow him to reimagine these trains as different ones that, as a Jew, he would have been forced onto if he had been in Europe at this time. In making these connections, yet simultaneously sustaining the distinctions between these experiences, Reich produces transformative recognitions that shift not only his vision of trains, but of the American landscape through which he traveled as a child.

Though Attie's art and Reich's music differ dramatically, in reading them together it is possible to understand some of what it means to remember the Holocaust in America and how it is possible to do so. Moving between a European past and an American present, each imaginatively engages with the history of the Holocaust. In so doing, each makes visible and audible—if not quite tangible—the memorial residue of that haunting past.[11] As installations that can only be reconstituted through photographs and as a piece of music that cannot be represented visually at all, both Attie's and Reich's artistic media are in some way not quite tangible themselves. This, in itself, says something about what it means for American Jews to remember the Holocaust: though this history may haunt our imaginations, it is not something that we or this place can hold.

Nevertheless, Attie's and Reich's work enable us to see what it means to "bump into a rememory that belongs to somebody else." A careful reading of Attie's European and American installations suggests some of the ways in which the Holocaust may be relevant in this place and this time. And, even more explicitly, Reich's music demonstrates how the Holocaust resonates with the histories native to this American soil and how a specific engagement with one history can open up an engagement with the other. Highlighting these resonances serves not, as some might fear, to obscure the memory of the Holocaust but demonstrates why it may be important to remember this history here, a place in which the Holocaust, though it seems not to belong at all, has become part of our cultural and social consciousness.

NOTES

1. The Scheunenviertel was called the Finstere Medine (dark quarter) by its Yiddish-speaking, Eastern European inhabitants, who are represented in the archival photographs used by Attie in his installations.
2. While Attie's projections were on display, he also photographed his installations. The resulting photographs have been exhibited widely in galleries and museums and were collected in the volume entitled *Sites Unseen* (Attie 1998).
3. This East Berlin neighborhood has also been marked indelibly by the communist regime. At the time the installation was being projected, 1991 to 1993, it also reverberated with the implications of the recent fall of the Berlin Wall. Although Attie does not allude directly to this more recent past, his installations cannot be unaffected by the historical import of a newly unified Germany.
4. Beginning on November 9—a date particularly evocative of the Nazi era (Kristallnacht, the Munich Putsch, the Nazis' annual Nuremberg rallies)—comprised part of Attie's confrontational strategy.
5. *Untitled Memory* was produced as an installation from 1996 to 1997 but was only put into its final representational form in 1998 (Kleeblatt 2000, 102).

6. In writing these sentences and trying to differentiate between the projected images and the surfaces on and against which they are projected, I found myself struggling to find the appropriate words to describe them. For the former, I tried "ghostly," "ethereal," "facsimile"; for the latter, I tested out "real," "actual," "concrete," "substantial." These words set up a binary that is not really there, given how embedded these projected figures and images are in the space they occupy. My difficulties finding the appropriate language thus resonate with the installation's effective blurring of distinctions between past and present, used to illustrate the temporal connections invoked by and within a physical place.

7. Norman Kleeblatt points out that, in these installations, Attie "articulates his position as a gay man" for the first time (2000, 102). Attie does not overtly make connections between the traumatic losses made visible by his earlier works in Europe and the traumatic losses that belong to the gay community in San Francisco. Nevertheless, *Untitled Memory* evocatively encourages these connections. The empty chair and the vacant space in front of the sink can also be seen as symbolic of the absent members of a community ravaged by the AIDS epidemic.

8. Discussions with Laura Levitt about her current project, *Ordinary Jews*, have helped me to think about the differences between these different kinds of histories and losses.

9. Attie's grandparents had lived briefly on the Lower East Side when they first immigrated to this country.

10. For authenticity in creating what he calls "documentary music," Reich uses collected recordings of American and European train sounds from the 1930s and 1940s.

11. I thank Oren Stier for helping me envision and define ghosts as such an intangible, memorial residue of the past that continues to be felt in the present.

REFERENCES

Attie, Shimon. 1994. "The Writing on the Wall Project." In *The Writing on the Wall: Projections in Berlin's Jewish Quarter.* Heidelberg: Edition Braus.
———. 1998. *Sites Unseen: Shimon Attie European Projects; Installations and Photographs.* With an Introduction by James Young. Burlington, Vt.: Verve.
Carr, C. 1998. "The Memory Wall: Shimon Attie Reveals the Collective Unconscious of the Lower East Side." *The Village Voice* (online). Published November 3–9.
Freud, Sigmund. 1953–74. *The Standard Edition of the Complete Psychological*

Works of Sigmund Freud. 24 vols. Translated and edited by James Strachey. London: Hogarth Press.

Gordon, Avery F. 1997. *Ghostly Matters: Haunting and the Sociological Imagination.* Minneapolis: University of Minnesota Press.

Kleeblatt, Norman L. 2000. "Persistence of Memory." *Art in America* 88 (June): 96–103.

Morrison, Toni. 1987. *Beloved.* New York: New American Library.

Novick, Peter. 1999. *The Holocaust in American Life.* Boston: Houghton Mifflin.

Reich, Steve. 1989. *Different Trains.* Performed by the Kronos Quartet. New York: Elektra/Asylum/Nonesuch.

Schreiber, Rachel. "Seized Images: Photography, Memory, and the Holocaust." *New Art Examiner* 24 (April 1997): 22–25.

Shimon Attie's Between Dreams and History, presented by Creative Time. 1998. <http://www.creativetime.org/between/>

Silberman, Steve. 1998. "New York Stories, with Lasers." *Wired News.* October 12. <http://www.wired.com/news>

Young, James E. 1993. *The Texture of Memory: Holocaust Memorials and Meaning.* New Haven and London: Yale University Press.

———. 1998. Introduction to *Sites Unseen: Shimon Attie European Projects; Installations and Photographs,* by Shimon Attie. Burlington, Vt.: Verve.

Chapter 3

A House for an Uninhabitable Memory (The Center for Holocaust Studies at Clark University)

Julian Bonder

The ocean of pain, past and present, surrounded us, and its level rose from year to year until it almost submerged us. It was useless to close one's eye or turn one's back to it because it was all around, in every direction, all the way to the horizon. It was not possible for us nor did we want to become islands; the just among us, neither more nor less numerous than in any other human group, felt remorse, shame, and pain for the misdeeds that others and not they had committed, and in which they felt involved, because they sensed that what had happened around them and in their presence, and in them, was irrevocable. Never again could it be cleansed; it would prove that man, the human species—we, in short—had the potential to construct an infinite enormity of pain, and that pain is the only force created from nothing, without cost and without effort. It is enough not to see, not to listen, not to act.

—Primo Levi, "Shame"[1]

The uncanny is really nothing new or alien, but something which is familiar and old—established in the mind and which has become alienated from it through a process of repression. . . . (According to Schelling) the uncanny is something which ought to remain hidden but has come to light.

—Sigmund Freud, "The Uncanny"[2]

The project for the Center for Holocaust Studies was completed in November 1999.[3] Dedicated to an unprecedented program in Holo-

51

caust studies, with a mission based on scholarship, research, study, and public service, and set in a distant and removed site in Worcester, Massachusetts, the project dealt not only with physical complexities, but raised questions about the nature of architecture, landscape, and memory in relation to the Holocaust and its representation. The project involved working on a particular site that plays a pivotal role between Clark University's historic Main Campus and the Woodland Street neighborhood, which is listed in the National Register of Historic Places (which meant that we had to navigate the project through many agencies for approval, such as the Massachusetts Historical Commission, the Worcester Historical Commission, and Preservation Worcester, among others). It called for the extensive renovation and adaptation of a preexisting structure, a Colonial Revival house built in 1899 by the firm Frost, Briggs & Chamberlain, including a systems and accessibility update; the addition of a new structure, which would include the new library; and the creation of a small memorial garden. In addition, the building program included offices for faculty, graduate students, and staff, meeting and seminar rooms, and an exhibition area.

The project's unprecedented nature called for a very precise conceptual framework in order to establish its position vis-à-vis the myriad of Holocaust-related projects dotting American, European, and Israeli landscapes at the end of the twentieth century. As such, the task of designing and building the Center raised issues and questions that were not merely architectural, but indeed moral, ethical, and philosophical—questions exposing a complex task: constructing a "house" for an uninhabitable memory.

Some Questions

How can an uncanny, unhousable, "foreign," and enormously loaded subject like the Holocaust be landed, grounded, and anchored in an untainted, "innocent" site in Worcester? How can this particular site be transformed into a dedicated place, a "Holocaust site"? How can it be made resonant of the fatality, the uncanniness, the territorial extension, and vastness of the Holocaust? Can—or should—this project attempt to embody a sense of uncanniness and unhomeliness in a medium like architecture, which is based on the premise or promise of creating shelter and homeliness?

Furthermore, as the very presence of the program of studies and its building would necessarily challenge, disrupt, and transform both the academic environment and the cozy and happy normalcy of the Historic District, and as the Holocaust presents only questions, how could the core questions be presented or suggested, architecturally or metaphorically, without resorting to any direct representation? How could I, through the project, attempt to address the paradoxical relationship between the impossibility of representing the Holocaust and the utmost necessity for its re-presentation within the public sphere? Moreover, how could I position myself as designer of the project without transgressing the boundary between personal self-expression and the creative distance arising from ethical restraint and self-deferral—an economy of architectural utterances?

On History and Memory

The relation between memory and commemoration on the one hand and history and education on the other is fraught with tension: silence and repose contrast with words and movement. As a Center for Holocaust Studies, its mission is based on the principle that Holocaust memory and learning from and about the Holocaust should be rooted in questions and memory-work as an attempt to construct an understanding of history. Meant to be neither a museum nor a memorial, it was built for a generation that will have to negotiate the twilight zone between the Holocaust as a recollected background and the Holocaust as a historic event, potentially open to dispassionate inspection. This time, as Eric Hobsbawn has observed, is a no-man's-land, characterized by obscurity and fuzziness, resulting from a mixture of second-hand memory shaped by public and private tradition, and dispassionate scholarship. It is by far the hardest part of history to fathom: still part of us, but no longer quite within our personal reach. "It forms something similar to those parti-colored ancient maps filled with unreliable outlines and white spaces, framed by monsters and symbols," Hobsbawn states. "The monsters and symbols are magnified by modern media, because the very fact that the twilight zone is important to us makes it also central to their pre-occupation."[4] Indeed, thanks to the media (*Holocaust, Shoah, Schindler's List*), the Holocaust has become a pivotal image and key marker of contemporary global civilization and culture[5] and has strongly impacted historiography, psychoanalysis, the visual and performing arts, as well as urban studies, public art, landscape design, and architecture.

No longer in it, but part of it, the generations to come can only acquire a provisional identity in relationship to the Holocaust, as it is only the generation of the survivors, saturated with memory, that bears personal witness to the events. With their passing, the ensuing void will begin to haunt the imagination of future generations facing the inaccessible fact of a Holocaust not experienced. Thus, for these new generations, to whom the Holocaust is a mediated experience—a received history constructed primarily through the activation of image-memory—new questions arise. In his recent book *At Memory's Edge*, James Young, in discussing the problems of artistic practices about the Holocaust, expresses three preoccupations that I deeply share:

> First, memory-work about the Holocaust cannot, must not, be redemptive in any fashion. Second, part of what a post-Holocaust generation must ethically represent is the experience of the memory-act itself. Last, the void left behind the destruction of European Jewry demands the reflection previously accorded the horrific details of the destruction itself. [For these artists it] is the memory-work itself, the difficult attempt to know, to imagine vicariously, and to make meaning out of experiences we never knew directly that constitutes the object of memory.[6]

In that light and following an enormous eruption of Holocaust-related art, museums, and memorials based on figural and/or abstract representations of death, despair, destruction, pain, and horror, new attitudes may be possible. While acknowledging the impossibility of representing the Holocaust experience, the generational differences, the limitations of our practices, and the difficulty of proposing meaningful answers to an absent meaning, these new attitudes may sustain the dilemmas of representation, the uncertainties, the necessity for more questions, and the resistance to closure.

The project for the Center for Holocaust Studies is grounded in such attitudes, as neither art nor architecture can—nor should attempt to—compensate for mass murder.[7] What the project does attempt to do, through its architecture and landscape, is to establish a dialogical relation with the Holocaust and its study. As an architectural project, it hopes to suggest and elicit a variety of themes and questions—questions about dwelling and habitation; questions about publicness, tradition, exile, and homecoming; questions about time and space, history and memory, reality and imagination; questions about the Book, the Word, the Other, and the Face;[8] and, perhaps, questions about life and death.

To do so, it was crucial to conceive and construct the Center for Holocaust Studies as a road map, as a spatial topography, condensing voices, opening up spaces for study and dialogue with a measure of spatial clarity and architectural depth. It was also crucial to attempt to inhabit the uninhabitable distance between ourselves and the "Holocaust as a Question," while offering the prospect that this chronological limbo, this no-man's-land, the space between the tomb of memory and the womb of history, may be traversed with generational piety, intellectual honesty, and ethical respect (see Fig. 1).

Boundaries

Architecture is an inherently practical and public art. It is a practical art insofar as purpose is its driving force, the reason why this work was called into being. It is a public art in that the "presence" of the work of architecture, its thingness first and foremost, constructs the space for public appearance, thus helping to "frame the public realm." Architecture operates first as desire, then as intuition and anticipation, and then gets translated and transformed into presence. It involves the poetic reorganization of matter to form purposeful inhabitable space, mediating between the earth and the sky, as setting for life to occur—a tectonic transformation of energy into matter, of image into built form, of site into place. Projects and buildings, while becoming catalysts for the process of memory, bring forth the depth of continuity as well as the desire for ethical transformation. In that, they establish multiple conversations in space and time.[9]

The making of boundaries, which is a fundamental role of architecture, entails constructing new frames for dialogic exchange—framing "presences"; for the boundary (peras), as the Greeks recognized, is not only that point at which something stops, but also the point at which something begins its presencing. This particular project entailed conceiving and constructing a new "presence": a spatial framework for the study of the Holocaust, thereby "framing the presence of Holocaust Memory"—a subject as elusive as the unanswerable questions it proposes. The project thus called for the reconceptualization and transformation of a number of traditional concepts, including those of boundaries and thresholds. Framed by catastrophe, boundaries and thresholds—and their memories in space and time—certainly acquire a different and uncanny dimension. Examples of this dimension may be found in Jean Améry's "Torture": "Although you may previously have walked by the gate of the Gestapo headquarters countless times, it has other perspectives, other ornaments, other ashlars when you cross its threshold as prisoner."[10] Or in Primo Levi's account of the experience of the threshold upon entering the camp, "Whereas for each one of us the moment of entry into the camp acted as the wellspring of a different sequence of memories, closer and sharper, constantly confirmed by present experience, like wounds daily opened."[11]

Accounts like these make clear that the memory of catastrophe, re-presented and brought to presence through writings, testimonies, film, or photography, is tied to real spaces that are no more. These real spaces, like the lager, the ramps, the forest, the tracks, the factories, and the showers, "frame" the remembrance of the "ocean of pain" and constitute a phenomenological backdrop for Celan's *Grave in the Air*, Delbo's *Voices and the Skin of the Memory*, Wiesel's *Endless Night*, or Pagis's *Cloud*. These real spaces have become mythical sites for memory and, in their ruined and estranged condition, have contributed to the construction of a collective imagination of a Holocaust that we can never know or fathom. Neither storytelling nor visits to sites of memory can begin to unfold the inarticulable reality of those boundaries, thresholds, and landscapes present in memory. For as Andre Schwartz Bart has eloquently remarked,

> this story will not finish with some tomb to be visited in pious memoir. For the smoke that rises from crematoria obeys physical laws like

any other: the particles come together and disperse according to the wind, which propels them. The only pilgrimage, dear reader, would be to look sadly at a stormy sky now and then.[12]

Or as Simon Schama—when addressing the unfathomable reality of those horrific landscapes—has clearly reminded us:

> In our mind's eye we are accustomed to think of the Holocaust as having no landscape. Or, at best one emptied of features and color, shrouded in night and fog, bracketed by perpetual winter, collapsed into shades of dun and gray, the gray of smoke and ashes, of pulverized bones, of quick limes. It is shocking to see that Treblinka too belongs to a vivid countryside.[13]

Landscape, Architecture, and Memory

Landscapes and buildings have always been sites for memory, from ruins and mythical gardens to cities and places encompassing diverse cultures and civilizations. For Jewish life in the Diaspora, the absence of "proper locus" involved the construction of a culture of Exile,[14] which, as part of its diasporic sensibility and in response to catastrophe, found expression in "building mimetic sites out of the ruins of original space."[15] It is a culture in which, as Sidra DeKoven Ezrahi observes, "The centrality of 'the Book' entails a wide culture of substitution for or imitation of the territorial dimension; in its devotional procedure and performative substitute for Temple rites, it created the rationale and the instruments for a mobile civilization."[16] References to the spatial and topographical characteristics of mythical places, cities, gardens, landscapes, and territories, which occur throughout the Book, become reenacted through reading and ritual remembrance. As the sense of place was located in the Book, the notion of the "public," or publicness, in Jewish culture, history, and religion, was—before Israel—related not directly to the construction of public space, but rather based on *time in the form of memory and narrative*, and framed by the presence of imagined and mythical mimetic sites.

In order to further some arguments related to the significance of the work of architecture, let us turn to a more specific discussion about architecture and memory. The architectural theorist and historian Stanford Anderson suggests that social memory *through* architecture—as distinct from memory *in* architecture[17]—refers to the uses and typological repetition of built form. An example of this is the repetition of chapels, monuments, sacred places, and domestic architecture, whose forms—their intrinsic form as human institutions, not their specific design—are legitimized by their use and historical continuity. In the aftermath of the Holocaust, Holocaust memorial spaces—and I mean to include all museums, memorials, study centers like the one at Clark, landscapes, remnants of camps, and more—have become a new kind of project. They are an utterly unprecedented type, not bounded or legitimized by use, habitation, or historical continuity, but originating thematically in memory—thematization that adds philosophical and ethical problems to those of representation. They are unprecedented in that their intrinsic qualities should speak to and about an absent meaning, a nonhousable memory, a rupture in history.

As agents of memory, these heterotopic places—constituting places within other places—may operate like literary figures, saying one thing by means of another, acting like tropes of the memory discourse they engender. Their "difference" enables architecture to speak a specific and limited truth, in a space between the question, the public, and the instruments of our practice/art. Social and communal memory *through* architecture may thus work in closer cohesion with memory *in* architecture, while referring directly, indirectly, indexically, analogically, and/or metaphorically to the void left by the destruction, to the absence of tombstones, to Holocaust memory.

The Tomb and the Monument

> When we find a mound in the woods, six feet by three feet, raised to a pyramidal form by means of a spade, we become serious and something in us says, someone was buried here. That is architecture.
> —Adolf Loos, "Architecture"[18]

At the beginning of the twentieth century, Adolf Loos claimed that only a small part of architecture belongs to art: the sepulcher and the monument. Released from the burden of function, the monument is true art, yet if the sepulcher and the monument were to be understood thematically, they would not, in fact, escape the universe of function. What Loos meant to assert, according to Massimo Cacciari,[19] is that art takes place in the idea of sepulcher and monument: the idea of a place of exception, to which life has led, but that transcends or reopens life's function. If considered as an aesthetic object, the mound in the forest would hardly qualify as a piece of art or as a work of architecture. But as Karsten Harries observes, "More important to Loos is the ethical function: the confrontation with death prevents us from going on with the usual business of life and carries us to another place, a place that lies, usually well submerged, within the self."[20] What matters is not who lies buried, but that a human being lies buried. Thus, genuine art, as Loos understands it, invites us to take leave of what we usually call reality, to free us to return to our true selves.

More permanent than ours on earth, houses of the dead demonstrate the continuity of those dead in the minds of the living. In that, and as the boundary of life, death continues to offer the living intimations of a personal self-transcendence, for while a house gives shelter and signifies life and habitation, a tomb signifies a world beyond. Thus the significance of the tomb proceeds both from the knowledge of an inevitable death in which the secret of space reveals itself, and from its action as a reminder of that inevitable condition.

Alois Riegl claimed that "a monument in its oldest and most original sense is a human creation, erected for the specific purpose of keeping single human deeds or events . . . alive in the mind of future generations."[21] Since "monument" derives from "monere," meaning "to remind, to warn, or to advise," we may perceive that instead of a form, a shape, or an image, monumentality is a quality—the ability that some places or objects have to evoke something beyond themselves, something much larger, related to our own humanity in the form of questions.

So, following Loos, it could be argued that Holocaust memorials and Holocaust-related projects may entail that paramount condition for artistic practice in architecture, for they are places of exception, to which life, or better, the destruction of life, has led. They are places of exception, for *in the absence of tombstones, Holocaust memorials can function as a mourning site.* They exist to remind us of that absence; as agents carrying the burden of this specific historical memory or trauma, they may be considered a *radical negative, both the nontomb and the nonmonument.* They may be conceptualized as "countermonuments,"[22] as James Young puts it, presenting extremely difficult yet interesting challenges for architecture and public space.

Charged with combining memory, remembrance, and mourning, these places are produced to be historically referential. Public Holocaust monuments and related projects refer to past events *because* they are no longer present.[23] Their material presence is meant somehow to turn invisible, transparent, bridging between the individual memory-work and the events they recall. As *embodiments of memory through art in the public realm, their value is not based on the public artwork, but in a certain point beyond themselves;* it lies in the public dimension and "dialogic character of memorial space."[24]

As an expression of an ultimate aspiration for permanence and durability transcending mortality and charged with the task of enabling and fostering questions in space, projects like the one at Clark may emerge as a paradoxical architectural statement: one that may speak about the impossibility of Holocaust representations, while at the same time affirming their necessity in the public sphere.

The Center for Holocaust Studies (Figs. 1–5)

The Site

Any architectural endeavor is an interference with its site, with a previous reality, a material geography, an archaeological foundation that hands down its memory through traces in transformation into architectural substance. Thus, the import and subsequent anchoring of new significations to the site at Clark University required that one be respectful of the preexisting, paired with the radical circumstance of this particular "innocent" site being charged with an enormous new task. This site, which paradoxically includes a paradigmatic image of the American nineteenth-century "homely," would be asked to "welcome" the most abhorrent of all crimes in human history and become a host for the memory of the Holocaust.

Fig. 1. Host house and Library/Reading Room addition. Photograph by Tom Lingner/Vanderwarker Photographs.

So again, how can an uncanny, unhousable, "foreign," and enormously loaded subject be landed, anchored, and "housed" in an untainted, "innocent" site in Worcester? How can an existing site, which includes a preexisting Colonial Revival structure never intended to "house" a subject like the Holocaust, be transformed into a Holocaust site?

At the sites of destruction, Holocaust memory becomes a kind of "object" that needs to be found, excavated, reenacted, and evoked, requiring a deliberate act of memory, for, by themselves, these sites lack the will to remember.[25] Without this deliberate act, the ruins remain little more than inert pieces of the landscape. Remnants of the camps tend to negate the distinction between themselves and that which they evoke. As James Young warns, "They invite us to mistake the debris of history for history itself."[26]

Still in—yet removed from—Worcester, this particular site becomes an imaginary landscape, transporting visitors, scholars, and students to distant places and landscapes. As the project's ultimate function is to "host" and "house" the study of something enormously disquieting—a tragic memory around which we should never feel comfortable—the site becomes haunted from without, with new stories, new displacements, new exiles, and, perhaps, new hopes. It is a host taken hostage by *different* ghosts.[27] Asked to "house" the memory of the Holocaust, Lasry House/the Center for Holocaust Studies is faced with the task of housing that memory that is neither "at home" with itself,[28] nor housable at all. Its domesticity, scale, and architectural qualities become alienated from themselves; it is no longer a "house" for domestic habitation, but a "house for an uninhabitable memory."

Estrangement

The very idea of the "haunted house," and in this case the "haunted structure," the "haunted site," the "haunted district," opens up questions about habitation (*Casa Tomada* by Julio Cortazar or any of Edgar A. Poe's haunted houses could serve as reference). This is not a haunted house per se; it is the relation to the story to be studied here, and how that story becomes part of the space, that makes the uncanny qualities of memory and architecture come to light. Anthony Vidler observes in *The Architectural Uncanny* that "for Freud, 'uncomeliness' . . . was the fundamental propensity of the familiar to turn on its owners, suddenly to become defamiliarized, derealized, as in a dream."[29] Approaching the uncanny as a metaphor for an unlivable modern condition—estrangement from the world, the world experienced as "not at home"—entails understanding that "the stabilizing function of architecture, by which the familiar is made to appear part of a natural—or conserved—landscape, will be subverted by the antithetical effects of the unfamiliar," as James Young observes.[30]

So, if the Holocaust represents the very paradigm of the Modern unhomely, and if the very idea and power of the uncanny to affect us arise from the transformation of something that once seemed familiar and homely into something strange and unhomely, as Freud suggested, part of this project's task was to make this transformation explicit in the form of architectural and landscape questions. To achieve this, a radical transformation was required to land and ground memories foreign to this site, a transformation that required a balanced action, treading the fine line between muteness and expression, between the familiar and the unfamiliar—while avoiding any romanticized version of history—in order to rethematize the existing historical context at Clark. Thus, it seemed appropriate to approach the conflicting relationship between "historic and imaginative narratives" through an interplay, integration, and intertwining of the preexisting historic structure and the new addition and garden,[31] a humble, nonredemptive, and respectful interplay framing the new architectural narratives within this specific historic context (Fig. 1 and Fig. 2c–2d).

The Project

The scheme proposes the integration of the old and the new beyond appearances, establishing a connection between the historic and the aesthetic filtered through multiple levels of intense ethical-architectural dialogue—a dialogue between the host house and the site—while adding a new layer to the historical record of the city. The different components of Lasry House—the preexisting structure, the library addition, and the Forested Mound in the Holocaust Memorial Garden—are to be seen as a new integral whole, while at the same time exposing a horizon of disconnections and absences. This new whole, called into being by insurmountable questions, hopes to suggest that the Question itself becomes *the* Architectural Theme.

The project presents what could be thought of as a multivocal history, in which no single, overarching meaning emerges unchallenged. Instead, the preexisting Colonial Revival house, the monolithic addition, and the Holocaust Memorial Garden seek to generate a "*frisson*[32] *of meaning in their dialogic exchange,*" suggesting a form of spatial and programmatic "integrated commentary." The presence of an alien that is never an alien in close relation to the defamiliarized host house, and the presence of new ghosts within the old host hope to suggest a strong yet balanced estrangement effect, expressive of a disquieting historical uniqueness. The attempt is to engage the observer in the search for memory through the absence of direct signs, making palpable the idea of space for memory-work, in opposition to memory-object, working "against the tendency of displacement,"[33] or the reduction of the viewer to passive spectator. Concepts such as difference, hierarchy reversal, iteration, displacement, and dialogism, utilized as design techniques, were used to expose continuities, ruptures, transformations, contrasts, extensions, and multiple levels of dialogue.

Movement through the site is radically transformed, as the new entrance goes through the garden, leading to the entry/exhibition area in the renovated basement. Rather than entering from the street to the "Piano Nobile" of the host house—a tradition of entrance that can be traced back to the Renaissance—the visitor walks around the site, which slows and delays both entrance and departure. Thus, the "welcome" into a seemingly familiar environment is paired with the estrangement of entering through the once totally derelict cellar or basement, creating a radical convolution of the historical hierarchy of the Victorian era. The memories of a Victorian domestic tradition are thus "shaken" through a slippage of the subject (the Holocaust and its study) onto the ground, which "haunts" the preexisting structure from underneath. The surface of the ground plane, the plane of human existence, is exposed to an estrangement process, and is disrupted through the landing, the slippage, and grounding of this particular additional layer of history. It is the ground, the wounded surface of the earth, that is the setting for the primary transformations; the new programmatic elements such as the garden, the exhibition area, and the library-reading room all occupy that space, creating "a new ground for Holocaust studies."

Memory Box

The project is constructed via a precise relation between the addition —the Memory Box—and the house through the use of materials, contrasts, textures, composition, proportions, and details (Fig. 1 and Fig. 2c–2d). The new addition does not seek to dominate, but rather retreats, complementing the preexisting structure in the creation of new spatial events. It appears as a "Memory Box," sitting on or "floating" above concrete walls emerging from the ground and sliding beneath the volume to form garden walls. These walls complement and complete the system of stone walls around the host house. The addi-

Fig. 2. Details of the Reading Room addition showing *(a)* desks and slot window (vertical cut) in axis with courtyard, *(b)* skylights ("cuts into the sky"), *(c)* lateral view of exterior (planes, continuities, dialogues), and *(d)* zinc-clad "Memory Box" on concrete walls. Photograph by Tom Lingner/Vanderwarker Photographs.

tion presents itself as familiar in scale, but monolithic in nature. Its proportions are 5:3:3. Materials such as zinc and glass that would offer the starkest contrast with the existing building were introduced in order not to compete with the old wood clapboard and details. The zinc-clad skin, consisting of preweathered zinc shingles, offers neutrality and a possibility of "mute" expression. It was intended to have a sort of "underdesigned" appearance, with minimal but sharp, complex detailing—a textured monolith.[34] The metal surface complements and contrasts, with its patina and blue-gray color, the wood clapboard of the house, enhancing the details of cornices, pilasters, trim, and windows. By contrast, windows in the addition are never windows in the traditional sense; rather they are cuts, ruptures, and punctuations.

As a key architectural element in the project, the wood watertable extends outward from the host house, "grabbing" the addition, and creating the new entrance canopy to the entry/exhibition room in the basement (Fig. 1 and Fig. 2c). It also serves as the horizontal datum from which all dimensions and measurements—structure, cladding, heights—in the addition begin. As multivalent architectural element, it connects yet separates the old and the new, suggesting both historical ruptures and continuities, while radically reversing, both formally and historically, the significance of the watertable line in the traditional New England house. Formally, the traditional relation between lightness and heaviness is based on a light frame sitting on a solid foundation.[35] Historically, the watertable signifies the "difference" between habitation in "the House"—which occurs above the watertable datum within the tectonics of the wood frame—and the derelict space occupied by storage and ghosts within the stereotomics of the stone found in cellars[36] and basements. The extension of the watertable into the addition not only becomes the entrance canopy, but also creates a horizontal line establishing continuities, as well as reversing and challenging traditional visual and structural relations. The traditional "wood sitting over stone"—color over opaque gray mass—becomes "zinc floating over glass"—gray metal over transparent or reflective material.

The addition sits close to the host house but is separated by a gap, a void, a rift at the core of the project. This gap, spatial evidence of the distance between the historical and the modern, creates a "zone in between" the old host and the new alien. It is a void, which allows both "histories" to coexist; it is a "silence in between architectural utterances" (Fig. 3). The key space in this zone is the small courtyard; within it, lifted from the ground on a concrete slab at seat level, a tree works as an inaccessible fragment of nature, inserted between the old and new structures. This gap or rift between the two serves both to link and to separate them: a present, yet denied, space. The compositional geometry, the organization of the plan, and the movement pattern of the building all revolve around that zone, more precisely, around the tree. Views to the courtyard and the tree from the exhibition room and the reading room are similarly framed, with large surfaces of glass and window seats, allowing for transparency and reflection. The low moment of passage (seven foot ceiling) between the library and the reading room is marked by views of the tree through a single vertical slot window, a cut between two work desks (Fig. 2a).

Fig. 3. Inside the "Memory Box" looking toward the host house through the courtyard with tree ("a silence in between" / "framing presences and absences" / "the zone of dialogue"). Photograph by Tom Lingner/Vanderwarker Photographs.

In the double height reading room (fifteen feet), space is defined by the presence of the "other." Its large windows "frame" views through the "zone of dialogue," calling up the presence of the past into the space of the present. Its limit, its boundary occurs at the "face of the architectural other" (Fig. 3 and Fig. 4a). Low windows "cut" the wood wainscot and the concrete walls. Skylights "cut" through the muted plaster surface and the zinc skin, capturing a portion of the sky (Fig. 2b). Transparency and reflection[37] blur precise volumetric and spatial boundaries and present questions about time and memory, not directly, but through intimation, needing to be read and interpreted. It is a new and humane place, in which a horrific story will be discussed, voiced, collected, and written about. It exists through light and for dialogue, filled with words, books, and ghosts: a Memory

Room. It opens to the courtyard, to the street, to the sky, and to the garden (Fig. 3 and Fig. 4a).

The Library: Paper and Stones

This scholars' library contains a special core collection of books about the Holocaust, placed mostly on the eastern wall, within the cellar of the host house (Fig. 4b). This small yet select collection, acting as both witness and testimony to be read, explored, and pondered, is kept mainly in the "Wall of Books," which extends throughout the length of the space. As a detail, the bookcases turn into desks, transforming the archive into reading space. Placed in the axis of the departure from the main reading room and framed by the Wall of Books is a sculpture by Joe Nicastri, consisting of a horizontal steel I-beam supporting a grouping of burned Hebrew and Yiddish books. It operates as a Memory Catalyst, opening an uncanny dialogue between the bluntness of the burned books in the sculpture, and the books about the "burning of the people of the Book."

It is not the direct bluntness of the sculpture, but its position in relation to the other books and its placement in the axis of the departure that acts as a reminder, as a witness, establishing a dialogical dimension with the study of the Holocaust, upon leaving. It is a direct and uncanny metaphor, perhaps quoting Heine's words in space, "Where books are burned, one day people will be burned as well." This uncanny and provocative dialogue acts as a Memory Catalyst and could also be considered a Holocaust effect, following Ernst van Alphen.[38] It is a Holocaust effect in the sense that, as a reenactment and not a presentation, "it does something instead of showing," as it transforms one's experience in space, as spectator, as user, as scholar, through the presence of the burned, the unreadable books, surrounded by readable ones.

The Ugly Garden

It is fair to say that to the general public, landscapes usually appear benign and passive. As images that evoke a virtuous-benevolent nature, they are typically viewed as a soothing antithesis to the sterile

Fig. 4. Interior spaces: *(a)* Library/Reading Room area (wood continui-
ties, window cuts) and *(b)* Bookcase area with Nicastri's sculpture on axis
("Burned Books" framed by readable ones). Photograph by Tom Lingner/
Vanderwarker Photographs.

frenzy of urban life. A combination of consumerism and nostalgia linked to the pastoral and the gardenesque drives this vision, suppressing invention and experimentation. A conservative attitude toward landscape may signify a loss of will to forge new landscapes, a distrust of innovation, or may simply be a sign of a culture seeking escape from the present in the idealized images of the past. Landscapes are not only the stewardship of the natural world, but are cultural constructs; therefore, they could be conceived as an innovative medium, dislocating regressive aspects of society and reorganizing nature in a life-enriching way.

In the aftermath of the Holocaust, and as Simon Schama observed, "after the confidence of the Enlightenment had been engulfed in catastrophe, after the picturesque and the sublime had been chewed up by war and fertilized by bones and blood of the unnumbered dead,"[39] we can no longer perceive the European territory as merely a series of scenic landscapes for pastoral picnics. So, in conceiving this small Holocaust Memorial Garden dedicated to the memory of the destruction of European Jewry, which is inextricably bound to a destroyed land, it became painfully clear that a different design strategy was required. Conceiving this Memorial Garden as evocative of the damaged horizontal space of history, evocative of the wounded crust of the earth and of the "ocean of pain," while anchoring the "subject" onto the site at Clark, called for a bold and strong landscape operation.

Landscapes have the capacity to critically engage the metaphysical and the mythical, not only because of their physical and experiential characteristics, but also because of their eidetic capacity to contain and express ideas and so to engage the mind. This Holocaust Memorial Garden was designed to become an active instrument in the shaping of our imagination of the Holocaust—an *ugly* garden. The Forested Mound—an essential component of the project as a whole—traced, condensed, and collapsed many historical and contemporary myths about territory and landscape (Fig. 5). It consisted of an egg-shaped earthform covered with ivy, twenty-five feet by fifty feet, and four feet high at its peak. Twenty-five young white birch trees were planted on top, creating a dense grove. In spatial terms, the Forested Mound occupied the center of the garden. In doing so, it displaced space, creating two zones of very different character: one

Fig. 5. Before and after: "Forested Mound" and "Erasure." Photograph by Julian Bonder.

leading to the street, and the other to the quiet courtyard. Coming to the fore, as a "landscape object," the Forested Mound produced an estrangement effect intended to provoke questions. These questions would challenge the observer's preconceptions about nature and artifice, Holocaust representations, landscape and memory, presenting a myriad of ideas—ideas that ranged from the relationship between artifice and nature to those about paradise,[40] the Mountain, exile, renewal, and displacement. Some have seen in it themes about the European territories, birch forests (Birkenau), persecution, escape, *ugliness*, beauty; while others have read in it an inaccessible core, an eruption of both pain and life, a deeper darker reality under the surface, under the skin of the earth, burial and regeneration, and more. By utilizing a very "innocent" but potent medium in a poetic way, we attempted to challenge viewers seeking a single overarching meaning or expecting "things" to "represent the Holocaust." If anything, it acted as a Memory Catalyst or, borrowing from Ernst van Alphen, as a Holocaust effect in that it did not seek "to represent," but "to do something."

A very important purpose of this "landscape-object" was to become a third object in space: a kind of a witness—in the sense that Levinas[41] suggests for the third in dialogue—balancing the architectural dialogue of the other components of the project, the house and the addition. It also belonged to or participated in an ancient tradition in landscaping, found in many cultures over many centuries, which understands landscape as *"the shaping of the land."* This Garden, while not designed as a representation of death, despair, and horror, was not about redemption through nature either—though as with any landscape, it could be suggestive of rebirth, growth, and healing in time. The hope was that it would have served as a metaphor for inclusive multiplicity and pluralism; that by being almost empty, it would have created a kind of synthetic overview enabling differences, controversies, and questions to play themselves out. In time, the Mound was to become green, covered with ivy; the very young birch trees were to become a grove, a knoll, a forest; and the hedge was to construct the limits this outdoor room needed. It would have become a room for memory-work in the form of multiple questions, a room to be read and interpreted in many possible ways. It would be a room that, by being almost empty, would have welcomed the voices of others.

Erasure/Destruction

Immediately after the building's opening, I was made aware that the Memorial Garden had caused discomfort:

> *"What does it mean?" "Is it really that?" "How could someone allow for such an ugly landscape?" "The building is the Anti-culture, the mound is the burial of culture!" "This is a burial mound and make no mistake, burial mounds look like burial mounds, even though they become covered with grass and flowers." "This is an art form and the intent is lost upon the viewer."*

Professors, donors, and the then-president of the university became engaged in a war against the Forested Mound, arriving all too soon to an ill-informed decision to erase it, with no official reason other than its appearance. Despite its approval and its construction; despite the numerous, and respectful, letters and calls requesting an explanation for the logic behind the destruction; despite the many scholars[42] and professionals who praised its evocative, poetic, and educative qualities, and raised concerns about the significance of destroying it; despite the very paradoxical fact that they would be destroying a landscape memorial designed to anchor the Holocaust story to this particular site, and to evoke the destruction of European Jewry; despite a number of professors who, aware of their previous mistake, called for a revision of the decision; nonetheless, on April 10–11, 2000, the trees were uprooted and the dirt removed. University officials had the "Forested Mound" leveled, leaving a scar where the forest was to have grown (see small image in Fig. 5). This act of destruction, committed in order to reclaim "their property," asserts a particular view of the notion of "appropriateness." What is "appropriate"—in light of a "garden dedicated to the victims of the Holocaust," as its dedication plaque reads—thus became a complex and central question, as the garden's removal entailed a paradoxically violent double erasure: erasure of the landscape piece and erasure of the ideas behind its creation.

Ugliness

What was so disturbing about this "innocent" landscape form? Was it its form, or its evocative power? Was it what some "saw" it may have represented? Was it its "ugliness"? Ugliness[43] can be thought of not simply as the negation of beauty, but as having a real, independent dimension. The ugly object is experienced as that which is there and should not be there, as an object in the wrong place. In Judaism, early ideas about sin were not described in terms of ethics, but as the material problem of the stain. The stain should not be there and must be removed. So it is the dirt, the dirt that must have crossed the boundary and been where it should not be. Dirt is an "ugly" deduction from "good" space and threatens to contaminate and disrupt.

Furthermore, ugliness transforms topological identities: the beautiful object retains its real size, while the ugly object becomes much larger than it is. Thus, the ugly object has spatial power quite lacking in the beautiful one. Rather than a lack (of beauty), it is an excess that threatens the subject. It exposes the precariousness of the subject, especially the subject's relation to objects in space. When exposed to the ugly object, one that is there and should not be, or one that is not there and should be, the subject's response is twofold: to destroy the object or to abandon the position of the subject.

The ugly object was destroyed, the dirt removed. The ideas behind the "Forested Mound" and its "threatening presence" were eliminated and transformed into memory. The "good" space was recovered, though the place was left with an evocative scar. As David Eisen, architectural critic of the *Boston Herald*, wrote:

> It is the scar left when Clark University officials had a mound sprouting a grove of trees ripped from the ground because [this] evocative landscape was deemed too powerful. One can hardly imagine a better reminder that intolerance for the new and different will always be with us. Although this destruction may diminish the strength of the Center's design, the addition remains a strong campus presence. Embraced by the earth around its solid concrete walls, yet floating free on ribbons of glass, it mirrors the complex relationship the Holocaust has with history.[44]

This mirroring continues through action, not through representation. Certainly, as the controversy over the Forested Mound and what it "could have represented, meant or signified to some" has shown, the piece has elicited strong reactions and violent responses. It is an unfortunate fact that part of its own history, as a project, includes such an unexpected and paradoxical episode: a garden designed to commemorate the Holocaust had become part of a story of destruction. But much more important than any controversy, without any doubt, is the fact that the building is being utilized quite successfully by the Clark community at large, as a Center for Scholarship and Holocaust Education. I say this with heartfelt respect and admiration for the academic undertaking—the "academic and the thinking action"—as well as with the proud joy of knowing that the spaces I created continue to elicit strong reactions and positive responses.

During the months of the controversy and after the erasure—as well as later, when the garden had been redesigned in an "unchallenging" manner—I asked myself on numerous occasions about the significance of such a paradoxical act of destruction. While many people have suggested that this act has proven that the piece produced a strong and disturbing effect, thus rendering its value—its "ugliness" —much larger, important questions will remain unanswered. Questions such as what constitutes "appropriate" work, or on what grounds the "appropriateness" of Holocaust-related art, architectural, and landscape works will be judged by users and the public, continue to be very important and difficult ones. For we have to remember that, as Michael Berenbaum suggested in his presentation at Clark University when discussing the building and the garden, "A subject like the Holocaust simply will not, and should not fit comfortably in academia—or in any other place—because there is nothing comfortable about it."[45]

Conclusion: Memory-Work

This project did not and does not seek to represent the Holocaust. As I mentioned earlier, the main intentions of the project were, first, to establish a place where scholars could gather together and study and, second, to propose questions in space, establishing a dialogic relation with the Holocaust and its study. As a work on the memory of the Holocaust *through* architecture, it has entailed and continues to entail an attempt to generate and foster dialogue, to present ethical questions and a mode of being in space that is in sharp contrast with the story at its core. Its ultimate task is to make room for the echoes of an uncanny past to be heard in a humane environment created for reflection, study, and dialogue: *a room for Memory-Work.*

If anything, the friction, the dialogic exchange, the material contrast, and the radical transformation seek to offer a spatial approximation—first, of the creative tension found in scholarly study and research, and second, of the complex relation between history and memory—the "twilight zone." It seeks to help illuminate in time and space the difficult questions to be continuously asked, while deferring any attempt to represent, through spatial gestures or dramatization, the Holocaust experience. For no matter how dark, vast, or complex spaces may be, the Holocaust doesn't fit in any space.

NOTES

1. Primo Levi, "Shame," in *Art from the Ashes*, ed. Lawrence Langer (Oxford: Oxford University Press, 1995), 117.
2. Sigmund Freud, "The Uncanny," quoted by Anthony Vidler, *The Architectural Uncanny* (Cambridge: MIT Press, 1992), 14.
3. Instrumental in the realization of this project were Dr. Deborah Dwork, director of the Center, who kindly invited me to give physical form to the Center, and whose enlightened guidance, clarity, and creative energy were paramount to its realization; Robert Jan van Pelt, who contributed throughout the process with very valuable insight and criticism; my associate architect David Honn, whose knowledge, friendship, and collaboration contributed enormously to the development of the construction aspects of the project; Paul Bottis, Physical Plant Director at Clark; and especially all the people who contributed with their hard work and skills to the transformation of ideas represented in drawings into material realities.
4. Eric Hobsbawn, *The Age of Empire, 1875–1914* (New York: Vintage Books, 1989), 5.
5. A culture that, since the 1980s, has developed an obsessive pursuit of memory, as attested by the large body of literature that has emerged in science and the humanities on the role of memory, commemoration, amnesia, and other related matters. It is also important to note that only in recent decades have ideologies of progress come to be seen as the dark side of modernity, and in most accounts of that darkness, the Holocaust, representing a paradoxical paradigm of progress, plays a central role in the crisis of modernity and memory. If modernity freed the West from the constraints of memory, during postmodernity it seems to be struggling between amnesia and obsession with the past. The concerns with memory can be seen as a defining cultural symptom at the end of the millennium; and the fascination with the past may perhaps be seen as a compensatory form in the fast process toward oblivion. In that, museums and memorials may be functioning as a key paradigm of contemporary postmodern culture. As Andreas Huyssen observes, "The newfound strength of the museum and the monument in the public sphere may have something to do with the fact that they both offer something that the television screen denies: the material quality of the object." See Andreas Huyssen, "Monument and Memory in a Postmodern Age," in *The Art of Memory*, ed. James Young (New York: Prestel, 1994), 16.

6. James Young, *At Memory's Edge* (New Haven: Yale University Press, 2000), 9.
7. Sidra Ezrahi writes, "Even or especially in the wake of catastrophe, a 're-demptive aesthetic' often emerges in the affected communities along-side public acts of commemoration to create regenerative spaces." She refers to the idealized function of art when discussing Leo Bersani's crit-ical reading of a crucial assumption in the culture of redemption, an as-sumption that proposes that "a certain type of repetition of experience in art repairs inherently damaged or valueless experience. . . . The ca-tastrophes of history matter much less if they are somehow compensated for in art . . . the redemptive aesthetic asks us to consider art as a cor-rection of life." Sidra DeKoven Ezrahi, *Booking Passage: Exile and Home-coming in the Jewish Modern Imagination* (Berkeley: University of California Press, 2000), 144.
8. Emmanuel Levinas writes,

   Knowledge seizes hold of its object. It possesses it. . . . Speech addresses itself to a face. The face, for its part is inviolable; those eyes, which are absolutely without protection, the most naked part of the Human body, none the less offer an ab-solute resistance to possession, an absolute resistance in which the temptation of murder is inscribed: the temptation of absolute negation. The Other is the only being that one can be tempted to kill. This temptation to murder and this im-possibility of murder constitute the very vision of the Face. To see a face is already to hear "you shall not kill," and to hear "you shall not kill" is to hear Social Jus-tice. "You shall not kill" is therefore not just a simple rule of conduct; it appears as the principle of discourse itself and of spiritual life. . . . Henceforth, language is not only a system of signs in the service of a pre-existing system.

   Speech, according to Levinas, belongs to the order of morality before belonging to that of theory. See Emmanuel Levinas, "Ethics and Spirit," in *Difficult Freedom: Essays on Judaism*, trans. Sean Hand (Baltimore: Johns Hopkins University Press, 1990), 8.
9. Other projects I have worked on around the subject of memory and ar-chitecture include a memorial for AMIA (Asociacion Mutual Israelita Argentina), bombed in a terrorist attack in 1994 in Buenos Aires; a proj-ect for a Holocaust museum in Buenos Aires (with M. Berenbaum and Y. Mais); a project for the Martin Luther King Memorial Competition in Washington, D.C.; and a memorial project for the Victims of State-Spon-sored Violence in Buenos Aires.
10. Jean Améry, "Torture," in *Art from the Ashes*, by Lawrence Langer (Ox-ford: Oxford University Press, 1995), 125.

11. Primo Levi, as quoted by Giovanni Leoni in "The First Blow," in *Holocaust Remembrance*, ed. G. Hartman (Oxford: Blackwell, 1994), 208.

12. As quoted by James Young, *The Texture of Memory* (New Haven: Yale University Press, 1993), 1.

13. See Simon Schama, *Landscape and Memory* (New York: Vintage Books, 1996), 26.

14. For a compelling work on architecture and exile, see Stanley Tigerman, *The Architecture of Exile* (New York: Rizzoli, 1988).

15. Ezrahi, *Booking Passage*, 145.

16. Ibid., 13.

17. Anderson distinguishes between "memory through architecture" and "memory in architecture." Put differently, the distinction is between "societal memory carried in architecture" as opposed to "the operation of memory within the discipline itself." Anderson argues that the advent of writing and history invites an increasing distinction between memory systems, while vernacular tradition (architecture without architects, or history without historians, or art without artists) represents a closer cohesion of social and disciplinary memory. Memory *in* architecture refers to the actual conception, creation, and translation of architectural ideas into architectural facts. It refers to both means and methods, as well as to the continuities and ruptures within the field of operation of architecture. Hence construction, invention, and uses direct us to the discovery of architecture as a discipline, whose forms and organizations are not deterministically derived from social forces. See Stanford Anderson, "Memory and Architecture," *Daidalos* 58 (December 1995): 22–37. For a discussion on the autonomy of architecture, see the seminal work by Manfredo Tafuri, *The Sphere and the Labyrinth* (Cambridge: MIT Press, 1987).

18. Adolf Loos, "Architecture," in *Spoken into the Void: Collected Essays* (Cambridge: MIT Press, 1993).

19. Massimo Cacciari, *Architecture and Nihilism: On the Philosophy of Modern Architecture* (New Haven: Yale University Press, 1993). See chapter 19, "On Loos Tomb," 195–98.

20. Karsten Harries, *The Ethical Function of Architecture* (Cambridge: MIT Press, 1997), 292.

21. Alois Riegl, "The Modern Cult of Monuments: Its Character and Origin," trans. Kurt Foster and Diane Ghirardo, *Oppositions* 25, as quoted by Vidler, *Architectural Uncanny*, 177.

22. James Young writes, "How to celebrate the fall of a totalitarian regime, which celebrated itself through totalitarian art like the monument than to celebrate the fall of the Monument? A monument against itself, a

'countermonument': memorial spaces conceived to challenge the very premise of the monument." He also suggests, with Horst Hoheisel, the notion that "better a thousand years of competitions than a single final solution to Germany's memorial problem." See the chapter on the countermonument in Young, *At Memory's Edge*, 90–119.

23. Young, *Texture of Memory*, 12.
24. Ibid., 11.
25. Young, *Art of Memory*, 23.
26. Ibid., 24.
27. I am making a somewhat ad hoc spatial-architectural interpretation of the words "host" and "hostage," following Derrida's reading of Levinas's discussion of the Face and the Welcome as it refers to Ethics and Hospitality. Derrida writes,

> We must thus think—and think as having, in the end, the same aim—this other way of inhabiting, of welcoming or of being welcomed. The Host is Hostage insofar as he is a subject put into question, obsessed (and thus besieged), persecuted, in the very place where he takes place, where, as emigrant, exile, stranger, a guest from the very beginning, he finds himself elected to or taken up by residence before himself electing or taking one up.

See Jacques Derrida, "A Word of Welcome," in *Adieu to Emmanuel Levinas* (Stanford: Stanford University Press, 1999), 56.

28. "It is that memory of historical events which never domesticates such events, never makes us at home with them, never brings them into the reassuring house of redemptory meaning." Young, *At Memory's Edge*, 155.
29. Vidler, *Architectural Uncanny*, 7.
30. Young, *At Memory's Edge*, 154.
31. It has been interesting to filter and see my work through the lens of concepts such as "Mimetic Approximation" as proposed by Andreas Huyssen and "Holocaust effect" as proposed by Ernst van Alphen. As Huyssen writes, "Mimetic approximation is a mnemonic strategy which recognizes the event in its otherness and beyond identification or therapeutic empathy but which physically relieves some of the horror and pain through the persistent labor of remembrance." Huyssen, "Monument and Memory in a Postmodern Age," 12.

    And, as Ernst van Alphen writes,

> When I use the term Holocaust effect, I do so to emphasize a contrast with Holocaust representation. A representation is by definition mediated. It is an objectified account. The Holocaust is made present in the representation of it by means of reference to it. When I call something a Holocaust effect, I mean to say that

we are not confronted with a representation of the Holocaust, but that we, as viewers or readers, experience directly a certain aspect of the Holocaust or of Nazism, of that which led to the Holocaust. In such moments the Holocaust is not re-presented but rather presented or reenacted.

Ernst van Alphen, *Caught by History: Holocaust Effects in Art, Literature, and Theory* (Stanford: Stanford University Press, 1997), 10.

32. Friction and dialogism were always key concepts in the design process. It was interesting to find Young mentioning the "frisson of dialogic exchange" when discussing historiography and meaning. See Young, *At Memory's Edge*, 15.

33. When transferred onto an object or icon, memory is placed outside ourselves, perhaps displaced altogether, thus relieving the viewer or community from the burden of memory-work. The massive repetition of memorials, words, and images about the Holocaust seems to be producing a "liberating" effect. As James Young warns, "under the illusion that our memorial edifices will always be there to remind us, we take leave of them and return only at our convenience. To the extent that we encourage our monuments to do our memory-work for us, we become much more forgetful. In effect, the initial impulse to memorialize events like the Holocaust may actually spring from an opposite and equal desire to forget them." See Young, *Texture of Memory*, 5.

34. In a very generous article, the architecture critic David Eisen wrote, "The addition is a somber metallic cube whose austerity challenges the cheerful normalcy of the neighborhood. Like a deep dark secret only partially masked by its neighbor's happy facades, it evokes the memory of civilization's darkest moment. . . . It strikes a compelling balance between the rationality of pure geometries and the evocative power of space and light. Walls of books wrapped in plaster, concrete and glass allow the Holocaust's unfathomable horrors to touch both the mind and soul." David Eisen, Architectural Section, *Sunday Boston Herald,* July 2, 2000.

35. I am alluding to the tectonics of the frame, a spatial matrix constructed through the assemblage of lightweight linear components, over the stereotomics (stereo, solid; tomia, to cut) of the earthwork, wherein mass and volume are constructed through the repetitious piling up of heavyweight elements or poured concrete. For a very complete discussion about architecture and tectonics, see Kenneth Frampton, *Studies on Tectonic Culture* (Cambridge: MIT Press, 1995).

36. See Gaston Bachelard, *The Poetics of Space* (Boston: Beacon Press, 1994).

37. Anthony Vidler argues, "Modernity has been haunted by a myth of trans-

parency, transparency of the self to nature, to the other, of all selves to society . . . both represented and constructed by a universal transparency of building materials, spatial penetration and flow of light, movement, and air." Transparency also functions to open architecture up to inspection. Its walls hide no secrets. Glass reveals its own opacity. Under the sign of opacity the universalism of modernity is constructed on the myth of the universal subject. Literal transparency is of course notoriously difficult to attain; it quickly turns into obscurity (its opposite) and reflectivity (its reversal).

Mirror reflection and its uncanny effects were noted by Freud. The proximity of the familiar and the strange causes a "profound modification of the object, which from the familiar is transformed into the strange, and as strange something that provokes disquiet because of its absolute proximity." Space itself is deformed by this experience. If, as Freud had implied, "the feeling of the uncanny implies the return to that particular organization of space where everything is reduced to inside and outside where the inside is also the outside, then the space of the mirror would meet this condition: a space of normal binocular, three-dimensional vision, modified by being deprived by depth. Leading to the conflation of the familiar (seen) and the strange (projected)." See the chapter on transparency in Vidler, *Architectural Uncanny*, 216–25.

38. See Ernst van Alphen, "Deadly Historians," in *Caught by History: Holocaust Effects in Art, Literature, and Theory* (Stanford: Stanford University Press, 1997), 93–122.

39. Van Alphen, *Caught by History*, 19.

40.

Eden the first and only paradise (a walled garden). Made by the hand of God, the garden has always been unknowable, though subject to speculation. Architecturally indecipherable, its boundaries limited only by imagination, it has perplexed geographers, philosophers, theologians, archeologists and, in particular, architects. The Garden of Eden is the natural resolution of a planet earth reduced in scale to palpable comprehension. The Garden of Eden, the first home of mankind, is the archetypal expression of the experience of the sacred geography in the Bible. It is comprised of various components, which appear in Genesis 2,3: 1. Eden is located on a Mountain, a mountain of God, a designation not explicitly stated in Genesis 2:4 bff., although Eden's elevation is suggested through the fact of downward coursing streams. Eden is characterized as a Mountain in Ezekiel 28:13, where this motif is used to satirize the king of Tyre's pretension to divinity. 2. This mountain is a center point in the cosmos of creation, a place where heaven and earth, God and Man meet. 3. At the center of the mountain is the Garden, in whose own center are the two magical trees containing the secrets of life and knowledge. 4. From this garden rises a stream, which flows, as from a navel, to the cosmic quadrants, thereby sustaining the earth.

Tigerman, *The Architecture of Exile,* 18.

41. The Third, as seen by Emmanuel Levinas, is the necessary witness and interruption of the dialogue with the other (the law). "If the illeity of the Third always marks the birth of the Question, at the same Time as the 'it is necessary' of justice, the word 'question' is forced to adapt to the situation of hostage: The subject is hostage insofar as it is less a question than in question." See Derrida, "A Word of Welcome," 56.

42. The *Forward* (April 28, 2000) published a report on the story. The reporter Ira Stoll interviewed people like James Young, Jo Noero (architect for the Apartheid Museum in South Africa), Wilfried Wang (then Director of the German Architecture Museum in Frankfurt), Stephen Goldsmith (director of city planning in Salt Lake City, Utah), and others.

43. I am indebted to Francisco Liernur, who pointed me to the writing of Mark Cousins on ugliness and architecture. See Mark Cousins, "The Ugly," Parts I, II, and III, in *AA Files* 28, 29, and 30 (autumn 1994, spring 1995, autumn 1995).

44. David Eisen, "Solemn Center for Holocaust Studies Celebrates Life," Architectural Section, *Sunday Boston Herald,* July 2, 2000.

45. Michael Berenbaum, panel discussion with Stanford Anderson and Julian Bonder at the Center for Holocaust Studies, March 2000.

Part II

ISRAEL AND THE POLITICS
OF MEMORY

Chapter 4

The Return of the Repressed

Ariella Azoulay

> I know when Hitler will die. I know the day. When the last Jew is
> dead. Then he'll shout once more, one last bellow, so loud that the
> mountains will crack, and he'll smile and fall dead on the stone
> table. But not until then. To be a Jew is to keep Hitler alive. (Steiner
> 1981, 47)

In 1997 Roee Rosen mounted his exhibition entitled *Live and Die as
Eva Braun* in the Israel Museum in Jerusalem. True to its name, the
exhibition invited the viewer to become Eva Braun, Hitler's beloved.
Three years later Boaz Arad showcased a series of video artworks in an
exhibition entitled *The Angel of History* at the Herzliya Museum of Art.
These works were based on historical film clips in which the figure of
Hitler plays a leading role.[1]

Rosen's exhibition opened up a new space for thought in regard
to the artistic, museological, and historical discourses.[2] Boaz Arad's
video artworks are testimony to the change effected by Rosen's exhibition, but they also provide us with an opportunity to rethink
Rosen's exhibition and understand its operation in the framework of
the various fields of discourse. I will conduct my discussion of these
two exhibitions on three levels: visual, textual, and acoustic (with reference to the voice that is speaking).This, then, is an essay on Hitler,
and on picture, text, and voice.

Albert Speer, official architect of the Third Reich, describes the
way in which Hitler planned his own grave:

> The party's conference room was supposed to be connected, in a vis-
> ible manner, to a round room as large and high as the Pantheon;

this room was meant to house Hitler's sarcophagus. At a fitting distance of 15 meters from the Holy of Holies of the party's future tradition, from this sarcophagus containing the body of the German "Messiah," the tens of thousands of adherents, his followers, who were located in the conference room, were supposed to grasp the importance of the coming of the political liberator and master of the world's fortunes. The party convenes in the place of its establishment. The founder himself remains present. (Speer 1979, 172)

The Pantheon served as Hitler's model. The dead man bestows of his virtue, sanctity, and value on the place in which he resides. During his last days in the Berlin bunker, when Hitler knew not only that the end was near, but that his ability to control his death and the management of his presence among the living after his death was about to be forfeited, he abandoned the grandiose Pantheon plan in favor of a more modest—but just as calculated—program of suicide and immolation of the body. In late January 1945 already, so testified his associates, he declared that "he had no intention of falling into the hands of the enemy" and that he "was not interested in having his body put on parade by a Jew or by a Communist."[3] Hitler's body did indeed disappear, and for the space of several decades it was paraded by neither Jewish nor Communist hands. This disappearance gave rise to various contradictory versions: rumors of an escape to a secret refuge in Argentina (that have never been substantiated); (bogus?) testimonies concerning the presence of charred skull fragments in Russian archives; a (forged?) photo of his body immediately after the Russians entered the bunker, which has been distributed in different ways and is currently featured on several Internet web sites. Each of these versions offers its own final solution of the mystery, and each additional solution expresses the missing body's potency and its ability to turn the wheels of science and imagination, manufacturing more and more presences, representations, and images.

Hitler's own desire to get rid of his body was met with a corresponding desire on the other side. Hitler's enemies unwittingly became his hidden partners on behalf of a common purpose. Although the reasons presented on either side were contradictory, they all nevertheless derived from a mutual cultural platform—not Nazi, but Western—based on a connection between an original (that can exist in the form of traces or remains), a place, and the authority responsible for preserving the place and its law.

The paradigm of a place that is constructed around the traces of someone, something, or a certain event, and that is endowed with its sanctity or significance due to these traces, has been typical of Western culture throughout its history. The standing of the original stems from its link to the place, while the standing of the place stems from the presence—or the traces of the presence—of an original. Hitler's Pantheon fantasy, which, as he neared death, was replaced by his horror at the Pantheon that his enemies—Jews or Communists—thought to administer, met its reverse mirror image in his enemies' desire to erase every trace of him, so that it could never serve as the foundation for establishing a Pantheon. The passion to erase his every trace engendered an opposite passion to manifest his every trace, and out of the meeting between the two a virtual Pantheon was formed, one in which Hitler's absent presence or present absence attracts viewers, producers, or intermediaries driven by the same passion: to dispose of or revive Hitler's body. The mutual assumption underlying both contradictory passions is that there is a necessary connection between a place and an original, whereby each bestows of its sanctity on the other. The two exhibitions with which I am concerned both seek, each in its own way, to resist these contradictory passions and undermine their common foundation: to stick a doubting finger into the original and desecrate the Pantheon.[4]

An exhibition generally consists of a series of items—images, objects, and documents—displayed beside a series of written captions, which are supposed to provide some information about the item to which they are attached. This museum convention makes it possible to draw a connection between the seen and the written, the relationship between the two dimensions changing in accordance with the type of museum, the nature of the exhibition, and the like.[5] The nature of the different series, or the principle according to which they are arranged, also changes in accordance with circumstances of time, place, or purpose. Nevertheless, there is almost always an additional element oscillating between the two series—the visual and the textual —that is as elusive as it is necessary for the exhibition to function; it ensures the proper relation between the two series, as well as their sense.[6] In its constant oscillation between the two series, this element breathes life into them and charts their paths. It itself eludes any view, identity, or stability. It can never be apprehended, its identity cannot be established, and its essence cannot be investigated; for, if these were possible, it would lose its standing and become just another element in one of the series. When it oscillates, it fulfills its function: it preserves the distance and distinctiveness of each of the series as well as the contact between them. It is entirely composed of movement and time. Without it, there is no plot and there are no characters, only dumb objects and dead pictures.

Roee Rosen's exhibition *Live and Die as Eva Braun* is also comprised of two series, one of images and one of written captions. They are organized as a route with ten stations. The visual series includes about sixty small- to medium-sized black-and-white pictures, each built on the pattern of a rebus. Most of the pictures are based on

Roee Rosen, *Live and Die as Eva Braun* (No. 1), 1995. Acrylic, gesso, and pastel on rag paper, 16" x 13.5". Courtesy of the artist.

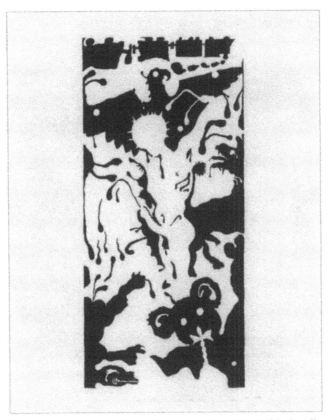

Roee Rosen, *Live and Die as Eva Braun* (No. 39), 1996. Acrylic on rag paper, 22" x 28.5". Courtesy of the artist.

religious and erotic scenes taken from the history of art, illustrations borrowed and adapted from German children's books, self-portraits of Rosen as a child and as a boy, architectural sketches, a portrait of Eva Braun, and a black rectangle whose shape is reminiscent of Hitler's mustache. These elements are interwoven into one another in an interchangeable manner so that the images that appear in the exhibition look like one long and twisting dance of black snakes, constantly assuming and changing shapes.

The textual series includes ten canvas sheets imprinted with texts describing each of the exhibition's stations. The ten stations are "The Waiting Period," "Arrival," "Control," "The Bed," "The Dream,"

Roee Rosen, *Live and Die as Eva Braun* (No. 8), 1995. Acrylic, gesso, and pastel on rag paper, 13.5" x 17". Courtesy of the artist.

"Tears," "The Gunshot," "Angel's Wings," "Wax," and "The Gift." Both series are exhibited under the general title of *Live and Die as Eva Braun*, which is not another item in the textual series; it stands outside the series and distinct from it, and it holds the key to locating and identifying the oscillating element (to which I shall immediately return).

The title is phrased in the imperative. It posits an addressee, aims at him or her, and imprisons him/her in the space it creates. It commands the viewer to be someone else. It employs the imperative although it is not delivered from a position of authority. Neither the museum institution, the standing of the artist or curator, nor the exhibition space are sufficient to command compulsory obedience, except for commands regarding the behavior of visitors to the museum and their attitude toward the objects exhibited in its framework ("Keep quiet," "Do not touch the exhibits," "To start, press the red button," and so on). The command to "live and die as Eva Braun" supersedes the museum's mandate, not because the museum does not take part in shaping the identity of the visitor in its gates (it does), but because that mandate calls for the shaping of a *universal* identity: "viewer," "visitor," or "connoisseur." To the contrary, *Live and Die as Eva Braun* commands the viewer to become a particular person—in other words, to change shape, appearance, image, identity, sex, race, language, and name[7]—to live her life and die as she died. The biography of the character that the viewer is being commanded to be is associated with the biography of someone who wielded the power of life and death over millions of human beings, and this character—Eva Braun—and he himself were among those he sentenced to death.

The title of the exhibition, then, commands you the viewer not just to become Eva Braun, but to live and die as Eva Braun, which means to live and die by Hitler's side: to survive as a Jew and to die —at Hitler's hands—as Eva Braun, or vice versa, first to die as Eva Braun and then to survive as a viewer.[8] The imperative provides no details on how to become Eva Braun; there are no accompanying instructions to grow or shave hair, to dab on or remove costume paint, to perform a sex-change operation, to fill in an application for a name change, to change feeding habits, or to perform physical exercises to lengthen the arm and leg muscles. The positing of the viewer as a direct addressee continues and is maintained from the title of the exhibition to the last of the exhibits in it; progressing through the exhibition, between the two series, the viewer is transformed from an addressee into the exhibition's hero:

> He comes toward you with such warmth, his smile tired, his arms are open to embrace you. Remember—you are Eva. When Hitler closes his arms around you, the view darkens and you are surrounded by his presence. . . . You relish the sour smell of an old man's sweat contained within the manly uniform. . . . The new, sharp sourness, the flabby waist, the recently formed, sagging male breasts—those are the bitter fruits of global defeat. (from the text of the exhibition's second station)

Without viewers having given their explicit consent to it, they are transformed into Eva Braun and their characters are alternately interchanged with hers:

> Eva is asleep and you dream her dream. But whence this perverse scene, so strong you realize it must be a recurring dream, even though this is the first time you sleep as Eva. . . . You see his face from high above as your pudenda slowly descend to kiss his gaping orifice. You look at the visage of the dictator. (from "The Dream" station in the exhibition)

There is no imposition here. Viewers can abandon their new character, leave the exhibition space, and forget the whole thing. But if they stay in the exhibition, look at the pictures, and read the texts, they discover that they have been transformed into Eva Braun. They can still get away from themselves as Eva Braun and say that it is all just twisted imagination, vain delusion, or cheap allegory, but in this case they will have already completed the course set for them by the exhibition—to become Eva Braun. To become Eva Braun necessarily also means to manufacture Hitler out of the same texts and images out of which you were manufactured. The deeper the spectator goes into the texts, the more she allows Eva Braun's view to adhere to her own eyes, the closer she draws to Hitler's body, examines the pores of his skin, feels his touch, responds to his breathing, and hears his voice:

> His power is perturbing, petrifying—and nothing is better emblem of that power than the magisterial veins along his neck. The swelling

of these blood vessels is awe-inspiring. (from the text of the "Control" station in the exhibition)

Viewers, who have formerly known Hitler as a historical character responsible for crimes against humanity, as the manifestation of evil, suddenly find themselves far detached from this image, in surprising propinquity to a body that they find to have no connection with this image. Becoming Eva Braun exposes the illusion of closeness and distance; it shows to what extent identity—any identity, even Hitler's—is fragile, illusory, and fantastic, and to what extent the effort to overcome the otherness of both the other and the self, just like the attempt to control or understand them, merely strengthens its elusiveness. However, this game of closeness and distance does not take place outside you, the viewer, just as the games of life and death are not a play performed for your benefit, leaving you a passive spectator. From the moment you first shared the privilege, with others of your kind, of taking and giving life,[9] it was only a matter of time until your, Eva Braun's, turn came:

How odd it is, really, that you do not expect to die. You always trusted his power to decide on deadly matters—it has been infallible. (from the "Tears" station in the exhibition)

Live and Die as Eva Braun is not an exhibition about Eva Braun. Eva Braun is the spectator's possibility of contemplating Hitler, his death and hers, which is also his own, for s/he too has been rescued (meanwhile) from Hitler's hands. Eva Braun is the viewers' point of view on Hitler, a platform that enables their views to linger on Hitler; she is a pair of eyes, a prism, closeness, and intimacy. But it is not an exhibition about Hitler either. Although Hitler seduces the gaze and leads it in circles, he is not actually present in the exhibition—there is no visual image of Hitler in it—and the gaze is unable to achieve its objective and remains dissatisfied. Hitler is that oscillating element that connects the visual and the written, breathes life into them, and eludes any fixed determination. Hitler is a distinctive nonportrait; any (visual or written) statement attempting to portray him would require another explaining the meaning of the former, forming a regressive chain of statements, each of them explaining the meaning of the one before it.

In this sense, Roee Rosen's Hitler is present inside the museum but denies Hitler's Pantheon project in the museum. The exhibition neither glorifies Hitler nor discredits him. It is not concerned with attempting to present and distribute a portrait—good or bad—of Hitler, nor with his biography or the history of the Third Reich. Nor does it propose a thesis concerning the banality of evil, even though the way in which it describes Hitler's daily life—talking on the telephone, raising his voice, the loving embrace, and so on—testifies to an affinity with this famous thesis of Hannah Arendt. The exhibition does not adopt psychological explanations of evil either, although traces of sexual perversions and emotional complexes are not missing from it. Such theses and explanations would have made the viewers passive addressees of the visual and textual information. *Live and Die as Eva Braun* utilizes a quality that is latent in the exhibition medium, but is usually left dormant—directly addressing the spectators and transforming them into active participants in the creation of the object of observation.

The exhibition is built as an open, transformational text—visual and verbal—the elements of which are in a constant process of change depending on the viewers and their point of view. Instead of a series of beings, the exhibition offers an endless process of becoming that grows out of an open latticework of images and texts, which are not committed to any historical, scientific, political, aesthetic, or ethical principles. The exhibition places the viewer in a special position. Someone in this position accepts responsibility for the figure of Hitler, and must deal with this responsibility throughout the exhibition. If the viewer evades this responsibility, the figure of Hitler will remain unseen, and the only thing left of it will be the portrait of Rosen as a child with a mustache adorning his upper lip. Hitler, who until Rosen's exhibition had remained outside the exhibition space and been strengthened in his standing as the one and only original, is here reproduced to infinity—morphing into the artist, threatening to conquer the viewer, spawning mustaches, and agitatedly waving his arms about as if he wanted to speak to his audience again.

All this takes place in front of the viewer, who participates in the play. There is something menacing about the return of the repressed (Hitler) to the exhibition space. Viewers are threatened and bear the responsibility. They can disengage and sweep him back under the rug —maybe it will work this time too—and avoid contending with Hitler face to face: with questions of responsibility, punishment, forgiveness, reconciliation, forgetfulness, and erasure. What viewers are obliged to contend with here is not the memory of the Holocaust and its victims but the figure of the hangman, the presence of evil among the living.

Rosen's exhibition was the first to manifest Adolf Hitler in a museum space in Israel and make the viewer responsible for his presence. When it was shown in the Israel Museum in 1997, the exhibition provoked extreme reactions of two kinds: On the one hand some argued that it was a contemptible exhibition and offensive to the memory of the Holocaust and its survivors. Others, on the other hand, claimed that the exhibition dealt with the instrumentalization of the memory of the Holocaust and that it accorded the genocide of the Jews a visibility and expression formerly denied to it in Israeli art. Both sides of the argument actually shared four assumptions with regard to art and the Holocaust:

1. Rosen's exhibition is concerned with the representation and commemoration of the Holocaust.
2. Art in general is a practice of representation.
3. The "Holocaust" is the organizing paradigm when dealing with World War II.
4. Dealing with the Holocaust always lies somewhere on an axis between identification and expression.[10]

These assumptions shape the field of vision and its boundaries in advance and obstruct any possibility of allowing the viewer to encounter what the exhibition offers beyond the label of "art dealing with the Holocaust," and beyond the intentions, actions, and representational practices employed by the artist. Such an encounter requires an undermining of the stability and distinctiveness of three conventions of museum display: the artist as an active and sovereign agent who controls his objects, the object as passive, controlled, and represented, and the medium (exhibition, painting, text, and the museum space) as a means of transmitting content.

I first wrote about Roee Rosen's exhibition in 1998. I then emphasized the fact that the exhibition is not concerned with representing the Holocaust. There are no representations in the exhibition that have actual referents, there is no image or text in it that mentions the genocide of Europe's Jews; therefore it is not concerned with the "Holocaust." In the same article I noted that Rosen's exhibition deals with the image of Hitler and offers the viewer—especially the Jewish viewer—a pair of gloves, seemingly taken from a virtual reality performance, with which to deal with the figure of Hitler. Thus, the exhibition in effect unwittingly implements the situation that horrified Hitler on the eve of his death: falling into the hands of a Jew. However, what I missed in that article was the fact that Hitler's presence in Roee Rosen's exhibition in the Israel Museum counted as his "premiere performance" in any museum exhibition space in Israel. This oversight—mine and that of others, including Rosen himself—is symptomatic with regard to the status of the figure of Hitler in Israel's public discourse. This image enjoys the standing of a sort of coat-lining in respect of the image, or complex of images, of the Holocaust—it is attached to these images that stand in the forefront, while it serves to line the back and is almost never exposed.[11] These images focus mainly on the transformation of the Jews into victims and rarely gaze directly at the victimizers or at Nazism's non-Jewish victims.[12]

This distancing of visual representations of Hitler from the museum space can be interpreted in several ways:

1. A continuation of Allied policy after the war (disposal of the body and eradication of Hitler's various residences and workplaces) to prevent the canonization of any pilgrimage site.
2. Fear of the contagious force of evil and its possible influence on its viewers.
3. Contending with the figure of Hitler directly could have opened the debate about the Nazi regime in general and the devastation it brought upon all Europe, not only the Jews; such a step might have undermined the Holocaust's special status.
4. Fear, intimidation, discomfort, or distress as a result of confronting this portrait face to face.

Hitler's absence from the visual space in Israel is not accidental, nor does it testify to a lack of interest in the matter. It is a structured absence, toward the production of which a special effort had to be made. In other words, Hitler's absence is no innocent oversight but a case of repression and denial; like any repressed content, it must eventually rise to the surface again. It is not a total absence either, but only an absence from museum spaces. The presence of representations of Hitler in spaces for exhibiting art would have required the view to linger and ponder (as did indeed happen in Rosen's and Arad's exhibitions), prompting a type of face-to-face confrontation from which some sort of emotional regard toward the figure must emerge. Likewise, the presence of representations of Hitler in the exhibition space of a museum of history might have necessitated the rewriting of the historical narrative.[13] All the same, despite this striking absence, Hitler's portrait has become one of the most famous and familiar of all, to the point where almost any child (at least in Israel) can easily identify it.[14] Hitler is recognized primarily by his mustache (an adornment he deliberately chose himself), and its dominant presence in the center of his face has become its hallmark. But it is not just the mustache that makes his figure so easy to recognize. The mustache is complemented by the stylized gestures and carefully orchestrated looks that Hitler often rehearsed to perfection,[15] and his supervision over the selection of still photos of him that were to be distributed in public (shot by his personal photographer Heinrich Hoffmann) and of the camera angles in his films (entrusted to his personal filmmaker Leni Riefenstahl). Thus, even though Hitler's portrait was denied a place of its own on which to stamp its imprint, it has left an indelible mark.

Hitler's portrait appears in ritual fashion in the life of the State of Israel once a year on Holocaust Day—on the flickering television screen, in short clips of documentary footage. Because of the characteristics of the cinematic medium, three additional dimensions accrue to the portrait: time, movement, and voice. The fact that this portrait is so familiar primarily means that people can easily recognize it, without really bothering to take heed of it. Correctly identifying the face is tantamount to erasing the face or turning your back on it, looking away and turning it into a mask. The mask, writes Elias Canetti, is a "seal and end of the matter. . . . Once the mask has been put in place, there can be no more beginnings, no groping toward something new" (Canetti 1978, 278). In the process of correct identification, specific facial features are recognized, linked together to form a stable and fixed matrix—a mask—and confirmed by a "yes" or "no." This type of identification eliminates emotional regard for the other. Any regard for a face that is based on identifying the portrait manufactures the face as mask, icon, label, or concept, maintaining a stable distance from it.[16]

Rosen's exhibition, as well as Arad's video artworks, to which I shall shortly refer, manifests this "automatic" procedure of identification and draws our view to it. But they do more than that. They impose on the viewer an encounter of a different kind, which is not based on identification, an encounter that undermines the iconic standing of the figure that functions as a mask. Rosen's exhibition demonstrates that a black rectangle on a human scale is enough to identify the traces of the Hitlerian portrait. When this black rectangle is located in the center of the face, almost any face—the different pictures of Rosen are a case in point—it stamps the Hitlerian visage upon it. The mustache, which is detached from Hitler's actual portrait, is thus present numerous times in the visual series of Rosen's exhibition but is almost entirely absent from the verbal descriptions presented in the parallel textual series. In this way the figure of Hitler emerges and oscillates between the two series: present here and absent there, signifying here and signified there, missing here and superfluous there. In its wake the viewer progresses through the exhibition, oscillating from here to there between the two series, trying not to lose Hitler, striving to overtake and capture him and to attach a shape, appearance, or portrait to him.[17] But Hitler's portrait continues to elude the viewer: when s/he thinks s/he has captured it, it changes shape and is discovered again by its absence. The Hitler flickering between the two series does not resemble the Hitler any of the viewers might have seen before, but all the same everyone knows of a certainty that it is Hitler.

The visual sign, the identified and identifiable sign, the distinctive portrait, the difference that turns one portrait into another, and all of these with respect to the particular portrait of Hitler—in other words, the identifiable quality of Hitler in a portrait or of something as Hitler's portrait—are part of the exhibition's obsessive preoccupation with various models of morphological transformation: metamorphoses of the painted figures, which change shape inside the picture itself (a teddy bear's mouth turning into a little girl's braid), at its margins (animated objects), in the passage from the visual to the verbal (the oedipal pair of scissors hovering above the portrait of Rosen-Hitler), or in the relation between picture and viewer (the mirror). The process of metamorphosis swallows up the visitor to the museum. An initial transformation is effected by means of the customary museum convention, whereby the anonymous private individual is transformed into someone who will assume the position of a universal spectator and accept this identity; this identity is then replaced by Eva Braun's particularistic identity.

The verbal series, in which Hitler is described during his last days in the Berlin bunker, presents Hitler's body through the intimacy of the eyes of his beloved, who desires him even though she recognizes the signs of decay and weakening in him. His body is a sort of quivering mass of decaying flesh that has lost its strength and serves as a tablet on which to write "the world's defeat," the leader's body as the face of the nation. Hitler assumes the form of the nation and feels its distress and pain.[18] In his body Hitler feels what the German nation feels, and in her body Eva Braun feels what Hitler feels, and now you the viewer are invited to feel in your body what Eva Braun feels when Hitler feels what the nation feels. In this way Hitler is drawn into the circular motion of metamorphosis and is separated both from the stable portrait that he sought to bestow upon himself in his lifetime and the fantasy of preservation in the Pantheon, as well as from the portrait that was bestowed upon him after his death by his distancing from the museum space and the avoidance of any face-to-face confrontation with his portrait.

In other words, the exhibition removes the mask from the figure of Hitler not in order to expose the truth behind it or to expose another mask beneath it, but in order to retrieve Hitler from his external place—one reserved for those for whom metamorphosis is prohibited and who are also capable of preventing others from changing shape[19]—and return him to all the exchange networks. The exhibition does all this without displaying even a single portrait of Hitler. Viewers are invited to wait with Eva Braun for Hitler's coming, to progress through the length of the exhibition's ten stations, and to find themselves anew in the last-first station, "The Wait," though the portrait tarries and fails to arrive at the Israel Museum. Instead of a ready-made portrait, the exhibition offers the viewer the practice of creating a portrait, the portrait as an elastic experience, as the experience of a virtual facelift, as a transformational game.

Both series, the visual and the written, are animated by means of two oscillating elements—Hitler and the viewer—who are now entirely dependent on one another. Without the viewer the figure of Hitler would not be in the exhibition; without Hitler viewers could not become Eva Braun and faithfully fulfill their role as visitors to the exhibition *Live and Die as Eva Braun.* Both Hitler and the viewer, in their pursuit of each other, give the exhibition life, time, and movement. What transpires in this time and in this movement is the transformation of the spectator's view. This view undergoes serious turmoil; it is fed on bits of information and fragmented images. The exhibition gives this view a good toss and tumble and injures it, leaving a painful, open wound. The obstinate search for the oscillating element—Hitler oscillating between textual fragment and pictorial detail—is never satisfied because it cannot find the object of its desire. It is a gaze sentenced to intermittence and is therefore repetitive, on alert, and distracted. It is a traumatic gaze that the exhibition engenders in the viewer, who suffers like a wound that refuses to be healed. In paradoxical fashion, Hitler—icon, mask, or stable portrait—would be the treatment for this wound, but he endlessly eludes the gaze, thus substantiating again his escape from all the blows and punishments that he rightfully deserved, his escape in life and his escape after he was defeated and died, his escape from his own death at the hands of others.

Three years after the exhibition *Live and Die as Eva Braun,* Boaz Arad exhibited a series of video art that employed Hitler's image and voice.[20] These works, in their relation to Rosen's exhibition, remind one of the story about Old Man Proteus of the sea, lord of the seals, who had the prophetic gift. On his way back from the Trojan War, Menelaus landed with his men on Egypt's shores and was unable to sail back to Greece for several years. Proteus's daughter, who took pity on Menelaus, told him what he must do to capture her father and force him to talk. Menelaus and his men disguised themselves as seals, waited until Proteus fell asleep among his seals, and fell on him and captured him. Proteus, a master of disguise, rapidly changed shape into a panther, a gigantic guinea pig, a tree, and a snake, but Menelaus and his men held on and would not let him go. When Proteus tired, he reassumed his human shape, asked Menelaus and his men what they wanted, and answered their questions.[21]

Until Rosen's exhibition, the abstention from exhibiting Hitler could be described as a pursuit of him in order to exorcise and expel him. Rosen's exhibition offers viewers a different endless pursuit that takes place between knowing and seeing, between presence and traces, between the verbal and the visual. Viewers come to the exhibition equipped with a certain image of Hitler. The exhibition does not reflect it back to them, just as it does not propose an alternate image instead. The exhibition robs viewers of the fuzzy image they have of Hitler—an image that is both controlled and repressed by their knowledge about the Holocaust—and leaves them in a state of discomfort, with a desire for an image that remains unsatisfied. Three years after Rosen's exhibition, when Hitler—the oscillating image— has been worn out and the viewers are exhausted, Boaz Arad's works arrive on the scene. In seeming innocence they point to Hitler's face as the first place to which the gaze must turn in order to contend with his figure and focus on the mouth as the source of every answer. Arad's video art takes Hitler's cinematic portrait, opens its mouth, and forces it to speak. Arad does not understand or speak German, and the German spilling from Hitler's throat sounds to him—as it does to many Israelis—like the soundtrack to the Holocaust. He exiles Hitler from the German—his own language—and immerses him in Hebrew. He ignores the content of the speeches in German and treats it as acoustic raw material, which he uses to splice together a Hitler who speaks Hebrew.

It was only when Hitler appeared in the museum space and began to talk with Boaz Arad's tongue that that it became possible to understand what Roee Rosen's exhibition had accomplished. In this sense, even though Rosen's exhibition preceded Arad's and in many ways made it possible, its full significance could only be appreciated in the wake of the latter.[22] The image of Hitler, which stands at the center of Boaz Arad's exhibition, supplies (ostensibly, of course) the gaze that was gouged out at Rosen's exhibition with its object and assuages its pain by means of a portrait. Arad's exhibition focuses more

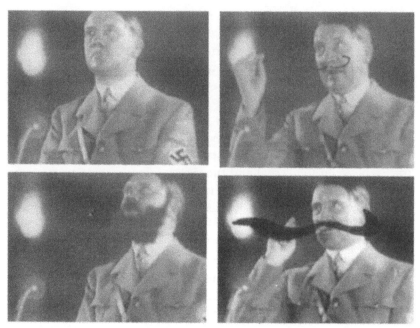

Boaz Arad, *Marcel Marcel*, 2000. Video, 27 seconds. Courtesy of the artist.

on the object of the gaze, on the semiotic signs offered to the gaze or those it organizes, and less on the gaze itself. To viewers, Arad offers a portrait of Hitler in several different states, a sort of consecutive series of faces. But each one is immediately replaced by the next sign, and viewers do not have time to capture it.

For example, Hitler's mustache first appears as a thin line along his upper lip, which thickens slightly and curls at the sides, then grows larger and larger until it bursts the boundaries of the face; then with a little twist the tips of the mustache curl downward, join over the chin, and swiftly grow into a beard of Theodore Herzl's magnificent proportions. But then, before viewers can digest the resemblance, the beard disappears all at once. This is followed by the disappearance of the grandiose mustache, and Hitler's upper lip is suddenly revealed, like exposed genitals. And the portrait remains that of Hitler, over and over again: once again hirsuteness proves its potency. In this way the face of Hitler that Arad presents to the viewer turns into content, a sign, identifiable marks that can be grasped, characterized, and named.[23] But in Arad's videos the sign itself—the mustache—turns into a face. It loses its quality of masquerade and begins moving in small gestures such as facial expressions, alternately becoming angry, happy, merry, evil, monstrous, Jewish, and German. Thus the mustache—the facial feature that contributed so much to the making of Hitler's face into a mask—is given not only an independent life, as happened at Rosen's exhibition too, but its very own face as well.

Arad succeeds in taking the distinctive, cartoonlike, masquerading sign and liberating it from its fixation, forcing the gaze desirous of capturing and fixating the figure to become liberated too. When it deviates beyond the masquerading mustache and the texture of the "Nazi regime," Hitler's face—from which the command "Thou shalt kill" came forth—places spectators in a surprising and unexpected position, which undermines the distance they have always maintained from Hitler. "Consciousness," writes Levinas, "is posed with a question mark by the face" (as quoted in Taylor 1987, 210). In this case consciousness is knowing who Hitler is: the hated and despised figure who was responsible for the deaths of millions, and who left his imprint on millions of others who survived the machinery of genocide.

But this knowledge is in need of a mask rather than a face. The face, says Levinas, "leads you to the beyond. The significance of the face extricates it from experience as being connected to knowing. Whereas *seeing* is nothing other than the *search for consonance.* It actually *swallows* experience. Indeed, regard for the face is *ethical in principle*" (Taylor 1987, 210). Levinas clearly strikes an opposition between seeing, which swallows and devours its object, and the ethical, which recognizes boundaries, does not transgress them, and delays and conquers the view in order not to conquer its object. Arad's work, like that of Rosen, rests on this opposition and alternates between ravenous, overpowering, denominative seeing and contention—their own and their viewers' in their wake—with the unconquerable otherness of the face, which imposes an ethical regard on those who contemplate it. Hitler's face imposes an ethical regard on the viewer.

With Levinas, the ethical is not just the denial of seeing. The ethical is involved with the appearance of speech, or, to be more precise, the acoustic space, the space of the voice: "Opposite the face I do not just stand to contemplate it—much more so, I respond to it. . . . Thou shalt not kill is the first commandment of the face. It is a directive.

In the appearance of the face there is an imperative, as if a master is speaking to me" (Taylor 1987, 69). In the encounter between myself and the other, between myself and what I am not able to grasp, see, or signify as nose, mouth and eyes—in this encounter that eludes any fixation, all I can do is respond to the other, to the other's imperative. The other commands me not to kill. He or she appears before me—twinkling from behind a face—and signifies by means of it what lies beyond it, which I am unable to grasp: something fragile for which I become responsible, responsible also for its preservation as such—as that which cannot be poured into a mold, for that would kill it (Levinas 1982).

The ethical, Levinas says, eludes any mold, regulation, or law. The ethical is the face, and the face is the imperative. The face is the voice of command even if no voice issues forth. In other words, the ethical is the place where the eye and ear are transformed from alert instruments trained to identify words and pictures into attentive (visual and auditory) monitors that absentmindedly receive a command, which does not even have to be voiced.[24] The retardation of the eye and ear's overmastering action suffices for it to get through.[25] Levinas does not repudiate seeing, but he would like to retard it and combine it with other mediums, just as he would like to retard the text, the spoken word, articulate speech that describes and explains. The ethical lies beyond the seen and beyond the text that could describe it. The ethical cannot be reduced to either the visual or the spoken. The ethical is the real—that which appears outside any order (Levinas 1982).

This movement of the ethical between three dimensions can be paralleled to the three types of order formulated by Lacan (1977). The symbolic order is language and law, which are based on an array of differences between different signs. The imaginary is appearances, the picture, the images I create out of what appears before my eyes. And the real is everything that is not grasped by either the symbolic or the imaginary. In Levinas the real is the ethical: nothing but a bare remnant, a commanding voice that is no voice but only unadulterated appeal. It is an appeal without a subject, it lacks intention or consciousness—it is "ça parle," as Lacan (1977) says with regard to the real. The ethical speaks through the apersonal unconscious that belongs to nobody, which precedes any subjectivity.[26]

The avoidance of Hitler's image for several decades by means of removal or its assimilation into the symbolic order has been overcome by Rosen's and Arad's exhibitions. However, it is not their intentional treatment of his figure, oscillating between the imaginary and the symbolic, but Hitler's own irruption into and out of the museum space—out of the symbolic order into which he has been stitched—that resembles an outburst of the real that speaks through the unconscious. The museum space and the mediums of cinematography and sound recording serve as the unconscious.

In the chapter in *Mein Kampf* that deals with "the significance of oratory," Hitler strikes an opposition between the written and the spoken text:

> As the orator takes in from the crowd in front of him he estimates what needs to be corrected in his lecture, and uninterruptedly gauges, according to the crowd's expression, to what measure his remarks are understood, if they are leading to the desired object. The writer, on the other hand, is completely unfamiliar with the readers of his writings. He will therefore not appeal to the crowd in front of him from the start and his explanations will be of a more general nature. As a result he loses psychological subtlety to a certain degree and his flexibility will also be reduced. (Hitler 1985, 179–91)

It is not the metaphysics of presence that underlies Hitler's differentiation between the written and the spoken text but a differentiation between conscious and unconscious, as manifested in the modern age by the encounter between technology and the masses.

> The era of private elation is over. . . . What we offer in its stead is the aspiration for the community's elation. Can anything express greater elation than a national-socialist gathering in the framework of which everyone is vibrating in harmony, orating and listening?[27]

The vibration of which Hitler speaks is not that of the spoken word but of the preverbal and the presemiotic. It is the vibration that the instrument—both optical and acoustical—knows how to record. The instrument does not record the human voice and its words but different frequencies of voice and light. The frequencies imprinted on photographic film or recording tape combine the conscious and the unconscious—one beside, with, and on top of the other.

The appearance of the pictorial and acoustic unconscious at the end of the nineteenth century lies at the basis of Freud's formulation of the relation between the conscious and the unconscious, which he often likened to the working of a camera (Freud 1950). The unconscious has universal laws and does not belong to a subject, who will someday expose its materials to consciousness. The unconscious is prior to the subject and a necessary condition for his or her appearance. "The subject emerges," writes Taylor, "by means of a process of differentiation in the framework of which he struggles to build his identity by separation from otherness" (Taylor 1987, 93). This otherness is the unconscious. The Hitlerian fantasy—as extrapolated from his speeches, actions, and writings—is not that of constituting the self out of otherness but that of subduing the unconscious at all three levels—verbal, optic, and acoustic—and reconstituting the figure of the omni-orator who has the capability to hypnotize, domesticate, control, and tame the otherness of the other, of the other planted in the mass, of the mass as other, and of the unconscious as the absolute other:

> [The orator] has always known how to ride the wings of the crowd's responses so that his sensitivity is aroused to the fluent words he requires in order to convince his listeners. However, if he makes the slightest inadvertent mistake, there is always someone in front of him to correct this mistake. As has already been said, he can take stock of the expression on his listeners' faces, to feel in the first place whether they are indeed capable of understanding what's being said. . . . If he sees—first of all—that they don't understand him, he will present his explanations in such a simple and clear manner that even the last of them could not do otherwise but fully fathom his meaning . . . . Until at last even the last group of resisters reveals through behavior and facial expression its capitulation before his incisive proof. . . . Once again it was the huge demonstrations, processions of hundreds of thousands, that impressed on the awareness of the small and mean individual the faith that has been given to him, despite the insignificance of his own existence, to belong like a link in a chain to a great dragon, the flame of whose searing breath shall someday annihilate the hated world of the bourgeoisie. (*Mein Kampf*, "The Significance of Oratory")

Hitler describes his encounter with the mass in three stages, although their order is not always maintained. One stage is the imaginary, in which Hitler and the mass meet face to face, as if they were a figure and its reflection. This is the stage at which the mass listens to Hitler, contemplates him, while he in turn gazes back at it. A second stage is the symbolic, in which Hitler employs language as an argumentative linear medium to advance his contentions and messages. The third stage is that in which the real appears, the preverbal and presemiotic stage, the stage in which the voice issues forth from Hitler's throat with no relation to the meaning of the spoken words. His throat serves as a medium through which "it is spoken" ("ça parle") and the mass becomes synchronized to its sounds, receives and manufactures the frequencies, vibrations, rustlings, and whisperings—everything that lies beyond the symbolic order and the imaginary order. It is a flaming, disembodied, and senseless voice that erupts thus from the throat of nothingness, hypnotized and hypnotizing, strewing fear and terror.[28]

As stated above, Hitler's voice, like his image, is absent from the museum space in Israel. Nevertheless, it is very familiar to many.[29] On first viewing Boaz Arad's video artworks, in which Hitler is seen orating, it appears as though their main thrust lies in Hitler's transformation into a flickering image, an effect achieved by means of "jittery" editing. On second and third viewing, having also noticed the names of the works that appear in captions on the wall ("Shalom Jerusalem I apologize" and "Drink water"), viewers begin to realize that something about the oratory they are hearing is irregular. Does the irregularity lie in the sentence, in the written or spoken text—"Shalom Jerusalem I apologize"? Has someone counterfeited Hitler's voice? Has someone discovered previously unheard and unreleased speeches of Hitler? No. The irregularity does not involve an act of counterfeiting or rediscovery. It stems from the fact that Hitler is speaking Hebrew. The fact of the matter is not that Hitler knew Hebrew without spectators ever having been aware of it, but that it has been proved possible to coax Hitler into speaking Hebrew, out of Hitler himself, in adherence to his own authentic voice.

In order to understand Arad's video art, it is necessary to take into account the three stages described earlier—according to Hitler's text on "The Significance of Oratory"—and to be familiar as well with the technical procedures involved in their preparation.[30] Arad uses filmed segments of Hitler's speeches, which he dissects on his computer. The process of dissection is dictated by technological and linguistic constraints determining the minimal acoustic unit that can be preserved. Although this vocal fragment is detached from the sequence of sounds, it constitutes a distinct phonetic unit. Arad classifies these vocal units and stores them in memory together with each one's visual "hanger-on"—the few filmed frames equivalent to the duration of the vocal unit. Arad then uses these units as raw material, putting them together painstakingly into Hebrew sentences.

This, then, is a case of *Hebrew lessons.* The lessons actually took place in the course of preparing the works between the keyboard and mouse, between the PC screen and the loudspeakers in Arad's home, between the written text and the phonetic traces. The Hebrew lesson is Arad's attempt to overcome the appearance of the real, the emergence of the naked voice—Hitler's presence erupting on the screen and out of the loudspeakers. After months of painstaking effort, Arad succeeded only partially in his attempt, coaxing from Hitler only a very few Hebrew sentences.

The difficulty Arad met with is surprising only if we regard language at the symbolic level, as a storehouse of phonetic units that can be assembled in countless combinations. Arad is attempting to uproot Hitler's voice from one symbolic order to which it is indentured and implant it in another—the symbolic order of Hebrew. This exchange does not take place without remnants, traces, friction, and dissonance. These are not missing from the museum exhibition and prevent Hitler from speaking in fluent Hebrew. While Arad was giving Hitler Hebrew lessons—so Arad relates—the sentences that blared out of the loudspeakers in his home became to him a part of the new fabric of the Hebrew language and a part of Hitler's vocal texture. In their move to the museum, they regained their foreignness. On the opening night of the exhibition, the videos were screened at the amphitheater in the museum courtyard before hundreds of viewers as part of a movie, in which Hitler's speeches in Hebrew were interwoven with Arad's remarks as a sort of Hebrew teacher.[31] The audience's response was unexpected and not entirely comprehensible.[32] Time after time the audience choked back its thundering laughter, only for it to be reignited through contagious infection. From an audience of individual spectators visiting the museum, pre-

Boaz Arad, *Hebrew Lesson*, 2000. Video, 12 seconds. Courtesy of the artist.

serving an individual regard for the work displayed before them, it turned into a crowd watching a movie.[33]

From the movie, the first and last portions of which dealt with characters and with other subjects, the figure of Hitler suddenly burst forth; and beside it—in peculiar proximity to Hitler and bathed in the light reflected from the flickering image—stood Boaz Arad. The movie showed an interview with Arad in which he describes the months of teaching Hitler Hebrew, while on a large screen in the background of the frame were shown the results of those lessons. Every few seconds, as Arad described his efforts to extract Hebrew from Hitler's mouth, and as Hitler spoke the rather halting sentences in the Hebrew imposed on his tongue, the mass burst into paroxysms of laughter. The on-screen Hitler—struggling to pronounce the Hebrew, but doing it nonetheless in the thundering and assertive voice left to him from the German—appeared human, tongue-tied, ridiculous, and perhaps even pitiful.

If the audience's laughter can be explained, then it must be connected with Hitler's appearance. But it also has to do with the discomfort felt by the audience: distress, confusion, perhaps rejoicing at the misfortune of others, relief, acceptance, and perhaps pain as well. In any case, the laughter gave expression in a nonverbal and unformulated manner to an uncanny encounter. Seeing Hitler this way was unlike aloofly looking at him as a portrait in a book, on the television screen, or on the museum wall; for a moment it turned the audience into a mass listening to Hitler's speeches. The audience at the Herzliya Museum made an intent effort to understand the words that Hitler was speaking, having realized that they were these words' addressee, for the Hitler that now appeared on-screen was speaking to them in Hebrew. Involuntarily, without meaning to, they were hypnotized by the wonder and magic of it, and embarrassed by this mesmerization, by its setting in the crowd united around Hitler at the moment of speech. It is the moment when what is spoken is no longer important. Here, too, it is not what is spoken that is important but the fact that it is spoken in Hebrew. The speech event itself is what is important.

Both exhibitions, Rosen's and Arad's, present to viewers open works. Both go beyond the visual dimension into the textual and acoustical dimensions as well, and both deviate from the dialectics of remembrance and forgetfulness. But what they are is not works of art. Rather, they are manifestations of the work (of art) in the museum space. In Rosen's case, the onus of performing the work is borne by the spectator—to become Eva Braun, or to re-create Hitler. In Boaz Arad's case, the work consists in the first place of a Hebrew lesson as a commonplace practice and only subsequently of *Hebrew Lesson* as the title of a video. Both Rosen and Arad are in effect challenging viewers to annul the conventional distance between Hitler and them. Neither exhibition is afraid of reviving the fantasy of the Jew through Nazi eyes or of the mimetic relations between Jew and Nazi. In Rosen's exhibition the Jew's shadow appears in the form of the hands that are supposed to grope at Hitler. Arad signals his traces through the agency of the fleeting image of a bearded Theodore Herzl.

It is as if the two exhibitions are closely examining, though unknowingly, an option proposed by George Steiner in his book *The Portage to San Cristóbal of A.H.* (1981). At a certain point one of the book's heroes reflects on the possibility of punishing Hitler by sending him to the State of Israel, with a mark of Cain branded on his forehead that is supposed to protect him and prevent the local inhabitants from killing him. However, this proposal—a sort of "final solution" for Hitler himself—remains undeveloped in the book, whose plot goes off in a different direction.

This laconic proposal is rather surprising because it deviates from any of our familiar models of crime and punishment, gaze and contact, strike and parry, freedom and arrest, victim and hangman, remembrance and forgetfulness, ruler and ruled, and speech and silence.[34] According to the most familiar model, the crime is adjudged in conformity with an accepted standard and its perpetrator is suitably punished in keeping with a standard penal code that includes distancing the felon from society in various ways (through compulsory service, through imprisonment, to the death penalty itself). The assumption is that distancing felons from society will enable society to reestablish the order that was disrupted by their crimes, and will help felons mend their ways before returning—if they ever do—to society. Steiner is not concerned, however, with reestablishing the social order. According to Steiner's proposal, it is forbidden to erase the crime that Hitler committed. But just the same, it is also forbidden to remember it, or at least to remember it in the manner in which the State of Israel managed the remembrance of the Holocaust at the Eichmann trial and has been managing it ever since.[35]

Putting felons into tables of crime and punishment is a type of erasure—it grants us permission to forget. The episode in Steiner's book can also be interpreted as a proposal to deal with the Nazi crime in a different way: by means of trauma. In this form of treatment both the felons and their victims take part. The trauma is the moment of the accident, the convulsive moment that was erased and subtracted and went out of control, which belongs to nobody. This missing moment keeps coming back. It relentlessly stalks the individual, reappearing time and again like something alien, never becoming integrated in the narrative molds familiar to the individual, always eluding them and retaining an indecipherable quality. To make this moment possible—that is the function of Hitler's presence among the Jews, his imprisonment in a society of Jews. Trauma, writes Caruth (1994) following Freud, is not just the encounter with death but the survival of that encounter as well. Hitler—who, among his other crimes, began purifying Europe of Jews in order to live in a space free of them—is sent to Israel, the Jewish state, and is sentenced to see only Jews wherever he turns, to listen to their language, incomprehensible to him, to be exposed to their touch, and to be saved at each and every moment from a sentence of death due to the mark of Cain that identifies him as the other, as a "Jew."

In this description, what the Jews are to Hitler is the return of the erased image and the missing moment, that foreign element that cannot be controlled, assimilated, or eliminated. And vice versa: for the Jews, Hitler serves in the same function as the return of the erased image and the missing moment, that foreign element that cannot be controlled, assimilated, or eliminated. This bare remnant should not be allowed to turn into a signifier of repression and silencing—"the Holocaust cannot be compared to anything else" or "the Holocaust cannot be represented"—but into one, disturbing and productive, that serves to stimulate an ethical regard in people for all horrors in general.

NOTES

1. To these exhibitions we might add the translation of Hannah Arendt's *Eichmann in Jerusalem* into Hebrew and the translation of Hitler's *Mein Kampf* (excerpts) into Hebrew in 1995. In 1994, Michael Shafir showcased a photograph of Hitler's hand in an exhibition entitled *Third Person* at the Bograshov Gallery. But this information was withheld from visitors to the gallery, and most of them remained completely unaware of the fact that it was Hitler's hand. Roee Rosen drew my attention to the presence of Hitler's mustache, detached from his image, in an exhibition by Uri Katsenstein that was shown at the Artists Workshops in Tel Aviv during the 1990s.
2. In this essay, I am not going to deal with the impact on the artistic discourse, which I discussed in my book *Death's Showcase* (Azoulay 2001).
3. Hitler's own remarks as quoted in *The Death of Hitler* (Petrova and Watson 1996, 25).
4. They do not attempt to provide an ultimate version of his fate or try to explain him and his actions either.
5. In a museum of art, for example, the function of the text is external and secondary to the exhibit—merely to provide information. In a museum of history, however, the text has a constitutive standing with respect to the exhibit: it authorizes the exhibit as authentic and original. In the

framework of these two paradigms, there are additional variations that I shall not touch upon here.

6. In his book *The Logic of Sense* (1969), Gilles Deleuze, following Jacques Lacan (1949; 1977), presents this oscillating element as a paradoxical element that is always present in one place while it is missing in another.

7. On the universal spectator at the museum in the context of Rosen's exhibition, see Azoulay 2001.

8. For a more extensive treatment of why Roee Rosen's exhibition cannot be said to deal with "the representation of the Holocaust," see Azoulay 2001.

9. See Michel Foucault's discussion on the modern right to take and give life in *The History of Sexuality* (Foucault 1996).

10. In his article "Mourning and Mania," which appeared in the catalog to Rosen's exhibition, Roger Rothman proposes an organizing scheme for representations of the Holocaust featuring the opposition between "identification without expression" and "expression without identification," with Rosen located—according to him—in the second category. Rosen's exhibition undoubtedly stands in opposition to all the art that preceded it and was cataloged under the title of "art dealing with the Holocaust," but this is because it does not deal with the Holocaust at all. Rothman too fails to notice the difference and, therefore, accepts the assumptions I have noted, which are common to all those who have written about Rosen's work to date. See Rothman 1997.

11. Here and there may be found small pictures of Hitler whose purpose is informative: they visually signal the presence of Hitler at some event or occasion. This is the role played by the small and isolated images of Hitler that appear in the Ghetto Fighters Museum or at the Yad Vashem Memorial.

12. In the Ghetto Fighters Museum in Kibbutz Lochamei HaGetaot, there is a photograph of Hitler receiving the surrender of France in 1940. In Yad Vashem Museum of the Holocaust, there is an early photograph of Hitler receiving his appointment as German Chancellor in 1933. In this context, note that Hannah Arendt's important book on Eichmann, *Eichmann in Jerusalem*, was not translated into Hebrew until recently, as well as the surprising cover photo chosen for the book. In this photo Eichmann appears without his dark glasses, his gaze distracted, and with his top shirt buttons undone—nothing in it reminds one of either the Eichmann of the death machine, evil incarnate, or of the Eichmann exposed to Israelis in the photographic images from his trial in Jerusalem (Arendt 2000).

13. In this context, it will be interesting to see the tenor of the new exhibition that is to open at Yad Vashem in a few years, and whether Rosen's and Arad's exhibitions will have had any impact on it.

14. As I prepared to write this article, I asked several of my acquaintances how they actually came to be familiar with Hitler's portrait. Most of them mentioned Charlie Chaplin half jokingly (*The Great Dictator*), but when pressed could not point to the place where they had seen Hitler's picture or a place (even a book) to which they could return to retrieve it.

15. Hitler learned the art of oratory and the psychology of the masses from Hamissen in Munich. From the psychological profile of Hitler (Part 1), to be found at the Internet site http://www1.us.nizkor.org/hweb/people/h/hitler-adolf/oss-papers/text/oss-profile-01.html.

16. The frequent use of the term "Hitler" to describe other leaders or tyrants—including Yasser Arafat, Slobodan Milosevic, Saddam Hussein, or Yitzhak Rabin—as well as the avoidance of this usage on the basis of the contention that there is no place for comparison because Hitler's actions and those of the designated leaders are incommensurable, is one indication of the transformation of Hitler's face into a mask.

17. For a more comprehensive discussion of the relation between the series, see Deleuze 1969, and Azoulay and Ophir 2001.

18. In *Crowds and Power* (1978), Elias Canetti differentiates between different stages preparatory to metamorphosis. The first stage is imitation, the second is simulation (suppression of the character or masquerading as it), and the third is metamorphosis in the framework of which one body becomes equal to another in at least one dimension, enabling it to feel what the other feels.

19. In this context, see Canetti's (1978) illuminating discussion on the two forms of power that were dominant in civilizations of the past, both of which he analyzes in connection with metamorphosis: on the one hand the figure of the shaman, who can metamorphose unendingly and whose power stems from this capability, and the dictator on the other, who cannot change his shape and who is able to prevent his subjects from doing so. In the context of Rosen's exhibition, it is hard not to think of Hitler's attitude toward the Jews, and the reversal that is effected in the museum by the exhibition.

20. *The Angel of History* exhibition, curated by Ariella Azoulay, at the Herzliya Museum of Art, October 2000.

21. For a discussion of the story, see Canetti 1978.

22. In this sense I propose reading the relation between the two exhibitions in connection with the concept of trauma—the appearance of a later

image that retrospectively endows with significance an earlier image that was missed, which had not been fully experienced. On the concept of trauma, see Caruth 1994.

23. The video of the metamorphosing mustache is called *Marcel Marcel* after Marcel Duchamp, who not only added a beard and mustache to Leonardo's *Mona Lisa* but also enjoyed changing his own portrait on occasion. Norman Kleeblat, in his chapter in this book, points out that Hoffmann, Hitler's personal photographer, also photographed Duchamp.

24. See Crary's discussion on attention and distraction (Crary 1999).

25. The escape of the ethical from the picture and from the law, from the view and from the voice, takes place only in a face-to-face encounter. The presence of a third person makes it necessary "to moderate that privilege of the other," in that it makes it necessary to equate what is incomparable, or in other words overcome the face that resembles a discovery —an incomprehensible eruption—and transform it into an object of view, speech, and intervention. The presence of a third person moderates my violence toward the other, as well as the violence in the discovery of the other, which affects me and, as Lyotard says, jolts me from my position as an "I," an addresser, into the position of an addressee, a direct object (see Lyotard's remark on Levinas, following paragraph 170). The eruption of the other is violent because it exposes me with no delay, removing me at once from my position and placing me in the position of an obligated addressee—"the obligation is immediate," writes Lyotard (1983).

26. On the unconscious as a universal structure, see Lévi-Strauss 1967, and Taylor 1987.

27. Hitler speaking before the Rauschning, as quoted in Speer 1979, 175–76.

28. In the book of interviews with him, Albert Speer (1979) puts forward two contentions with regard to Hitler's cinematic presence. First, in principle any movie made about Hitler is immoral because there is no raw material available of Hitler showing him somehow in connection with his work of destruction. Second, all the movies and programs that have used Hitler's speeches have missed the point, namely, the way these speeches were constructed around a "delicate psychology" of intensification. All the movies, Speer contends, show only that portion of his speeches culminating directly in open and loud belligerence, thus entirely missing the opportunity to understand Hitler's hypnotic sway over his listeners. In this context, it may be useful to note that the segments of Hitler's speeches that are broadcast on Israeli television on Holocaust Day, which are chosen for didactic purposes, focus mainly on passages

enforcing the particular message being broadcast. This choice of selections ignores the role of the unconscious in Hitler's oratorical doctrine, with which this essay is concerned.

29. As opposed to the U.S. Holocaust Memorial Museum in Washington, D.C., where the central axis of the exhibition is based on video screens, in the two primary museums of the Holocaust in Israel, Yad Vashem and Lochamei HaGetaot, video displays (with no connection to Hitler's speeches) are almost entirely absent.

30. Several years before Boaz Arad, Doron Solomons, an Israeli video artist, exhibited video art that was based on the same principle of dissecting filmed raw material into phonetic units and reassembling them into sentences with a different meaning. Arad borrowed the technique and applied it to Hitler's speeches.

31. In the framework of the movie *The Angel of History*, which accompanied the exhibition of the same name.

32. Both to me, as the director of the movie, and to Boaz Arad, who had created the video art.

33. See, in Benjamin's essay on the work of art, the distinction he makes between looking at Picasso and looking at Chaplin (Benjamin 1978).

34. The proposal deviates from any causal logic contending that if Hitler committed a crime, he should be punished; if he is dangerous, then he should be locked away; if he is bound to hurt Jews, he must be kept away from them; if the words from his lips turn corruptive, they must be avoided at all cost and he must be prohibited from speaking; if he ruthlessly subjugated the Jews, he must be subjugated and his movements restricted, and so forth.

35. Toward the end of the book, when its characters are wondering what to do with Hitler, one of them says: "The Jewish organization must not be allowed to claim rights over his person [Hitler], let alone transport him to Israel. Which had no status either *de jure* or *de facto*, at the time of the said crimes or of the Nuremberg trials" (Steiner 1981, 103).

REFERENCES

Arendt, Hannah. 2000. *Eichmann in Jerusalem* (in Hebrew). Tel Aviv: Bavel.

Azoulay, Ariella. 2001. *Death's Showcase: The Power of Image in Contemporary Democracy*. Cambridge: MIT Press.

Azoulay, Ariella, and Adi Ophir. 2001. "We Are Not Asking What It Means, But How It Works: Introduction to *A Thousand Plateaus*." *Theory and Criticism*, No. 17.

Benjamin, Walter. 1978. "The Work of Art in the Age of Mechanical Reproduction." In *Illuminations*. New York: Schocken Books.

Canetti, Elias. 1978. *Crowds and Power* (in Hebrew). Tel Aviv: Gome sifre mada ve-mehkar, Ts'erikover.

Caruth, Cathy. 1994. *Unclaimed Experience*. Baltimore: Johns Hopkins University Press.

Crary, Jonathan. 1999. *Suspensions of Perception: Attention, Spectacle, and Modern Culture*. Cambridge, Mass.: MIT Press.

Deleuze, Gilles. 1969. *Logique du sense*. Paris: Minuit.

Foucault, Michel. 1996. *History of Sexuality*. Tel Aviv: Hakibbutz Hameuchad.

Freud, Sigmund. 1950. *Moïse et le monotheisme*. Paris: Gallimard.

Hitler, Adolf. 1985. *Mein Kampf.* Jerusalem: Akademon.

Lacan, Jacques. [1949] 1977. "The Mirror Stage as Formative of the Function of the I as Revealed in Psychoanalytic Experience." In *Écrits: A Selection*. Translated by Alan Sheridan. Reprint, London: Tavistock.

Lévinas, Emmanuel. 1982. *Ethique et infini: dialogues avec Philippe Nemo*. Paris: Fayard.

Lévi-Strauss, Claude. 1967. *Structural Anthropology*. New York: Doubleday.

Lyotard, Jean-François. 1983. *Le Différend*. Paris: Les Éditions de Minuit.

Petrova, Ada, and Peter Watson. 1996. *The Death of Hitler*. New York: Norton.

Rosen, Roee. 1997. *Live and Die as Eva Braun*. Jerusalem: Israel Museum.

Rothman, Roger. 1997. "Mourning and Mania." In *Live and Die as Eva Braun*. Jerusalem: Israel Museum.

Speer, Albert. 1979. *L'Immoralité du pouvoir*. Paris: La Table Ronde.

Steiner, George. 1981. *The Portage to San Cristóbal of A.H.* London and Boston: Faber & Faber.

Taylor, Mark C. 1987. *Altarity*. Chicago: University of Chicago Press.

Chapter 5

Racism and Ethics: Constructing Alternative History

Sidra DeKoven Ezrahi

In his presentation at the Notre Dame Holocaust Project conference, Saul Friedlander suggested that "it may be that, beyond traditional religious categories . . . what our contemporaries are seeking to discover in the Shoah is a new definition of Evil." And, inevitably, a redefinition of the very "nature of human nature"—or, as he rephrased it, "the nature of *all of us.*" This essay responds to that challenge. My fundamental working premise is that both the challenge and the response are compatible with a postmodern moral discourse that is constructed of radically new possibilities for empathic acts of imagination, for embracing "all of us."

Such a discourse is evolving in a polarized cultural environment that extends to every public space—literature, theater, cinema, commemorative rituals and sites, oral histories, and theory. The reverberations of this polarity are epistemological, aesthetic, and ethical. The examples I will draw upon here come almost exclusively from literature and the performing arts, primary nonpolitical sites in which secular societies negotiate their moral profile.

One extreme end of this polarity rests on the referential status of the Shoah as an—or *the*—*Event*, the place or entity to which our historiographic or artistic reflections do—or do *not*—correspond. (We never say *the Event* when referring to World War I or the French Revolution or the Civil War.) The Holocaust is represented by the exponents of this position as the epicenter of an earthquake or as the center of a volcano or as a black hole. It is the *unsayable*, that which swallows up all the words, all the colors, and even the instruments that would measure the damage. The many elaborations of this position take on a theological cast as the approach to the Center becomes a kind of pilgrimage. The closer one is to the Center—the place, the person, or even the story itself—the more authentic the representation. In its most extreme articulation, writing poetry or narrative constitutes a transgressive, barbaric activity to the extent that it takes place outside the vortex leading to the epicenter and maintains linguistic and conventional connections with the world beyond.

Let me acknowledge at the outset that in referring casually to "barbarisms" and "earthquakes" I am taking liberties with two of the most ubiquitous tropes in the critical discourse on representation of the Shoah. Loosely co-opted by the culture industry they helped to define, T. W. Adorno and Jean-François Lyotard have provided the signposts for a symbolic geography in which the place that swallows up everything—all words, all life, all structures, all meaning—is indexed metonymically as "Auschwitz" or, more precisely, the *crematorium* of Auschwitz. Assuming that *any* language survives the earthquake, goes this reasoning, only the most transparent or positivistic writing would be adequate to the mandate to represent *that* place. All other forms of aestheticization occupy some barbaric space outside the consensual community of rememberers. This is of course a gross simplification of the profoundly ambiguous and dynamic elaborations of Adorno's and Lyotard's philosophies, which have been submitted elsewhere to more subtle critical analyses; I am deliberately focusing on this rarefied symbolic geography as the apocalyptic ground on which the most polemical expressions of the position I am describing rest.

At the other end of this polarity is a radically different landscape. Located in the periphery, *back turned toward Auschwitz*, it unfolds as a vast terrain punctuated with potentially infinite points of access. Words and stories that were "swallowed up" in the epicenter or black hole may appear in the "barbaric" periphery, in the place where fictive possibility may even defy historical representation. In their protean and mobile forms, they subvert any and all apocalyptic or redemptive schemes.

There is a constant, unresolved tension between center and periphery, between the gravitational pull of the black hole, of Chaos as

a parody of the Sacred Center, and the cosmos-building of more distant places, local shrines, that manage to free themselves from the
pull of the center and set up alternative sites and alternative scenarios. The distinction is between static and dynamic approaches to
history and its moral and social legacies, between a premise of in-
communicability and incommensurability on the one hand and communicability and commensurability on the other. And it revolves
around the privilege granted to or withheld from those who are survivors—either because they didn't die or because they were *not there*—
to write themselves (ourselves) into *and out of* the past.

I am attempting to explore here the ethical implications of a typology I developed elsewhere. In that essay I argued that one cluster
of cultural impulses is absolutist and the other relativist in regard to
the same historical stimuli:

> The absolutist approach locates a non-negotiable self in an unyield-
> ing place whose sign is Auschwitz; the relativist position represents
> the memory of that place as a set of strategies for an ongoing *re-
> negotiation* of that historical reality. For those I will refer to as the
> "relativists," the immobility of the past is mitigated, at times under-
> mined, by the very conventions mobilized to represent it. For those
> I will call the "absolutists," an invented language grounded in a
> sense of sustained "duration" or unmastered trauma prevents con-
> vention and commensurability from relativizing the absolute reality
> of the place.[1]

All works of historical representation and interpretation are being performed in the aftermath, at a distance, but it is distance itself
that is at stake. The language of the absolutists is frozen in a mythical
replay of inexorable forces yielding either an empty and silent, or
noisy and apocalyptic, vision. The psychological dimensions of this
position were most explicitly defined by Lawrence Langer and have
been adapted by those who refer to the "deep memory" that is inarticulable and incommensurable. One of the first writers to offer a
model for "re-*present*-ing" Auschwitz was Tadeusz Borowski. In "This
Way for the Gas, Ladies and Gentlemen," all mention of a world outside, beyond, before, or after Auschwitz is effaced. "All of us walk
around naked," is the way this story begins. Consider, further, Paul

Celan's "black milk of daybreak": "we drink it at evening / we drink it at midday and morning." It is a world replayed *sub specie aeternitatis.*

The material expression of this frozen world can be found in the architecture of our memorial sites, most starkly in the reconstruction of Auschwitz and Birkenau and the various attempts to establish where IT happened (at the railroad platform? at the gate with its lacerating message like a wound on the human landscape? at the crematorium? in Birkenau II?). The paths leading inexorably to *that place* are reenacted kinetically in the railroad tracks in Claude Lanzmann's film *Shoah* and in the testimonies to the lives and the words that were swallowed up in its center. The presumption is that an aura of authenticity emanates from the gas chamber and the Sonderkommando who operated it. By extension, there are concentric circles of authenticity, stretching from the body of the survivor to his/her postwar family, and from there to the nonparticipants and nonwitnesses, and for each of these circles there is an appropriate language, beginning with the witness or documentary report closest to the Event Itself.

An example of the other—the dynamic, centrifugal, or relativist posture built of the same materials—may be found in Primo Levi, as early as his *Survival in Auschwitz* and in his own survival *after* Auschwitz, the long productive years that followed his liberation and preceded his putative suicide. In the most celebrated chapter in his memoir, "The Canto of Ulysses," what is most significant is that there remains a world out there . . . not only a world of poetry and beauty encapsulated in the memory of Dante's verses, but also the *otherness* of the Christian vision of cosmic order.

I want to submit that it is only the relativist position that provides enough space to re-create a real moral discourse—a discourse based on the legitimacy of great acts of projection. Such attempts are more than a search for memory sites and points of origin and reference, something other than the locus of absolute, unspeakable evil. They serve to create points of departure for the construction of alternative histories, of a "history that might have been," in the language of Eric Santner: the identification for postwar Germans, for example, of moments where moral decisions might have been made and were not.[2] Of course, the artistic imagination is the only place where counterhistories, even counterfactuals, are legitimate. Although nodding acknowledgment of Aristotle's distinction between history and poetry is made by participants in the debate on the limits of representation —from Hayden White to James Young[3]—their emphasis on narrative forms and conventions and the subject position of the witnesses and participants obscures the fundamental license that free societies have always accorded their artists (and that totalitarian societies have always rescinded): to carry on the moral debate through *argument* with history and its "successes."

Literary examples of the construction of alternative sites of memory that prompt a new moral discourse include Shoshana Felman's provocative reading of Albert Camus's *The Fall* (the absences in the Jewish Quarter of Amsterdam as analogues of the unremarked suicide of an anonymous woman from a bridge in Paris—that is, revisiting the place where you personally or collectively failed to take a stand). Alternative scenarios for reengaging with the past take place *anywhere*, but the ghetto and even the concentration camp serve as common venues: the Lodz ghetto (in Jurek Becker's novel *Jacob the Liar*, and in its film adaptations), the Warsaw ghetto (in Jaroslaw Rymkiewicz's narrative *Umschlagplatz: The Final Station*), a generic concentration camp (in Roberto Benigni's film *Life Is Beautiful*).

Alternative history is based on the presumption of a normative world outside Auschwitz and an untouched "age of innocence" as primary references. In all the above evocations of ghettos and camps as alternative sites of memory, children are the touchstone and target of major acts of "revisioning" history. Jacob the "Liar" engages in the most outrageous fabrications of a "better world" for the preservation of the innocence of his young ward, Lena, much as Guido does for his son in Benigni's film; in a verbal photomontage, Rymkiewicz positions his own childhood self vis-à-vis the iconic boy in the Warsaw ghetto to give him respite from the burden of raising his arms for an eternity. Saul Friedlander's ability to reconstruct his childhood out of a cup of hot chocolate with his mother at the Café Slavia, out of his father's copy of Meyrink's *The Golem*, is the counternarrative to his more mature historical consciousness of imminent doom. He admits at the beginning of his memoir that he was born in Prague "at the worst possible moment, four months before Hitler came to power." But even if the historian acknowledges with nearly forty years' hindsight that "the way of life of the Jews in the Prague of my childhood was perhaps futile and 'rootless,' seen from a historical viewpoint," the child in him insists that "this way of life was ours, the one we treasured."[4] This is the beginning of all narrative, the "petite madeleine" of all memory banks, the platform for the victims' voices he will introduce in *Nazi Germany and the Jews*—and the points of departure that, however short, make every post-Holocaust journey possible.

Childhood becomes necessary as a nature preserve with no back-shadows[5]—analogous, perhaps, at the individual level, to mediated access to faith in the Enlightenment ("the discourse of modernity," in Friedlander's words) at the collective level. We are presented in these cultural productions with another set of "concentric circles," with the *self* in the center, safe even for a brief moment in the bosom of family and nature—as counterpart to the concentric circles with Auschwitz at the center. The difference between those survivor memoirs and fictions with the protected self at the center, providing a ground of reference for the construction of postwar identity, and those for which the protected self is so occluded as to be missing as primary reference is the structural representation of the difference between the possibility and the impossibility of narrative itself and the construction of an ethical discourse on this subject at century's end.

This point is driven home dramatically if one considers how lionized Binjamin Wilkomirski was when his book *Fragments* first appeared; it may very well be that he provided the text that the absolutists were waiting for, the most harrowing of all texts to have emerged from the black hole. This self-declared memoir begins: "I have no mother tongue." It follows from this that the narrator has no *mother* either—no mother, or father, or nature preserve to which he can reliably refer:

> My earliest memories are a rubble field of isolated images and events. Shards of memory with knife-sharp edges, which still cut flesh if touched today. Mostly a chaotic jumble, with very little chronological fit; shards that keep surfacing against the orderly grain of grown-up life and the escaping laws of logic.[6]

The debate over the authenticity of Wilkomirski's narrative is as germane as the book itself to the argument I am making here. Whether or not this document is authentic, or some fantastic creation of a deranged mind, or simple fraud, it speaks a language for which the only possible "objective correlative" is Auschwitz, the *logically necessary* language of a survivor with no reference to a world beyond or before such total chaos. The apocalyptic landscape preempts any language of one's own, any private territory of the self, and any narrative that is not already invaded and fragmented by a trauma that began before one could formulate a nature preserve, before one could even construct a family album.

In the imaginative reconstructions represented in work as diverse as the "fictions" of Borowski, the testimonial film of Lanzmann, and the "memoir" of Wilkomirski, Auschwitz is the terminus of a *centripetal* imagination, wholly transcendent and therefore wholly unrepresentable. The *centrifugal* narrative, on the other hand, provides an infinity of mobile points of departure and access.

In conclusion, I would like to explore the ramifications of this argument in one arena in which a centrifugal, open-ended, ironic, and self-critical discourse is struggling against a centripetal, totalizing, formulaic, or mythic one: Israel in the aftermath of 1967. The three decades that have elapsed can be defined as an era in which fundamentalist and expansionist definitions of the collective self and absolutist definitions of excluded and inimical others have competed with inclusivist definitions of self and porous definitions of geographical and cultural boundaries; what have evolved are two diametrically opposed worldviews and political platforms. The more inexorable or absolutist the representation of the Holocaust becomes in the rhetoric and thinking of certain sectors of Israelis infected with toxic doses of "Post-Holocaust Stress Disorder" the more unyielding and archetypal the definition of the ongoing encounter between Israelis and Arabs and the more mythical the internal debate with "Jewish Destiny."

Y. H. Yerushalmi defined Jewish collective apprehension of historical events from the postrabbinic period till the modern period as a pattern of archetypes derived from biblical prototypes. While this position has been challenged by other historians and certainly deserves to be more inflected and nuanced when examining the intricacies of Jewish historical consciousness over many centuries, the logic that locks Israel into an internal theodicy between God and His chosen people has resurfaced in the essentially premodern attitudes of enclaves of contemporary Jews who perceive historical realities as replays of basic mythic patterns. The pageant that represents the

Arab-as-Nazi-as-Amalek is the Jewish version of apocalyptic or absolutist thinking, of a discourse that totalizes, constituting its own form
of "deep memory." It traps us in paradigms that are morally self-con-
gratulatory and yield lethal forms of "repetition-compulsion." If Jew-
Nazi is just the most recent incarnation of the eternal, inexorable
enmity between Jews and Others, then by definition we remain stuck
in a reductive pattern that can admit no free acts of moral imagination. Since it is unimaginable that the Jews could behave like Nazis,
since the Jews are always already Jews—that is, victims—then the
Arabs must be Nazis and everything we do is a form of self-sacrifice at
worst and self-defense at best.

For a long time after the Shoah, representations of the Holocaust in Israeli literature banished the Nazis, making them either
demonic ("Ha-German," in the words of the Hebrew poet Uri Zvi
Greenberg) or invisible (effacement as a form of revenge—a curious
reading of Deuteronomy 25:17: *"timheh et zekher amalek mi-tahat ha-
shamayin"* [thou shalt blot out the remembrance of Amalek from under heaven]). Such representations allowed for essentially no open
ethical debate. The literature that emerged through the 1960s was
with few exceptions a literature of either elegy or trauma, but it fit too
unfortunately into the theodicy of the Jews as God's eternal victims—
a form of essentialism and predestination that today continues to
gain strength among Israel's ultraorthodox and many fellow-travelers
who do not bother to examine its political and moral implications.
The Nazis in this scheme are simply the agents of an eternal cosmic
enmity.

"Imagining the Nazi" is the beginning of a new ethical rhetoric
in the culture in Israel that is broadly referred to as "post-Zionist";
going so far into unexplored, unimaginable territory as to imagine
the Jew as Nazi is to finally come to terms with the Jewish self in its
most aggressive alterity. David Grossman's *See Under: Love* ponders
"the Nazi within onself" and fantasizes about "Sondar," the heroic
leader of the "Commandos."[7] The imagination of alternative histories leaves narrative space in which the Jew can imagine him/herself
as both hero and aggressor. One of the first poetic sites to reflect
this was Dan Pagis's Cain and Abel poems, in which the two brothers
serve as universal—and interchangeable—referents for fratricide, in
place of Abraham and Isaac and the covenantal model (the Jew as

the sacrifice that God wants, and the hand that wields the knife as incidental to the act).

In the 1980s and 1990s this new relativism was largely manifested in the performative arts, challenging the rituals of consent in the commemorative spaces. The distance from commemorative to theatrical performances in Israel is the distance between the consensual, ritual affirmation of a relatively fixed, if largely secularized, theodicy and the ongoing reflexive encounter with the past as moving target. Examples of the latter include Arbeit Macht Frei (Acco Theatre group), Yehoshua Sobol's dramatic trilogy on the Lodz ghetto, and Shmuel Hasfari's play *Tashmad* (1984). Hasfari's drama focuses on the fantasies of a group of settlers living on the West Bank as their settlement is being emptied of its Jewish inhabitants by the Israeli army; the stage business employs the symbols and gestures of a swastika and a "Heil Hitler" salute.

But the most powerful expression of this sensibility is Hanokh Levin's play *Ha-Patriot*, defined by the playwright as a "satirical cabaret." Mahmud, the Arab boy, assumes the iconographic capitulary pose of the little boy with hands raised in the Warsaw ghetto. Lahav, the main Israeli character, addresses his own mother while aiming his revolver at Mahmud's head:

> He will avenge your blood and the blood of our murdered family, as then, mother, when your little brother stood alone in front of the German at night, in the field, and the German aimed his revolver at his head, and your little brother, trembling with fear, said (and he sings as he aims the revolver at Mahmud):
>
> > Don't shoot.
> > I have a mother.
> > She is waiting for me at home.
> > I haven't eaten yet. Dinner. Don't kill me.
> > I am a child.
> > I am a human being like you.
> > What did I do?
> > What difference would it make to you if I yet lived?
>
> (from the program notes of *Ha-Patriot*)[8]

The fate of this passage reflects the perceived threat that such daring acts of representation evoked in the Israeli public sphere: it was excised from the play by the board of censors (which was still operative in those years in Israel, under a code inherited from the British Mandate) and remained only in the program notes.

While performances like this inaugurated a new moral discourse, they were only the beginning of the process; with the Intifada, the Palestinians became subjects in history, in their own eyes as well as in the eyes of their Israeli "interlocutors." The representation of the Arab as "Jewish" object of history in Levin's play is, then, still part of an *interior* dialogue in which the Arab is a projection of the Israeli psyche. The decade that has elapsed since the Intifada, the era of the Peace Process, is one of greater parity between two subjects acting in and writing history.

All versions of monolithic memory and identity fixed either in the disconnected present or in the traumatic past deny the capacity of the human soul to regenerate after trauma and to contain past and present without killing either one. The price that Jews and especially Israelis pay as a collective when they are too obsessed with the past is that although the disembodied or bodiless victims, with their silences and their black holes, may provide great photo opportunities for the apocalyptically minded, they now stand in the way of present- or future-oriented, demystified meditations on the connection between collective trauma and collective power.

A "new definition of evil" in Israel would be an affirmation of a "universal" discourse that is external to the theodicy that explains Jewish history as an internal dialogue and a series of fixed archetypes. The license to imagine history as either an iconography with *interchangeable* players or as one scenario in an infinitude of *possible* histories could be the greatest contribution that free artistic representations of the Holocaust could make to the moral discourse that will cross the millennial divide.

NOTES

This essay appears in *Humanity at the Limit: The Impact of the Holocaust Experience on Jews and Christians,* edited by Michael A. Signer (Bloomington: Indiana University Press, 2000), and is reprinted with permission of the publisher.

1. Sidra DeKoven Ezrahi, "Representing Auschwitz," *History and Memory* 7, 2 (Fall/Winter 1996): 122. Many of the cultural texts that are mentioned here in passing are analyzed in greater detail in that essay.

2. Eric Santner, *Stranded Objects: Mourning, Memory, and Film in Postwar Germany* (Ithaca: Cornell University Press, 1990), 152–53.

3. See the essays by them and others in *Probing the Limits of Representation: Nazism and the Final Solution*, ed. Saul Friedlander (Cambridge: Harvard University Press, 1992). For an overview and attempt at a different approach to this ongoing debate, see James E. Young, "Toward a Received History of the Holocaust," *History and Theory* 36 (December 1997): 25–26.

4. Saul Friedlander, *When Memory Comes* (New York: Farrar, Straus, & Giroux, 1979), 9. See on this Sidra DeKoven Ezrahi, "See Under: Memory," *History and Memory*, Special Festschrift in Honor of Saul Friedlander's Sixty-Fifth Birthday (Fall/Winter 1997): 364–75.

5. On "backshadowing," see Michael André Bernstein, *Foregone Conclusions: Against Apocalyptic History* (Berkeley: University of California Press, 1994).

6. Binjamin Wilkomirski, *Fragments: Memories of a Wartime Childhood* (New York: Knopf, 1996), 3–4.

7. David Grossman, *See Under: Love*, trans. Betsy Rosenberg (New York: Farrar, Straus, & Giroux, 1989), 29. The "Jewish self as Nazi" has already been explored in other cultural contexts, most notably in American fiction after the Eichmann trial.

8. Quoted in Sidra DeKoven Ezrahi, "Revisioning the Past: The Changing Legacy of the Holocaust in Hebrew Literature," *Salmagundi*, Special Issue on *A Sense of the Past* (Fall 1985–Winter 1986): 268.

Chapter 6

"Don't Touch My Holocaust"—Analyzing the Barometer of Responses: Israeli Artists Challenge the Holocaust Taboo

Tami Katz-Freiman

> The national museum in the eternal capital of the Jewish people should encourage many exhibitions attesting that we are indeed liberated from the traumas of the past. If the Israel Museum could get hold of the bones of Holocaust victims, they could invite kindergarten children to build castles. Perhaps the Israel Museum should also import hair from Auschwitz to hang on it postmodern works.[1]

This sarcastic and radical response, published in *Ma'ariv* on January 19, 1997, by Holocaust survivor, Knesset member, and journalist Joseph Lapid, following the controversial exhibition of Israeli artist Ram Katzir at the Israel Museum, reflects the problematic nature, the hypersensitivity, and the intricacy of the current Holocaust discourse in Israel.

In this essay, I delve into the pressing issues of this highly delicate discourse. I attempt to locate the very root of its problematic nature, wherefrom all taboos and paradoxes stem pertaining to the discourse of Holocaust representation in contemporary Israeli art. The Zionist ethos is informed by two fundamental notions—"Holocaust and Heroism" and "Negation of Exile"—that are crucial to the understanding of the problematic nature inherent in Holocaust representation in Israel. In the following paragraphs, I trace the implications of these two perceptions on Holocaust representation in art, and attempt to categorize and classify modes of Holocaust representation in contemporary Israeli art in light of, or in relation to, the public sensitivity toward the manipulative use of the Holocaust. In order to elucidate some basic concepts relating to the Israeli "black hole," I examine some strategies employed by current Israeli artists who are "communicating Auschwitz"[2] in their work. Thus, the essay explores several artistic projects executed in recent years and attempts to scrutinize and analyze "the barometer of responses"—that invisible imaginary super-apparatus that measures the sensitivity of the Israeli public and determines what is included in and what is excluded from the canon of Israeli art.

The first part of the essay provides historical background to help us understand the paradox, the taboo, and the turning point that occurred in the 1980s, when the maturation of Israeli society led to a readiness to reopen the wound and second-generation artists began to break the conspiracy of silence. The second part of the essay focuses on various artistic strategies, discussing specific recent projects that challenge the Holocaust discourse. I raise basic questions pertaining to the boundaries of representation: What kind of artwork makes people lose their temper to the point where they protest, demonstrate, and create road blocks, and what kind of project goes down quietly, stirring up no storm at all?

I present eight artistic approaches: estrangement, humor, and irony (Ram Katzir and Roee Rosen); identification with the victim (Shimon Attie); emphasis on the biographical element (Haim Maor); emphasis on sentimentality and protest against the commercialization of the Holocaust (Natan Nuchi); the conceptual (Simcha Shirman); spirituality and the Jewish link (Moshe Gershuni); the model of denial and negation of the very option of "Holocaust art" (Joshua Neustein); and the radical model (*Arbeit Macht Frei*).

The heated debates revolving around the work of these artists and the spectrum of responses they evoked led me to examine the three greatest taboos of the Holocaust discourse in Israeli society: linking the Holocaust with the Israeli-Arab conflict, employing humor and irony in the context of the Holocaust, and shifting the gaze from the victim to the victimizer. This essay sets out to measure the endurance and flexibility of the yardstick of acceptance or rejection as it applies to Holocaust representations in art.

The Holocaust and Israeli Art: The Paradox and the Taboo

There is no denying the sweeping presence of the Holocaust in Israeli public life—on television, in ceremonies, memorials, books, political demagogy, and even on the street.[3] As an Israeli and as the daughter of Holocaust survivors, I can attest that the Holocaust has always been there, breathing down our necks, as a looming threat that may descend upon us once again, and after 1967 as a pretext for Israel's military power and its charged relations with the Arab world. Over the course of time, the official memory of the Holocaust, supplemented by the trauma of local wars, has intensified the country's anxiety, transforming it into an ideological instrument justifying the oppression of others.[4]

In light of the overwhelming presence of the Holocaust in Israeli cultural and political life, it is surprising that up until the early 1980s the Holocaust was entirely excluded from the canonical and hegemonic discourse of Israeli visual art.[5] Much has been written in recent years about this paradox and about the taboo regarding Holocaust representation.[6] Theodor Adorno's famous aphorism, "there can be no poetry after Auschwitz," is one of the most widely cited phrases in this context, which indicates how problematic silence is and how complicated it is to break that silence. Moshe Zuckermann, an Israeli historian who has studied the public discourse of the Holocaust and published numerous essays about the difficulties inherent in representation of the Holocaust in Israel,[7] focuses on three obstacles:

> First, the risk of hurting survivors' feelings. When the act of representation goes beyond the survivor's private experience, or as may be the case within the framework of artistic representation, when the historical inferno is subordinated to modes of structuring and modeling relying on principles of alienation, aesthetic estrangement, and irony; naturally, this is a particularly sensitive nerve in Israeli society. Second, there is the danger (just as typical in Israeli society) of the horror's inflationary use for various purposes, inappropriate usages, which, due to their vulgar instrumental nature, desecrate the memory of the dead, and in a political context—also the memory of their status as the victims of extreme oppression. Third, the paradox emerging from Adorno's very words: How can

there be cultural representation of that which culture itself col-
laborated in generating or at least failed to prevent. Not to mention the fact that such representation . . . embeds some measure of
pleasure?[8]

Up until the early 1980s, Adorno's assertion appears to have been
carved in stone in the visual arts in Israel, providing a good pretext
for avoiding the subject. Representation of the Holocaust was perceived (by the elitist milieu) as trivialization and erosion of its memory. The main argument was that the documentary images of the
horror were all too familiar and all too accessible. Why would one
choose to represent it in art?

Reluctance to touch upon this sensitive nerve has to do with the
fact that for many years the words "Holocaust and heroism" were virtually inseparable in Israel. Our Independence Day is part of a sequence of three days during a single week: Holocaust Remembrance
Day, IDF Memorial Day, and Independence Day. The linear arrangement of these three days was aimed at producing a narrative structure
with a clear message and a happy ending. The sequence—Holocaust,
heroism, and revival—corresponds to the historical record as follows:
The nearly annihilated nation defended itself, defeated its enemies,
and built its own country. This was the ideological formula in the days
following the establishment of the state, heroic days of nationality
and patriotism. In order to raise the people's spirit during the country's early days, it was necessary to repress individual experiences of
the Holocaust. Instead, it was perceived as a time of national destruction, a genocide that resulted in redemption. The memory of the
Holocaust became a ritual aimed at uniting the people and not a tool
for historical understanding.[9]

Another crucial concept for understanding the problematic nature of Holocaust representation in Israel is the "Negation of Exile,"
as discussed by historian and scholar Amnon Raz-Krakotzkin.[10] Kra-
kotzkin's major argument is that the ideology of the negation of exile
has guided the Zionist approach toward various aspects of the extermination of European Jewry. The preoccupation with Jewish identity
was considered obsolete. In Israel, the notion of the "Jew" is associated with the concepts of "Diaspora" and "Exile," representing the
negative aspects of our history. The Israeli is the positive "new Jew,"

the "ex-Jew," an antithesis to the image of the passive, Diaspora Jew, who went to the slaughter like a lamb.

This ideology, which nurtures the Zionist ethos, may also account for the exclusion of the Holocaust from the discourse of Israeli art.[11] Likewise, the desire to construct and establish a distinct Israeli identity unrelated to the Diasporal identity, underlay the hegemonic ideology of the artistic avant-garde. An absurd situation was created—the extreme manifestation of the destiny of the Jewish people is entirely absent from the canon of Israeli art. For Israeli artists to this very day, the term "Holocaust artist" is derogatory, smacking of kitsch, sentimentality, and anachronism (unless the artist employs post-Zionist critical strategies such as humor and irony—a recent trend).

In other words, the Holocaust touches upon such a sensitive public nerve in Israel that discussion of the quality of works dealing with it has been virtually absent. The difficulty and pain involved in the very preoccupation with the trauma have made discussion of the works problematic as well. A matter-of-fact critique of a work which makes an explicit statement of pain or memory was considered insensitive. Thus, the art created by survivors was pushed to the margins and was never accepted as legitimate by the elite. It was "not modern enough": neither abstract nor conceptual, neither sophisticated nor universal. Rather, it had narrative, figurative, and symbolic ("too Jewish") content and had not dealt with the language of art itself. It was regarded as obsolete.[12]

The Turning Point

Since the 1980s there has been a shift, and the Holocaust now makes a strong showing on the Israeli cultural agenda. A new understanding of the Holocaust seems to be in evidence, judging by the considerable increase in academic research alongside various productions in theater, film, television, literature, and popular music. Several factors have come together here. With the fall of the Soviet bloc, increasing numbers of Israelis started going on "root trips" to Eastern Europe. For more than fifteen years now, youth expeditions have been sent annually to the concentration and death camps in Poland. Many Holocaust survivors have begun telling their stories. This need to talk corresponds to the need to listen. With the publication of the testimonies of survivors who have written their own personal stories, the Holocaust has acquired autobiographical features. Specific details have gradually emerged from the black hole. No longer a silent, faceless crowd, its victims are actual people—my grandmother, your aunt.

The taboo was gradually challenged in the visual arts too.[13] Second-generation artists began expressing their anxieties. By 2002 they had already taken the subject to different realms, deepening the Holocaust's layers of meaning and linking them to other fields of discourse such as memory, racism, and the body. During the 1990s, in line with postmodern and post-Zionist trends the Holocaust has ceased to be repudiated as subject matter; it has a new legitimacy, as can be seen in the way it is confronted by second-generation artists.

This readiness to reopen the wound must be perceived as an integral part of the maturation of Israeli society. It is a sign that society is no longer perceived as monolithic. Art is no longer expected to speak on behalf of the national collective whole. Its voice has split into a multiplicity of personal, individual, stratified, dynamic, conflicted, and contradictory voices.[14]

However, the subject is still not the *bon ton* in art. There has not yet been a single large-scale group exhibition in a major Israeli museum dealing specifically with the Holocaust. To date only one book by an Israeli has been published about art and the Holocaust,[15] and a mere fifteen of the artists mentioned in it are Israeli.[16] One feels that preoccupation with the Holocaust leads down a dark road, which only a handful have managed to cross safely. The fact that the conference for which this essay was written took place at Lehigh University in Bethlehem, Pennsylvania, rather than at the Israel Museum in Jerusalem reaffirms that we are probably not ready yet.

The Barometer of Responses

Over the past fifty years the threshold marker, the barometer that measures the sensitivity of the Israeli public, seems to have become more flexible, changing in response to the spirit of the times and circumstances. The dynamic of the responses, both those of the general public and of the art world (which are generally opposed to one another), is like a seismograph reflecting trends and the national mood. Where exactly does one cross the line? Which image is permitted and which forbidden? What is considered disgraceful and what decent? What is desecrating and what purifying? At what point does the threat of censorship or loss of public support loom? And, conversely, what ensures acceptance by the elitist Israeli art establishment?

Two recent projects at the Israel Museum in Jerusalem offer a principal test case, having triggered passionate responses and challenged the status quo regarding Holocaust representations in Israel. The first was Ram Katzir's site-specific installation *Within the Line* (winter 1997), based on the concept of coloring books with Nazi images; and the second was Roee Rosen's interactive installation *Live and Die as Eva Braun* (fall 1997). By critically viewing the importance of the Holocaust in the formation of Israeli identity, both shows caused a scandal and infuriated many Holocaust survivors to the point that the Minister of Education was called upon to cancel the exhibitions.

One of the most radical responses is quoted at the beginning of my essay. The other, by Haim Dasberg, a Holocaust survivor who responded to Ram Katzir's project, reflects the difficulties in turning the gaze from the victim to the victimizer:

> What do I care about the murderer? After all that I have been through, do I still have to explain, understand, and relate to the way the poor bastard became a murderer? If the museum wants to deal with the lesson of the Holocaust, let it screen documentary films, display authentic photographs and paintings inspired by the horror. But where do they get the nerve to make playful use of a picture where a Jew's side-locks are being shaved off? . . . They are taking our open wound and treating it lightly.[17]

An analysis of the response to these installations raises several questions and quandaries:

> Was it the fact that these exhibitions were presented at the Israel Museum, the very heart of the establishment, the official national museum of the State of Israel, that triggered the public response? At the same time, another artist, Orchedea Yemnfeld, exhibited in the Jerusalem Artists' House a swastika made of human hair, eliciting no response whatsoever.

Who is allowed to touch upon the subject at all? Who has the license to represent the inferno? Does the fact that an artist belongs to the group of "second generation"—that someone in his/her family "was there"—automatically grant him the right to speak?[18] Does a non-Jewish artist have the right to deal with the Holocaust?[19] And what is the "boiling point"? What is most infuriating? What makes people lose their temper?

It seems that the three taboos that may not be broken (as far as the general public is concerned) are: (1) making an analogy between the Holocaust and the ongoing Israeli-Arab conflict;[20] (2) employing rational unsentimental strategies, such as humor and irony; and (3) turning the gaze on the victimizer rather than on the victim. Ram Katzir and Roee Rosen's projects forced the viewer to participate in a dialogue (in Rosen's case, an erotic dialogue; in Katzir's case, an ostensibly innocent one) with the victimizer. The disapproval of these works was based on the perverse relations forced on the viewer, an objection to the manipulation that has transformed viewers into "Nazi collaborators," so to speak.

Shimon Attie: Rejection of the Non-Israeli

In 1991 the American Jewish artist Shimon Attie slide-projected portions of pre–World War II photographs of Jewish street life in Berlin in their present vicinity. Screened for an evening or two, these projections could be seen by local residents, drivers on the street, and passers-by. By using slide projection on location, fragments of the past were introduced into the visual field of the present (for a discussion and illustration, see Michelle Friedman's essay in this volume). Thus, parts of long-destroyed Jewish community life were visually simulated, momentarily re-created. By attempting to renegotiate the relationship between past and present, the project sought to violate the collective processes of denial and forgetting.

This project, entitled *The Writing on the Wall*, was shown in major museums worldwide, among them the New York Museum of Modern Art,[21] and yet it was rejected by all the major Israeli museums. Since arguments about quality are not relevant here, this puzzling rejection raises the question of "license": Who is qualified to touch *our* Holocaust? I can only conclude that the project was perceived by Israeli museum curators as "too Jewish," "too Diasporal," "too sentimental." Attie's point of view and the representation of the victims were inconsistent with the perception of "Holocaust and Heroism." Moreover, the project requires no ironic or subversive post-Zionist gaze. But most of all, Attie's project clashes with the "negation of Exile" ideology. Israel prefers to remember the gas chambers rather than the richness and intricacy of prewar Jewish life in Europe. And—beyond all this—the fact that Attie was not Israeli disqualified him, as if to say, "We don't need any external experts on this matter" (in other words, in Israeli terms he had no "license").[22]

Haim Maor: Qualified Acceptance

Haim Maor, the son of survivors, began dealing with the Holocaust as early as the late 1970s. He was not really accepted into the canon, although he was born in Israel (1951) and has even exhibited his work at the Israel Museum. For more than twenty years, he has been delving intensively into the black hole of the Israeli collective consciousness, extracting materials for his art. In his oeuvre he combines these materials with biographical elements.

Maor first referred to the Holocaust—directly and chillingly—in an installation he mounted in a bomb shelter in Tel Hai in 1983 entitled *Message from Auschwitz-Birkenau to Tel Hai.* Tel Hai is a settlement in the Galilee, in northern Israel, etched into the Zionist collective memory as the ultimate symbol of heroism and sacrifice. The installation was a walking tour from light into darkness: The viewer walked in through the entrance door of a school building under construction, passed through empty classrooms, walked down some stairs into a long and narrow corridor, and arrived at Tel Hai's central bomb shelter. The viewer experienced a sense of suffocation triggered by the descent into the unventilated shelter and seeing the image that appeared on the shelter's wall—a combination between Tel Hai's mythological courtyard building and the building through which one enters Birkenau. The surprising similarity between the buildings' silhouettes and the fact that on the way out the viewer noticed the showers, always found in Israeli bomb shelters, was highly disconcerting.

Haim Maor, *Light Number,* 1992. Detail from the installation *Disqualified Scrolls.* Brass, illumination, 41.5 x 60 cm. Courtesy of the artist.

In 1988, following a visit to Poland and Germany, Maor presented an exhibition at the Israel Museum entitled *The Face of Race and Memory,* where he first revealed his private history as a son of Holocaust survivors. It was a kind of private exorcism touched by a sense of persecution and humiliation alongside illuminating observations about how we imbibe racist prejudice. Maor displayed photographs of his family and himself alongside photographs of his German friend Susanna, her family, and friends. The use of visual conventions of frontal or profile portrait was reminiscent of mug shots, Nazi studies of racial theory, and the photographs taken by the Nazis in the camps. The similarity between the two families shattered the viewer's basic racial stereotypes.

The same portraits appeared in a separate room, this time painted on wooden boards, reminiscent of the painted portraits found in the ancient tombs of Fayum in Upper Egypt. Here he applied a different kind of classification based on transformation from realistic painting to broken, faded painting, from memory to oblivion.

One of Maor's most powerful works is the 1992 *Light Number*—the numbers tattooed in 1942 on the arm of his father, survivor of the Birkenau camp, engraved on a copper plate: 78446. The copper plate was illuminated from the back. The light emanated from the tiny holes, creating an aura around the entire plaque. Maor transformed the act of skin tattooing, intended to bestow a technical identity on the person while eliminating his or her singular human identity, into a metaphysical symbol with spiritual connotations associated with alchemy. By magnifying the private number and its tattoo in the copper, Maor created a magical object which projects the finite nature of mortality, while simultaneously hinting at the generation of new life.

No one in Israel was disturbed by Maor's work. But neither was he praised or considered a member of the elitist milieu. His work contained a harmless dose of biography and criticism. His point of departure was identification with the victim, and his "license" derived from the fact that he was the son of survivors.

Simcha Shirman: Documentary Manipulation

Simcha Shirman, a well-known Israeli photographer, was born in Germany in 1947 to Holocaust survivors of Polish origin. His work was also received in Israel without controversy. In the early 1990s, when he was forty-three, Shirman traveled to Poland and Germany and started exploring the effect of his parents' Holocaust trauma on himself. Only then did he begin to include images directly linked to the Holocaust in his works, signing them with his initials: SS. His works manifest a desire to transform the bleeding wound, the emotions, and shame into an unsentimental semiotic system.

In 1999 Shirman represented Israel at the Venice Biennial with an explicit Holocaust piece entitled *History as Memory*. In two of the four spaces allotted to the Israeli Pavilion, he constructed an installation combining objects and photographs. The subtitle of his installation was *Polish Landscape, German Landscape*. The space was split into two separate areas: the lower level was an area of purification, and the upper level, of hunting. The site of purification—the bathroom—was a white, sterile, alien space projecting claustrophobic medical sterility. Impressed on the tiles was the German sign from Auschwitz,

Simcha Shirman, *Polish Landscape, German Landscape: S.S. 470430-990613*, 1999.
General view of the upper level of the installation *History as Memory* at the Israeli
Pavilion in the Venice Biennial. Courtesy of the artist.

bearing the command "Be Civilized!" Three urinals were attached to
the shiny porcelain walls, and above them three portrait photographs
—two authentic, black-and-white portraits of the victims, and one
color portrait of the artist.

At the center of the upper level—the hunting ground—Shirman
mounted a sniper rifle cast in aluminum, its site aimed at three monitors projecting an image of the flow of visitors on the lower level.
Here Shirman employed role reversal between the hunter and the
hunted, between murderer and victim. The viewers photographed on
the lower level thus played the role of the hunted, and when they arrived at the upper level they became the hunters. In the same space,
Shirman also presented two series of black-and-white photographs,
German Landscape and *Polish Landscape*: hunting towers in Germany
and watchtowers from Auschwitz. Here too he was interested in the
point of view of the watchman/hunter as well as that of the victim/
hunted. These are images deeply engraved in the Israeli collective

consciousness, although the collective memory has been emptied of emotional content.

This, incidentally, was one of the objections of the Israeli art world to Shirman's project. Many rejected the very idea of presenting Israeli artists through the clichéd filter of "Memory and Holocaust." They maintained that it was tacky and sentimental and that it would further isolate Israeli art on the international art scene. Indeed, the exhibition received very little coverage in professional magazines in Israel. Thus, the exhibition in Venice does not necessarily indicate Shirman's acceptance into the Israeli canon.

Moshe Gershuni: Acceptance

An entirely different case, that of acceptance, is presented by Moshe Gershuni, who was among the first to link Israeliness and Jewish identity. The presentation of his works in the late 1970s and early 1980s relegitimized the connection between Israeli visual art and Jewish identity in general and with the Holocaust trauma in particular. Gershuni is neither a survivor, nor second generation. He is a *sabra* (born in Tel Aviv in 1936), a modernist with roots in the current Tel-Aviv-based artistic community, which speaks no Yiddish nor shows much interest in the Holocaust.

Gershuni's work deals with mourning, lamentation, consolation, and forgiveness, and the permanent presence of Jewish suffering and discussion of victims and sacrifice. In 1982 he was quoted as saying: "I am a Jew! Yes, with all the mystique that it may imply. I am Israeli because I am Jewish, otherwise there is no reason for me to be here of all places."[23] This was the first time a secular artist had identified himself in such a way, trying to articulate the connection between being a Jew and being an Israeli.[24]

Gershuni referred to the Holocaust via two key images: The swastika and the yellow Star of David. The swastika emerged in several of Gershuni's works during the 1980s. One of the first was *In My Heart's Blood*, an installation created for the 1980 Tel Hai Biennial, also shown at the Tel Aviv Museum of Art and later developed for the 1982 Venice Biennial. Gershuni filled the entire room with bloodstained

Moshe Gershuni, *Justice Shall Walk before Him*, 1988. Painted dishes, 60 x 65 cm. Courtesy of the artist and Givon Gallery, Tel Aviv.

plates arranged on the floor in the shape of a swastika. The accompanying plaque read, "My wonderful red is your precious blood." Throughout the 1980s, Gershuni challenged divine justice after the Holocaust. Thus, for example, in the 1987 work *Glory and Eternity, Mightiness and Majesty,* and a year later in *Justice Shall Walk before Him,* he displayed four cracked ceramic plates, on two of which he painted swastikas. On the other two he wrote, "Justice Shall Walk before Him" —a verse from a prayer recited at a Jewish funeral. By juxtaposing the reverent text and the swastikas, Gershuni undermined God's glory after Auschwitz. The same may apply to the 1988 work *And Where Are All the Jews?* in which he inscribed this horrifying question on a ceramic plate. Gershuni's later works, such as the 1995 *All-Merciful God,* with dark eye sockets next to the line from the Kaddish prayer, were similarly perceived as a lamentation.

Analyzing the barometer of responses, it is interesting to ask why Gershuni was accepted, even embraced, by the Israeli art world, without stirring up any antagonism on the part of the so-called "Holocaust protectors," despite his breaking of the taboo, and despite the distinct Jewish motifs, the discussion of Diaspora, and the use of Yiddish. The key to acceptance appears to be to find the right dose of sentimentality, complexity, and concept. In Gershuni's case, it helped that his work was not exactly "about the Holocaust," that it was intellectually layered, and, most importantly, that it was congruent with the spirit of the times. The change in Gershuni's work occurred at the right place at the right time: He reflected the values of the Israeli elite, representing the intellectual *bon ton* of the early 1980s.[25]

Joshua Neustein: Total Denial

Another response (in this case from the artist's point of view) is that of denial. *Domestic Tranquility, Bne Brak*, a site-specific installation made for the Herzliya Museum of Art by the New York-based Israeli artist Joshua Neustein in 1999 did not provoke any scandal. Moreover, it was never meant to be associated with the Holocaust. It was the fifth project in the series *Ash Cities*, which Neustein, a Polish-born survivor, started in 1996.[26]

Domestic Tranquility, Bne Brak was composed of ten tons of powdery moist ashes which covered the three-hundred-square-meter museum floor as a relief, forming a map of the orthodox city of Bne Brak, with all its streets and prominent *yeshivas*. The scale was such that it allowed viewers to walk through the city streets. A large crystal chandelier was suspended from the ceiling very close to the surface of the relief, and at the entrance was a monitor featuring a video piece in two parts: In the first part, Neustein himself was seen facing a field of sunflowers, reading an excerpt from a speech by President Yitzhak Ben Zvi in Hebrew, Arabic, and English.[27] In the second part, one saw a young woman in modest traditional attire diligently ironing scribbled pieces of paper, possibly those of the speech, bringing to mind the use of "laundered words," namely, euphemisms and, of course, "domestic tranquility."

As mentioned, Neustein's work, powerful and provocative, did not conjure up any demons. According to the artist, it had nothing to do with the Holocaust. I was fascinated by the consistent denial and the "laundered perceptions" Neustein himself enforced on his viewers.[28] After all, the installation was entitled *Domestic Tranquility, Bne*

Joshua Neustein, *Domestic Tranquility, Bne Brak,* 1999. General view of an installation at the Herzliya Museum of Art from the series of *Ash Cities.* Ashes, monitor and crystal chandelier. Courtesy of the artist and the Herzliya Museum of Art.

Brak. Bne Brak is the largest orthodox city in central Israel. It is often compared to the pre-Holocaust *shtetl*—the Eastern European Jewish village. Its numerous *yeshivas* bear the names of Jewish seminaries wiped out in the Holocaust. It is a city where the spoken language is still Yiddish. Neustein introduced a chilling link between a Jewish city made out of ashes, with the chandelier clearly invoking the Jewish-European context. Nonetheless, not a single word in the exhibition's textual material implied any connection with the Holocaust.[29] Only one critic read the work as directly linked to the Holocaust.[30] Other critics, following the artist's lead, preferred to read it as referring primarily to the current state of affairs in Israel, with Bne Brak symbolizing the polarization between the secular and the religious in Israeli society.

It is interesting to examine the artist's attempt to shift the reading of his installation from the historical to the political, from the local to the universal. In one of our recent (virtual) discussions, Neustein wrote to me:

Reading *Shlom Bayit Bne Brak* as a Holocaust piece would defeat the purpose of the installation that addresses current traumas and not history and memory. I am a supporter of Adorno's famous dictum. In a sense I am "anti-memorialist." . . . There is nothing in my lexicon that has privileged insight into the Shoa. Shoa has a rightful place in the study of history, sociology, politics and other disciplines. I do not make Shoa art, it is not do-able.

This attitude reflects the reluctance of Israeli artists to be associated with the label "Holocaust art" as well as their desire to speak in universal terms.

Natan Nuchi: Voluntary Exclusion

One who has entirely excluded himself from the canon of Israeli art, consciously and voluntarily, is Natan Nuchi—one of the few artists who has dared look at Holocaust representation straight in the eye, dealing with the subject in a direct, refined manner long before such discussion was possible. Nuchi was born on Moshav Nahallal in the Jezereel Valley and left Israel for the United States in 1969, when he was seventeen. He currently lives and works in New York. He is a quintessential second-generation artist. Observing his paintings from 1986 to 1994, one cannot misread the image, the theme, and the context—elongated nude figures, Giacomettian, as though hovering in midair, floating in thick dark space like ghosts, like *Muselmann*. These are meditative works calling upon the viewer to keep silent in the presence of a single central image—that which is left of the human figure: skin and bones.

In 1994 Nuchi wrote about the significance of the Holocaust in his work:

The Holocaust meant for me an authentic, primal realm, that as a subject matter for art defied prevalent trends of ironical and tongue in cheek preoccupation with appropriation and inauthenticity. The photographic imagery from the Holocaust seemed to me to be among the most extreme in the pool of images that exist in our culture . . . and although with the passage of time these photographs tend to lose their power to move us, my position as an artist is that images of human suffering are still the truest, most enduring and most honorable approach to the Holocaust in art. . . . The large scale image of the single naked . . . white skinned powerless male goes against consumerist and capitalistic ideals of optimism, and activism. . . . Mortality, vulnerability and being victimized are either repressed or kept in low profile, and can be generally tolerated in the art of this society, only if the aesthetic pleasure, such as metaphor, beauty, form, richness of texture and material etc. can surpass the harshness and pain of the subject matter.[31]

In 1997 Nuchi radically changed his artistic direction. In a project entitled *The Holocaust and the Market,* he expressed his discontent with the commercialized marketing of the Holocaust.[32] The installation consisted of two walls covered with photographs of book and video covers dealing with the Holocaust found in major book and video chainstores in New York. Along the wall, on a real shelf, the artist placed authentic photographs of the piles of corpses documented by the camera of an American soldier in Buchenwald. Through this juxtaposition, Nuchi strove to confront representations of the Holocaust at the national level in museums and official memorial sites and representations of the Holocaust on the market.

According to Nuchi, photographs depicting heaps of corpses and mass executions are immediately identified as belonging to the Holocaust; however, none of them appear on the book covers. They are usually concealed in the inner pages, if included at all. The competition for the consumer's attention and pocketbook transforms the book covers into ads designed to seduce the consumer. A book cover with the word Auschwitz written in elongated, embossed golden letters against a black background is as seductive as a pretty box of chocolates.[33] The typography and design are subordinate to the same marketing terms, the same advertising language and consumer ideology as other commodities on the market. The harsh images violate the rules of the marketplace and are perceived as emotional extortion, invasion of privacy, contempt of suffering, kitsch, or pornography.[34]

"The Holocaust has become yet another subject among other subject matters (Holocaust, sports, cookery, business), without any hierarchy of importance, or yet another holocaust among other holocausts, all equally significant—those of the Cambodians, the Armenians, the Gypsies, the homosexuals, the Jews, the Aztecs."[35] Thus, to

Natan Nuchi, *The Holocaust in Hollywood*, 2000. Digital print (variable size). Courtesy of the artist.

each of the two groups of photographs, Nuchi added a title, a label, as in a library index: The Holocaust as merchandise / The Holocaust for the middle class / The Holocaust for the rich / The Holocaust on sale / The Holocaust as best seller / The Holocaust as Oscar winner, and so on.

Nuchi's social critique escalated to such great anger and discontent that he himself crossed the line toward the very tactics of "ironic play and intellectual witticism" he had dubbed inappropriate. This is especially evident in his recent work, *The Holocaust in Hollywood*, 2000, in which he replaced the well-known Hollywood sign with a Holocaust sign. The underlying idea is that the capitalistic filter has transformed the Holocaust into the story of the individual fitting into the pattern of Hollywood action movies in which the individual triumphs against all odds. According to the capitalist myth, with initiative, effort, and a little bit of luck, anyone can become a millionaire. This formula is applied to survivors' stories too, as in Spiegelman's comics series *Maus* and Spielberg's *Schindler's List*. In both cases, the survivors, the story's protagonists, endure against all odds, while everyone around them dies.[36]

Arbeit Macht Frei: **Contradictory Responses**

I would like to conclude this discussion with the convention-breaking theater performance *Arbeit Macht Frei* from Toitland Europe by the Acre Experimental Theater Group, which was an extreme case of contradictory responses. More than any other artistic project, *Arbeit Macht Frei* is one of the most powerful experiences offered by Israeli culture in recent years,[37] conjuring up old demons.

It is a multimedia production that took three years of preparation, and is performed by a group of actors directed by David Ma'ayan—a five-hour performance without a script, based on the personal experiences and life histories of each of the actors. It is an overwhelming event, during which the audience participates, is led through narrow corridors, crowding into suffocating rooms and eating dinner.[38]

It begins with a visit to the Ghetto Fighters' Museum, a memorial museum on Kibbutz Lohamei Hageta'ot (Ghetto Fighters' Kibbutz) established by Holocaust survivors after the war. The participants are taken on a ride in a tourist bus, accompanied by an actress-soldier (from the "memory corps"). The leading characters in the scene are Zelma and Chalid, who guide the viewers on this museum visit. Zelma (actress Smadar Ya'aron) represents the victim, the one whose memory was excluded from Zionist discourse. In broken language, she comments on the exhibits in the museum, guiding the viewer toward new insights, as when she analyzes Fascist aesthetics or presents photographs of the ghetto, and asks the audience about other present-day ghettos. Later on Zelma is replaced by Chalid (actor Chalid Abu Ali), who guides the visitors on their tour of a miniaturized model of Treblinka. Chalid provides a meticulous explanation of the extermination procedure. The Palestinian actor's identification with the suffering of the Jews challenges the Zionist monopoly over the memory of the Holocaust. Chalid's participation in the ritual of remembrance furnishes it with an added significance, providing the viewer with a new perspective on various aspects of Israeli reality.

One of the outstanding parts of the performance, back in the theater halls, is the piano piece played by the same Zelma from the museum, now playing the role of a Holocaust survivor who raises her son, Moni, to be a living torch to Holocaust memory. In one scene she tries to trace the structure of German and Hebrew popular songs and children's songs. In a chilling manner, she demonstrates the psychosis of nationalism both in Germany and in Israel. Later the event evolves into a multimedia spectacle linking the commemoration ceremonies familiar to every Israeli with other ritual events associated with Independence Day celebrations and the Arab-Israeli conflict. The well-known narrative of Holocaust-heroism-revival is shattered. In the final climax Zelma and Chalid unite into a single memory, first in a torture scene where Chalid is riding a torture apparatus while one of the women from the audience is whipping him, and later in a moving Pieta-like scene.

Arbeit Macht Frei offers no single clear message, but rather introduces new ways of discussing the Holocaust as the most important factor shaping Zionist consciousness, as the root of our national neurosis. It demonstrates the paranoia fostered on the Israeli public, the cynical abuse of the Holocaust, and the moral permission it ostensibly gives us to abuse others. It criticizes the Holocaust industry, the obsessive memorization, and the imperative to remember, and discusses the danger of transforming preoccupation with the Holocaust into a ritualistic substitute.

Back to the "barometer of responses," *Arbeit Macht Frei* injected a new argument into the discourse: The play received the first prize in the Acre Festival and won sweeping acclaim, superlatives that have not been heard for years in the Israeli press. Public debate was triggered only when the group was invited to the Berlin Festival. The Ministry of Education, which also supported the theater financially, voiced its reservations about going to Berlin. This in turn triggered a wave of responses in the press. The usual voices were heard, such as: "Why air our dirty laundry in public, let alone in Germany!" The main argument was that we must appear "united" in a foreign setting. "The Germans will feast on it. It will clear their conscience." In other words, never mind such offensive talk at home, but why outside? In front of the Gentiles? Particularly the Germans? Most controversial was the association made in the play between the Holocaust and the ongoing conflict with the Arabs: "Why does the naked Jewish woman have to caress a naked Arab against the backdrop of television sets blasting Independence Day songs?" "I understand they wanted to torture us, but there is a limit."[39]

In conclusion, the projects, works, and cases presented here—
and many others which I could not include in the confines of this
essay—reflect the intricate discourse revolving around the manner in
which the Holocaust is presented in Israeli art, introducing new ways
of discussing the Holocaust as our national neurosis. These works
raise questions about the lessons of the Holocaust: how does it happen that instead of learning the lesson of human love and the struggle against racism and nationalism, the opposite lessons are drawn?
The dynamic barometer of responses highlights the problematic nature of these grave issues in Israel. What is accepted? What is rejected?
What constitutes the limit? Where exactly does one draw the line?

NOTES

English translation: Daria Kassovsky

"Don't Touch My Holocaust," the title of this paper, is drawn from a documentary by Israeli filmmaker Asher Tlalim about *Arbeit Macht Frei*, a theater
performance by the Acre Experimental Theater Group.

1. Yosef Lapid, "Museum Stupidity," *Ma'ariv*, January 19, 1997.
2. Sidra DeKoven Ezrahi, "Representing Auschwitz," *History and Memory* 7,
   no. 2 (winter 1995): 121.
3. For example, all the streets in my neighborhood bear the names of Jewish communities that were annihilated in Europe: Lodz Community
   Street, Warsaw Community Street, and so on.
4. The concept of the "perpetual victim" and the famous mantra "the
   whole world is against us" were fostered by the Zionist ethos and became
   a common cliché. Sitting with my family in my parents' home on the eve
   of Holocaust Remembrance Day, after watching a videotaped interview
   about my mother's life in Hungary during the war (produced by the
   Spielberg Archive), I realized that the message she wished to convey to
   her children and grandchildren was "Keep this country safe, don't let it
   happen again." For a profound discussion of the instrumentalization of
   the Holocaust in Israeli rhetoric, see Moshe Zuckermann, "On Anxiety
   in Israeli Political Culture," in *Anxiety* (Ramat Gan: Museum of Israeli
   Art, 1994): 77–81.
5. In this context I would like to clarify my use of the term "canonical art."
   There is a distinct hierarchy within the Israeli art world: two major mu-

seums, a single professional art magazine, and a handful of theoreticians and scholars outline the discourse's boundaries. Although Holocaust representations have been present in Israeli art throughout the years, they were excluded from the canon and considered inferior. The reasons why certain voices were silenced while others were encouraged are addressed later in this essay.

6. This essay does not purport to be a historical overview; rather, it is an attempt to clarify some basic concepts related to the current Holocaust discourse in Israel. For a comprehensive and current discussion of the subject, see Dalia Manor, "From Rejection to Recognition: Israeli Art and the Holocaust," *Israel Affairs* 4, nos. 3 and 4 (spring–summer 1998): 253–77. See also Roee Rosen, "The Visibility and Invisibility of Trauma: On Traces of the Holocaust in the Work of Moshe Gershuni and in Israeli Art" (in Hebrew), *Studio Art Magazine* 76 (October–November 1996): 44–62, and Sarit Shapira, "Scorched Link," in the catalog *Burnt Whole: Contemporary Artists Reflect upon the Holocaust,* curated by Karen Holtzman (Washington, D.C.: Washington Project for the Arts, 1994): 3–7.

7. For his major publication on the Holocaust in public rhetoric during the Gulf War, see Moshe Zuckermann, *Shoah Ba-heder Ha-atum: Ha-"shoah" Ba-itonut Ha-israelit Bi-tkufat Milhemet Ha-mifratz* (Shoah in the Sealed Room: The "Holocaust" in the Israeli Press during the Gulf War) (Tel Aviv: n.p., 1993).

8. Moshe Zuckermann, "Steven Spielberg: There Were No Rehearsals in the Death Camps" (in Hebrew), *Shishi Tikshoret/Tarbut,* February 16, 1996, 16–17.

9. On the dangers of nurturing the Holocaust myth, see Adi Ophir's essay, chapter 9 in this volume.

10. Amnon Raz-Krakotzkin, "Exile within Sovereignty: Toward a Critique of the 'Negation of Exile' in Israeli Culture (Part II)" (in Hebrew), *Teoria U-vikoret* (Theory and Criticism) 5 (fall 1994): 113–32.

11. In the historiography and criticism of Israeli art, there is another approach discussing, not the absence, but the presence, albeit implicit and subliminal, of the Holocaust in Israeli art. According to this approach, high-quality works of art created in Israel "infiltrated" the black hole of the Holocaust in spirit and atmosphere, rather than in specific images or metaphors. For this interpretation, see Shapira, "Scorched Link," 3–7.

12. For a comprehensive analysis of the exclusion of the Holocaust from the "modern" discourse, see Manor, "From Rejection to Recognition," 256.

13. There were certain Israeli artists who dealt with the theme of the Holo-

caust in their works even before the early 1980s. One of them is Yoche-ved Weinfeld, a second-generation artist, who in the late 1970s was the first to present feminist-oriented works saturated with Holocaust memo-ries and Jewish identity. At that time her work was not interpreted as Holocaust-oriented, but rather as a radical feminist statement.

Art historian and scholar Gannit Ankori was the first to take the "po-litically incorrect" direction, maintaining that "anything that smacked of the Eastern European Jewish Diaspora was considered regressive, virtu-ally taboo." For a further discussion of Weinfeld's work, see Gannit An-kori, "Yocheved Weinfeld's Portraits of the Self," *Woman's Art Journal* (spring–summer 1989): 22–27. On the gradual process of acceptance and legitimacy of the Holocaust as subject matter, see Manor, "From Re-jection to Recognition," especially 274 n. 18.

14. For Holocaust Memorial Day in April 2000, a group of young people conceived of a commemoration ceremony of their own as an alternative to the formal institutional ceremonies. The youngsters' need to create and constitute for themselves new, more critical, and more open frame-works for understanding the Holocaust and the very feasibility of such ceremonies indicate the extent and scope of recent change.

15. Ziva Amishai-Maisels, *Depiction and Interpretation: The Influence of the Holo-caust on the Visual Arts* (Oxford: Pergamon Press, 1993).

16. For this and other calculations, see Manor, "From Rejection to Recogni-tion," especially 273 n. 2.

17. Haim Dasberg, quoted in Yehuda Koren, "What's Wrong with This Pic-ture?" (in Hebrew), *Yediot Ahronot,* January 17, 1997.

18. Ram Katzir, for instance, had to harness his "license" and that of the other "license holders," who assisted him on his project, when respond-ing to the scandal created by his work: "Whoever thought this exhibition was a joke or a prank is very much mistaken, and this mistake offends me, insults the memory of my family members who perished in the Holocaust, and deeply hurts the feelings of many survivors who live in this country. During the work on the project I sought the assistance of dozens of survivors, historians and propaganda researchers." See Ram Katzir, "Who Refuses to Look?" (in Hebrew), *Kol Ha'ir,* January 24, 1997.

19. Public debate was recently provoked by a study that set out to prove that Roberto Benigni's film *Life Is Beautiful* is a quintessential anti-Semitic movie. This debate touched upon the question of whether a non-Jewish artist has the right to deal with the Holocaust. See Kobi Niv, *Life Is Beau-tiful, but Not for Jews* (in Hebrew) (Tel Aviv: N. B. Books, 2000).

20. A notable case where a possibly inappropriate analogy was made oc-curred when London-based Palestinian artist Mona Hatoum exhibited a

work made of bars of Nablus soap in the East Jerusalem Anadil Gallery. Nablus is known throughout the Arab world for its olive oil soap industry, and the most self-evident reference here was to Palestinian history. Still, Jewish Israelis who saw the work could not avoid making associations with the Holocaust.

21. For a comprehensive review of Shimon Attie's work, see Norman L. Kleeblatt, "Persistence of Memory," *Art in America* 88, no. 5 (June 2000): 97–103.

22. A totally different case is that of Christian Boltanski, whose works were shown at the Israel Museum in Jerusalem as part of the permanent collection in the International Art section for many years. Boltanski, the most celebrated contemporary artist whose oeuvre deals with the Holocaust, was embraced by the Israeli art community because his work alludes to the Holocaust in a nonspecific way and is universal in nature.

23. Moshe Gershuni, *Kav* 4/5 (November 1982): 18 (in Hebrew), as quoted in Manor, "From Rejection to Recognition," 263.

24. For a further discussion of Gershuni's Holocaust-related images, see Manor, "From Rejection to Recognition," 263–64; and Rosen, "The Visibility and Invisibility of Trauma," 45–51.

25. The popularity of German Neo-Expressionism, the yearning for authenticity, and the search for identity underlay the metamorphosis in Gershuni's work in the early 1980s. For a further explanation, see Rosen, "The Visibility and Invisibility of Trauma," 45.

26. The four previous *Ash Cities* were *Light on the Ashes,* at Southeastern Center for Contemporary Art (SECCA), Winston-Salem, North Carolina, 1996; Ash-Map of Poland and Germany, *Geographiestunde,* at Gropius Bau, Berlin, 1997; Ash-Map of Warsaw and the Wisla, *Polish Forests and Other Drawings,* at Zacheta National Gallery of Contemporary Art, Warsaw, Poland, 1998; and *River of Ashes,* Center for Contemporary Art, Cleveland, Ohio, 1998.

27. The speech, calling for brotherhood between different ethnic groups in Israel, was delivered by Yitzhak Ben Zvi in 1953 and appears on the 100 shekel notes.

28. In 1969, two years after the Six-Day War, Neustein presented an installation consisting of 17,000 pairs of boots piled in heaps at the Jerusalem Artists' House. They were Arab soldiers' boots bought from a merchant in the Occupied Territories. This project, undertaken in collaboration with Georgette Battle and Gerry Marx, was perceived as dealing with "the idea of displacement, of removal, transmission and migration" and vehemently denied any affinity or even the slightest association with the Holocaust. See Amnon Barzel as quoted in the catalog *Joshua Neustein:*

Polish Forests and Other Drawings (Warsaw: National Gallery of Contemporary Art, Zacheta, 1997), 76. Nevertheless, the exhibition was closed down because it was considered offensive to Holocaust survivors.

29. Wendy Shafir, ed., *Joshua Neustein: Five Ash Cities*, with essays by Arthur C. Danto, Hilary Putnam, and Kristine Stiles (Herzliya: Herzliya Museum of Art; Chicago: Olive Production and Publishing, 2000).

30. Smadar Sheffi, "The Center Is Shifting North" (in Hebrew), *Ha'aretz*, February 17, 2000, 3.

31. These quotes are drawn from an unpublished work by Natan Nuchi, "Statement about the Relation of My Work to the Holocaust," August 1994.

32. The installation was created for *Y-ZKOR: Shoah and Memory in Art*, a group exhibition (Ami Steinitz, curator) at Ami Steinitz Gallery, Tel Aviv, March–April 1997.

33. Paraphrase of an excerpt from an unpublished work by Natan Nuchi, "The Holocaust and the Market," 1997.

34. Ibid. Nuchi alluded to Susan Sontag, who wrote, "The display of atrocity in the form of photographic evidence risks being tacitly pornographic." See Susan Sontag, *Under the Sign of Saturn* (New York: Farrar, Straus, & Giroux, 1980), 139.

35. Nuchi, "The Holocaust and the Market."

36. Ibid. Historian Moshe Zuckermann also refers to the commercialization of the Holocaust, yet he questions the efficacy of "high art" (such as the "scientific knowledge or meticulous documentation à la Lanzmann's *Shoah*") in dealing with the memory of the Holocaust vis-à-vis patterns of oblivion and natural processes of forgetfulness. See Zuckermann, "There Were No Rehearsals in the Death Camps," 17.

37. *Arbeit Macht Frei from Toitland Europe* by the Acre Experimental Theater Group was presented in Acre between 1993 and 1996.

38. The following description of *Arbeit Macht Frei* is based on Amnon Raz-Krakotzkin's luminous analysis in "Exile within Sovereignty," 122–24.

39. For this and other responses, see Sarit Fuchs, "On the Ongoing Public Debate concerning *Arbeit Macht Frei* Traveling to Berlin," *Ma'ariv*, January 1992.

Part III

TRANSGRESSING TABOOS

Chapter 7

Holocaust Toys: Pedagogy of Remembrance through Play

Ernst van Alphen

In a 1994 interview French artist Christian Boltanski declared that all his work was "more or less about the Holocaust." This remark is not particularly revealing of his work from 1984 on. His installations generically entitled *Shadows, Candles, Monuments, Canada,* and *Reserve* compellingly evoke the Holocaust. But Boltanski's statement does not so obviously apply to his earlier work. For example, how does *Model Images* from 1975 or *Comic Sketches* from 1974 relate to the Holocaust? *Model Images* shows ordinary snapshots from the seventies, which can be found in photo albums belonging to almost anybody who lived in Western Europe, Canada, or the United States at that time. Their normality is in stark contrast to the apocalyptic horror of the Holocaust.

The Holocaust is also hard to see in the series of staged photographs entitled *Comic Sketches.* In these works Boltanski himself humorously playacts scenes from ordinary childhood. In *The Shameful Kiss,* for instance, he plays a young boy who meets a young girl at the beach whom he wants to kiss but cannot because he is too shy. In *The First Communion* we see Boltanski playing a young boy who receives a host from a priest at his first communion. In *The Doctor's Visit* we see him playing a young boy who is ill; his mother is worried and calls for the doctor. The latter comes and says that although the little one is very ill, the illness is not serious. This is a great relief to the mother.[1] In short, the series *Comic Sketches* shows scenes that can be recognized by almost everyone: they are the most ordinary and archetypal childhood scenes one can imagine.

There is, however, a remarkable difference between *Model Images* and *Comic Sketches*. For *Model Images* Boltanski used old snapshots. Moreover, the images we see are "serious" as opposed to comic. The scenes in *Comic Sketches*, in contrast, are playacted. Importantly, all the roles in the scenes are explicitly played by Boltanski himself only. He wears the same dark suit in all the roles he plays. He is able to distinguish between the different characters he plays by adding a simple attribute to this outfit: glasses for the doctor, a hat with a flower for the mother. This minimalist play of distinct characters, together with their facial expressions, makes the scenes comical.

It is this aspect of *play* that interests me. We could say that in *Comic Sketches* Boltanski, the child of a Jewish father who survived the Holocaust by going into hiding, foreshadows a younger generation of artists whose work deals with the Holocaust "playfully." These artists are second- or third-generation descendants of survivors or bystanders who represent the Holocaust or Nazi Germany in the form of play or toys. They make Holocaust toys. Among them is American artist David Levinthal, who, in his work *Mein Kampf* (1994–96), photographed scenes from Auschwitz staged by means of little dolls or figurines. The figurines remind us of the little tin soldiers, for decades a popular toy for young boys or a collectors' item for adult men. In a 1977 work that he made together with Garry Trudeau entitled *Hitler Moves East*, Levinthal represented Operation Barbarossa, Hitler's invasion of the Soviet Union in 1941, in the same way. The second artist in this grouping is the Israeli-Dutch Ram Katzir, who made a series of installations in which the audience was invited to color the images in a coloring book or to make additions to it. The images in the coloring book, however, were based on Nazi photographs. The third is Polish artist Zbigniew Libera, who made a "Lego Concentration Camp Set." This set consists of seven boxes of different sizes from which a miniature concentration camp can be built.

I will consider these artists as a group and their work as representing a particular genre. This genre has a specific epistemic-artistic thrust. Their artworks raise the following question: What is the function of play in Holocaust representation? Since Holocaust art centers on the question of remembrance, I rephrase this question more provocatively: Is there a place for Holocaust toys in Holocaust remembrance? In other words, do these toys embody a pedagogy of

David Levinthal, *Untitled*, from the *Mein Kampf* series, 1994–96. Color photograph. Courtesy of David Levinthal Studios. Photograph by Jason Burch.

Ram Katzir, *Your Coloring Book,* coloring plate, 1996. Courtesy of Ram Katzir. ©
Ram Katzir.

Ram Katzir, *Your Coloring Book,* installation view, 1996. Courtesy of Ram Katzir. ©
Ram Katzir.

remembrance through play? The issue of generation will be an important aspect of this question. It is striking that until these artists came along, representing the Holocaust playfully had been taboo, whereas suddenly it seems as if a later generation of artists can only relate to the Holocaust through play. Given the centrality of remembrance in all Holocaust art, I want to examine why this phenomenon—the toy as memory play—occurs at this time. What does it mean, and how can we evaluate this phenomenon in terms of remembrance?

I broach this issue through the question of Boltanski's playful *Comic Sketches*. Taking the artist up on his statement, I am interested in speculating in what way these pictures relate to the Holocaust. As I have said, the exaggerated poses of his characters and the rather silly events they enact evoke collective, ordinary notions of childhood and parenthood. They do not represent the specificity of Boltanski's autobiographical childhood or the situation of children in the Holocaust. I contend that their generic ordinary plots are exactly the point. For their point is replacement. These comic sketches actively

Zbigniew Libera, *LEGO Concentration Camp Set*, detail, 1996. Seven cardboard boxes. Edition of three.

and playfully replace the abnormality of "Holocaust Sketches" by sketches of ordinary childhood and parenthood. In an interview with Paul Bradley, Charles Esche, and Nicole White, Boltanski says the following about his work:

> CB: When I am doing art, I am a liar and I am mostly an awful professional artist, disgusting, it is my job. . . . it is true that I really wanted to forget my childhood. I have spoken a lot about a childhood, but it was not my childhood. It was a normal childhood. I never spoke about something that was true, and in my art at the beginning it seemed biographical but nothing was true, and I was never speaking about the fact that I was Jewish or that it was impossible for my mother to move because she had polio. I never spoke about that and I never spoke about my weird grandmother. When I spoke about my childhood, it was this normal childhood and when I decided to make a photo album, I chose the photo album of my friend called Durrant because Durrant is just Smith in England, Durrant is nobody, just a normal French man.
>
> NW: Is this a way to re-create a better childhood?
>
> CB: To erase and forget my own childhood. You know it was so tough, it was so awful, I mean all our parents are awful, but my father was so awful, my mother was so awful.
>
> NW: But it is not just to forget, but to make something better.
>
> CB: Yes, just normal.[2]

In this interview Boltanski again refuses to say anything specific about his childhood because, although his father was awful and his mother was awful, all parents are awful. Hence, for him art is a means of telling lies. Art does not represent reality, autobiographical or not. Instead, it is a means of transforming an insufferable reality into something normal, that is, something sufferable. In this conception, art is not mimetic, but performative. This explains how the *Comic Sketches* are works of art "about the Holocaust": in post-Holocaust culture they act upon an intense desire for normality.

Boltanski's remarks also make clear, however, that within his oeuvre the *Comic Sketches* are not at all unique. They are not different because of their playfulness. Rather, they are emblematic of all his work, including that of the late eighties and nineties. In another interview he explains how this is possible:

At the time of the *Saynetes Comiques* [Comic Sketches] I was asking myself questions about the nature of representation and the double meaning of the verb "to play." . . . In a small book of 1974, *Quelques interprétations par Christian Boltanski,* I ask myself what differentiates the act of someone who drinks a glass of water and an actor's interpretation of someone drinking a glass of water. I realized that art consisted of making something with the intention of demonstrating the reality of these two situations.[3]

Comic Sketches foregrounds an aspect of art that, for Boltanski, defines art as such. Art is "play" and "play" is its reality. The reality of play is fundamentally different from the reality art refers to mimetically. This early work, then, has an artistic manifesto inscribed in its silly childishness.

In the case of Boltanski, the notion of art as play has never led to controversy, because in the only work in which he turns this aspect of art into its theme, as happens in *Comic Sketches*, the reference to the Holocaust is totally invisible or at least implicit. But that thematic restraint is different in the case of the younger generation of artists, including Levinthal, Katzir, and Libera. These artists enact the Holocaust playfully with emphatic explicitness in the form of toys. Whereas in the context of modern art in general toys are already the kind of object considered bizarre or of marginal interest, in the context of Holocaust representation they are provocative or even scandalous.

The work of Katzir and Libera especially has led to great controversy. The controversy was enhanced by the venue of display, which further underscored the works' serious claims concerning Holocaust remembrance. When Katzir showed his installation *Your Coloring Book* in 1997 at the Israel Museum in Jerusalem, questions were even asked in the Knesset about the possibly shocking and hurtful effect of the installation. Some people wanted to close it down.[4] And when Libera showed and discussed his work in 1997 at a conference on contemporary art and the Holocaust in Brussels, organized by the Fondation Auschwitz, many people in the audience were scandalized by the work. Holocaust survivors present in the audience became so emotional that they had to leave the room. During the entire conference people kept discussing the controversial nature of Libera's work.[5]

Holocaust artworks in the form of toys seem to be controversial by definition. This is so because Holocaust art tends to be automatically reduced to the function of Holocaust education and remembrance. Art, teaching, and remembrance are thus unreflectively collapsed into one another. In this context it is an unassailable axiom that historical genres and discourses such as the documentary, the memoir, testimony, or the monument are much more effective and morally responsible in teaching about the Holocaust than are imaginative discourses.[6] Accordingly, art in general is already problematic because it is imaginative, not documentary. Obviously, if art is not "serious" enough in terms of historical reconstruction, within the realm of the imaginative toys are the lowest and least respected, for they can be seen as doubly imaginative—as things to play with and to play out, as toys and as art.

Fictional novels are also problematic, as the controversies around Kosinski's *The Painted Bird*, D. M. Thomas's *The White Hotel*, and Darville's *The Hand That Signed the Paper* have shown. But at least such novels can teach something about the past, even by the less reliable means of fiction. That is exactly why the hybrid genre of the historical novel has gained respect and popularity. But toys, what do they teach? Do they teach at all, or do they do something else?

Teaching as a Cultural Activity

In order to understand how toys teach and what they teach, some reflection on teaching as a cultural activity is needed. Therefore, I first briefly point out dominant conceptions of teaching and the role these ideas play in Holocaust teaching and remembrance. As Shoshana Felman has argued, "Western pedagogy can be said to culminate in Hegel's philosophical didacticism: the Hegelian concept of 'Absolute knowledge' . . . is in effect what pedagogy has always aimed as its ideal: the exhaustion—through methodical investigation—of all there is to know; the absolute completion—termination—of apprenticeship. Complete and totally appropriated knowledge will become —in all senses of the word—a *mastery*."[7]

Learning, according to this traditional conception, is linear, cumulative, and progressive, and leads to mastery over the object of learning. Mastery over the Holocaust, indeed, is one of the main motivations behind Holocaust education. In order to prevent something like the Holocaust happening again, later generations have to have as much knowledge as possible about the Holocaust. It is through knowledge of it that one can "master" the Holocaust.

But it is precisely this conception of learning as pursuing mastery over the object of learning that seems to fail in face of the Holocaust. For instance, Ram Katzir, who felt the need to revitalize Nazi photographs by using them as models for a coloring book, complained about overfamiliarity with Nazi and anti-Nazi propaganda in the Israeli schools he attended. Even the most shocking images have been robbed of the power to move or create serious attention by being turned into just another school subject.[8] Not mastery, but boredom seems to be the result of the Holocaust education Ram Katzir received. Holocaust teaching and remembrance in Poland had a similar effect on Zbigniew Libera. At the conference on contemporary art and the Holocaust organized by the Fondation Auschwitz in Brussels, he defended his art as follows: "Of course, I was born fifteen years after the war and sometimes people call my art 'toxic' and actually it is toxic. But why? Because I am poisoned, I am poisoned of it. And that's all."[9] Poisoning, like boredom, is the opposite of mastery. Instead, these conditions express a weakening of the subject who masters neither him/herself nor the object of learning.

I completely sympathize with this negative assessment of Holocaust education. Elsewhere I have written about the effect Holocaust education in the Netherlands has had on me.[10] As someone born in Holland in 1958, who passed through primary and high school in the 1960s and early 1970s in the same country, I had the memory of World War II and the Holocaust drummed into my mind. Or rather, the Dutch school system tried to do so. But they failed to have the required effect. I was bored to death by all the stories and images of that war, which were held out to me "officially" as moral warnings. At school we were shown documentaries of the war. Our teachers encouraged us to read books that informed us in great detail of what had happened not so very long ago. But I avoided my society's official war narratives. Until quite recently, for instance, I had refused to read Anne Frank's *Diary of a Young Girl.*

The failure of the kind of Holocaust teaching that Katzir, Libera, and I have been exposed to is caused by two misconceptions. The first concerns the goal of teaching: that goal cannot be reduced exclusively to mastery over the object of learning. The second misconception concerns the nature of the Holocaust: the Holocaust is not just a history of memory that can be mastered by memorizing it. It cannot be taught along traditional pedagogical lines; for, as we know, the traditional conception of learning implies remembering and memorizing first of all. In contrast, the Holocaust is foremost a history of trauma, that is, a history of nonmastery. This is in the most literal sense true for the survivors of the Holocaust, but in a more general sense it is also true for later generations or for post-Holocaust culture as such. Because although the Holocaust came to an end more than fifty years ago, post-Holocaust culture has not yet been able to work through the enormity of this apocalyptic event. Teaching a history of trauma means teaching knowledge that is not in mastery of itself. Felman's assessment of literary knowledge and its implications for teaching this knowledge applies equally to Holocaust teaching. This teaching "knows it knows, but does not know the meaning of its knowledge—does not know *what* it knows."[11] In other words, Holocaust teaching confronts us with the problem of how to master by means of teaching a past that has not yet been mastered and cannot be mastered.

Felman analyzes the dominant conception of teaching within the framework of a discussion about whether psychoanalysis has renewed the questions and the practice of teaching. She contrasts psychoanalysis to traditional methods and assumptions of education as a radically new pedagogy. But in light of the traumatic, hence nonmasterable, nature of the Holocaust, her remarks on psychoanalysis as a mode of teaching also provide a model for Holocaust teaching. It provides a model for teaching knowledge that is not in possession of itself. "Psychoanalysis is thus a pedagogical experience: as a process which gives access to new knowledge hitherto denied to consciousness, it affords what might be called a lesson in cognition (and in miscognition), an epistemological instruction."[12]

The mode of learning practiced by psychoanalysis distances itself from the view of learning as a simple one-way progression from ignorance to knowledge. It does not proceed through linear progression, but through "breakthroughs, leaps, discontinuities, regressions, and deferred action."[13] This teaching has nothing in common with the transmission of ready-made knowledge. Rather, it is the creation of a new *condition* of knowledge—the creation of an original learning disposition.[14]

This learning disposition is "new" in the ways in which it handles and structures repression. As those familiar with the psychology of childrearing know, repression is one of the most important strategies of traditional pedagogy. In Freud's words,

> The child must learn to control his instincts. It is impossible to give him liberty to carry out all his impulses without restriction. . . . Accordingly, *education must inhibit, forbid and suppress* and this is abundantly seen in all periods of history. But we have learnt from analysis that precisely this suppression of instincts involves the risk of neurotic illness. . . . That education has to find its way between the Scylla of non-interference and the Charybedis of frustration. . . . An optimum must be discovered which will enable education to achieve the most and damage the least. . . . A moment's reflection tells us that hitherto education has fulfilled its task very badly and has done children great damage.[15]

Freud's definition of overrepressive education as structured by prohibitions and suppression seems to have become the explicit guideline or epigraph for Holocaust education. In the education of the Holocaust, prohibitions usually take the form of their binary opposite: they are articulated as orders or commands.

The moral imperative of the prescriptions for "respectable" Holocaust education and studies is more than explicit in the formulations of Terrence Des Pres. Appropriating—in a nice case of interdiscursive heterogeneity—the voice of God in his use of the "genre" of the Commandments, he dictates

(1) The Holocaust shall be represented, in its totality, as a unique event, as a special case and kingdom of its own, above or below or apart from history.

(2) Representations of the Holocaust shall be as accurate and faithful as possible to the facts and conditions of the event, without change or manipulation for any reason—artistic reasons included.

(3) The Holocaust shall be approached as a solemn or even sacred event, with a seriousness admitting no response that might obscure its enormity or dishonor its dead.[16]

No wonder later generations get a bit restless under the weight of such regulation. The art of the Holocaust toys under discussion seems to be the result of a conscious violation of these commandments and their complementary prohibitions.

First of all, Levinthal, Libera, and Katzir do not represent the Holocaust as "unique" but as a historical object that can be toyed with, which is exchangeable with, let's say, the Wild West, knights and medieval castles, pirates and pirate ships. Second, accuracy and faithful representation do not appear to be a high priority in their artworks. This lack of representational truthfulness does not imply that these toy art works are the product of Holocaust denial. They are not untrue. In logical terms they are neither true nor false, for they are not propositional statements. But something other than accuracy or historical truth-value is at stake. Third, the seriousness related to the Holocaust as "solemn or sacred event" seems to have been actively ignored. Instead, these artworks make us imagine (and feel) the pleasure certain toys can provide. In this case the way the toys work implies pleasurable activities: identification, and impersonation or playacting. Thus they run against the grain of traditional teaching. But then, is this art at fault, or is the teaching?

Identifying with the Perpetrator

In order to further probe the relationship between toy art and pedagogy, a tension must be acknowledged between representation of documentation on the one hand, and identification on the other. Whereas representation often uses strategies that promote identification, the relation is not reversible. Identification can be brought about outside the realm of representation. Indeed, in the artworks under discussion, identification is solicited while representation is at best mocked or otherwise discarded. The issue of identification is doubly ticklish. First of all, identification is promoted at the expense of representation. Second, the target of identification has shifted in a drastic and rather shocking way, from victims to perpetrators. These two aspects of identification—its centrality and hence its precedence over representation, and its new target—are inextricably bound up with each other. Together, they change Holocaust remembrance, art's role in it, and identification itself.

Presenting these artworks as toys (Libera, Katzir) or as images of toys (Levinthal) encourages the viewer to envision her/himself in a situation comparable to the "real" one. Identification replaces mastery. The toys (or images thereof) facilitate this envisioning of oneself in the historical situation. These artworks provocatively challenge, rather than respect, *distance* from the past, the distance required for mastery which in Holocaust representation is so tenaciously guarded in the preference for historical genres and solemn tones—even, as we have seen, religiously so, speaking in a divine voice.

But the use of identification as a pedagogical tool is not problematic as such. Recently it has been applied in several Holocaust museums in order to make visitors imagine what it meant to be victimized. For instance, in the U.S. Holocaust Memorial Museum in Washington, D.C., the itinerary leads visitors through a cattle-car. The experience of being transported to the camps by cattle-car is not being talked about or shown—at a distance—but is thrust upon the visitor. For the few moments that one is inside the cattle-car, it is almost impossible not to identify with those who were transported to the camps in such cars during the Holocaust. In this museum, the kind of identification that is allowed, and even encouraged in this case, is identification with the victims, not with the victimizers. But, of course, in the context of an outing to a museum, such identification is not "real," not total, but partial. The goal of such rides in the museum is to get a small and short taste of the experience, a tiny bit of the poison.

But what if the object of identification consists of the victimizers instead? The toy artworks under discussion do not facilitate identification with the victims, but rather with the perpetrators. This is, of course, much more difficult to do as well as to justify. How do the toy artworks accomplish this, and how can it be considered helpful for the cultural remembrance of the Holocaust to do so? How can this unsettling kind of identification be an effective form of pedagogy? One way to achieve this identification with an undesirable position is by making, shaping, forming the perpetrators. The visitors of Katzir's installations were invited to color coloring plates based on

Nazi photography. We, as visitors, are coloring Nazi leaders or members of the Nazi youth: we are giving them color, form, and substance and in the process we "generate" them. This making of the Nazis is a convoluted yet real form of identification. As creators of the perpetrators the coloring visitors become complicitous in the possibility of the Nazis—not, of course, with the real, specific, and acting Nazis.

Libera deploys a different technique to achieve the goal of identifying with the perpetrators. Libera's *Lego Concentration Camp Set* asks visitors of the museum or the gallery to envision the possibility of *building your own concentration camp*. Again we are put in the shoes of the victimizers, not of the victims. Here, the identification concerns the acts perpetrated, the conception and construction of the material condition of the Holocaust. Levinthal's photographs are at first sight more ambiguous. His scenes of "playing the Holocaust" seem to facilitate identification with victims as well as with perpetrators. But the moment we start to take the title of these photographs into consideration ("Mein Kampf") the ambiguity evaporates and we end up with an enforced identification with Hitler, the author of *Mein Kampf.* We each have our own *Kampf*, our own ambitions that can be potentially catastrophic. Here the identification targets the conception of the ideological mind-set out of which the historical disaster sprang.

Art and Pedagogy

So far, I have argued that the traditional, dogmatic "rules" for Holocaust remembrance and education are inevitably a framing device for understanding Holocaust art that challenges those rules. The reason this frame is so powerful is that education—more than any other cultural practice—is the transgenerational tool for remembrance of the Holocaust. The danger of this view for art's specificity is that it results in the subjugation of art to the pedagogical pursuit of Holocaust education. Yet, toy art through its reference to childhood endorses this subjugation but changes its terms. This antagonistic pedagogy as a major feature of the toys suggests that Holocaust art is a special, negative case of aesthetics in its "interestedness." It is not autonomous, as art since modernism likes to see itself, but subordinated to the service of another—inevitably higher—goal.

In contrast, in the wake of Kant, art has usually been seen as disinterested, that is, free from educational ideals. The toy art I am discussing breaks through this binary opposition. Thus Libera's works seem to imply that Holocaust art and other kinds of art are not at all opposed categories. In this respect Holocaust art is not different from, but perhaps only a stronger, more evident case of the pedagogical ambition of art in general. Hence, the change of perspective this art brings to the pedagogy of remembrance also entails a change of aesthetics.

Libera's artistic interest focuses on those cultural products that serve to educate or to form the human being, and to "form" should be understood in the figurative as well as in the literal sense. The objects that he creates consist of appliances that already exist in the contemporary cultural world through their resemblance to toys or machines used in fitness clubs or beauty salons. These are not related to the Holocaust. Apart from the *Lego Concentration Camp Set*, for example, he made *You Can Shave the Baby*. These are five pairs of baby dolls, with a shock of red hair emanating from their heads and sprouting from their pubic areas, lower legs, and underarms. *Ken's Aunt* is a Barbie doll in the form of an overweight woman. These works have an upbeat tone to them that contrasts sharply with Rosen's suicide scene. But if we look back to that work, the positive quality of the earlier, erotic fantasies is also artificial. Libera's *Doll You Can Undress* is a doll that reveals her open stomach area with visible intestines. And *Eroica* is a set of fifty boxes of small bronze figurines, look-alike toy soldiers. This time not the army but civilians, women, the oppressed of society, are the toy soldiers to be played with. The tone here is more unsettling. Other works by Libera present themselves as "correcting devices" such as *Universal Penis Expander, Body Master,* and *Placebo.* "Forming" takes on a multiply layered meaning in these works. What matters in this non-Holocaust part of Libera's work is the foregrounding of correction or "forming." In light of this, the "making" that subtends them all is even more nuanced.

Libera's artistic oeuvre shows that although his *Lego Concentration Camp Set* is unique in having the Holocaust as subject matter, all his works foreground the issue of pedagogy, literally or figuratively, of the education of body and mind. In an illuminating essay, Andrew Boardman has argued that Libera challenges the contemporary belief that

aesthetic values are disinterested, fluid, or "freeform." On the contrary, contemporary Western art is essentially a remnant from an indelible nineteenth-century construct which holds that art and education go hand in hand with moral strength and prudence.

> Although art produced today likes to believe that it has shed the ma-
> jority of those stodgy nineteenth century precepts, it has carefully
> disguised them in the fine-woven cloak of pedagogy. The built-in
> assumption of art today is that it acts to inform us, develop our fac-
> ulties and therefore deliver us from a transgressive and earthly ig-
> norance into the safe arms of civilisation. . . . One might argue that
> Libera's work, because of its visual connection to child development
> and to learning, superficially epitomises this nineteenth century
> bourgeois outlook. In fact, by wrapping his work in this upright
> mode of educational discourse, Libera questions the sweet plati-
> tudes and patronizing certainties of art that adhere in our educa-
> tional aspirations for visual culture.[17]

From this perspective, the target of Libera's *Lego Concentration Camp
Set* is twofold. In addition to exposing the repressions and inhibitions
of Holocaust education and its conceptions of remembrance, he also
exposes the moral rectitude of (contemporary) art.

Combining these two conclusions, we cannot stop at the idea that
in modern Western culture, art unavoidably teaches and informs. For
the specificity of toy art remains *play*, which is also the tool for freedom from pedagogical lessons. The intricate relationship between art
and teaching can neither be dismissed nor endorsed. Before opining
on the desirability of art's pedagogical mission, then, the function of
play in relation to both art and teaching needs some consideration.
The question that is thrust upon us is also twofold: does *play* teach,
and how does play *teach* differently? Is the "mastery" provided by play
of a different order than that resulting from cumulative and progressive learning?

Holocaust Narrative versus Holocaust Drama

To understand how the mastery provided by toys differs from that
provided by "learnable" knowledge, we have to analyze both modes of

learning in terms of the generic discourse to which each belongs. "Learnable knowledge" of the Holocaust takes the form of narrative. Personal narratives in the form of testimonies, diaries, or memoirs are seen as particularly instructive as they can teach later generations not just the facts of the Holocaust, but more importantly its apocalyptic inhumanity. But the works of art by Levinthal, Libera, or Katzir do not tell us anything about the past. Like Boltanski's *Comic Sketches* before them, they envision playing the past. And I use the verb *envision* emphatically, because—with the possible exception of Katzir, who experimented with schoolchildren actually coloring the books— these works are not real toys. Instead, they are artworks in the form of toys. These artworks are meant to be processed by adults, not by children.

Processed, then, by adults acting—playacting—like children. In the art under scrutiny, a shift in semiotic mode is at stake. The Holocaust is not represented by means of narration but in the mode of drama. This is, of course, more literally true of Katzir's installation and Libera's Lego boxes than of Levinthal's photographs. But I will argue that Levinthal's photographs should also be understood as drama. James Young has remarked that the photographs of *Mein Kampf* generate a powerful sense of the past through a measured act of simulation. He uses the phrase "a sense of the past" to distinguish an effect from an actuality.[18] What strikes me most, however, and in analogy to Young's view, is how these works generate a "sense of the present." I do not see fictional, narrativized images of a concentration camp. What I see, imagine, or even *am*, is a subject in post-Holocaust culture playing with a concentration camp. The narrative images are embedded in, or produced by, an act that should generically be defined as drama. And, as I will argue, this difference between narrative and drama is of crucial importance for an understanding of what is at stake in the artworks under discussion.

Libera's Lego boxes cannot, of course, be played with, but they evoke the possibility of a scene in which somebody in post-Holocaust culture performs Holocaust events within the setting of a camp. Constructing the setting by means of Lego, the artist facilitates the articulation of playacting Holocaust events. They facilitate *envisioning* what making the Holocaust could feel like. Katzir's work does not just envision the dramatic mode of representation; it really enacts it. As I mentioned, in his installations *Your Coloring Book*, realized in different ways in Utrecht, Enschede, Jerusalem, Vilnius, Krakow, and Berlin, visitors were invited to color or draw in the coloring books, which had been put on classroom desks or tables. The visitors of his installations were drawn into a performance in which they actualized, shaped, and colored, in other words generated, Nazi characters.

In order to assess the crucial difference between works of art that narrativize the Holocaust and those that perform or playact it, the distinctions made by the French psychiatrist Pierre Janet between narrative memory and traumatic memory are helpful.[19] Narrative memory consists of mental constructs, which people use to make sense of experience. Current and familiar experiences are automatically assimilated or integrated in existing mental structures. But some events resist integration: "Frightening or novel experiences may not easily fit into existing cognitive schemes and either may be remembered with particular vividness or may totally resist integration."[20] The memory of experiences that resist integration in existing schemes of meaning are stored differently and are not available for retrieval under ordinary conditions. It is only for the sake of convenience that Janet has called these unintegratable experiences "traumatic *memory*." In fact, trauma is fundamentally (and not gradually) different from memory because "it becomes dissociated from conscious awareness and voluntary control."

Trauma is failed experience, and this failure makes it impossible to *voluntarily* remember the event. This is why traumatic reenactments take the form of drama, not narrative. Drama just presents itself, or so it seems; narrative as a mode implies some sort of mastery by the narrator, or the one who focalizes. This is a fundamental difference. In the words of Mieke Bal: "All the manipulations performed by a narrator, who can expand and reduce, summarize, highlight, underscore, or minimize elements of the story at will, are inaccessible to the 'actor' who is bound to enact a drama that, although at some point in the past it happened to her, is not hers to master."[21] Janet's clinical distinction between narrative and traumatic memory ultimately concerns a *difference* in distance toward the situation or event. A narrative memory is retroversive; it takes place after the event. A traumatic memory, or better, reenactment, does not know that distance toward the event.

This distinction between narrative memory and traumatic memory does not apply literally to the artworks under discussion. Although these works are not narrative, it is of little help to see them as instances of traumatic memory. These works are not involuntary reenactments of the Holocaust, but rather are purposeful attempts to lose the mastery that Holocaust narratives provide and to enter into an emotional rather than cognitive relationship with it.

As in the discussion of teaching, mastery is again at issue, but this time the methods for obtaining this mastery are totally different: not mastery through knowledge, but mastery by working through the emotions. To explain how these imaginative attempts to work through *work*, the distinction made by Eric Santner between "narrative fetishism" and mourning is helpful. He defines narrative fetishism as the construction and deployment of a narrative consciously or unconsciously designed to expunge the traces of the trauma or loss that called that narrative into being in the first place. The work of mourning, on the contrary, is a process of elaborating and integrating the reality of loss or traumatic shock by remembering and repeating it in symbolically and dialogically mediated doses. It is a process of translating, troping, and figuring loss.[22]

Of course, Santner uses Freud's discussion of the *fort/da* game in *Beyond the Pleasure Principle* to explain the mechanisms of mourning. The fort/da game was a game Freud observed in the behavior of his one-and-a-half-year-old grandson. In this game the child is able to master his grief over his separation from the mother by staging, play-acting his own performance of her disappearance. He does so by repeating and using props that D. W. Winnicott would call transitional objects. This game is based on a ritualized mechanism of dosing out and representing absence by means of substitutive figures. In the words of Santner,

> The dosing out of a certain negative—a thanatotic—element as a strategy of mastering a real and traumatic loss is a fundamentally homeopathic procedure. In a homeopathic procedure the controlled introduction of a negative element—a symbolic or, in medical contexts, real poison—helps to heal a system infected by a similar poisonous substance. The poison becomes a cure by empowering the individual to master the potentially traumatic effects of large doses of the morphologically related poison. In the fort/da

game it is the rhythmic manipulation of signifiers and figures, objects and syllables instituting an absence, that serves as the poison that cures.[23]

Similarly, in the Holocaust toys the poisonous (Libera's word) stuff needed in a carefully measured dose is the "Holocaust effect": to "do" the camps instead of talking "about" them. A double distance is produced: play instead of reality and in the context of "high art," play instead of an institutional frame that sets these toys apart. To "do" the Holocaust in this way is performed under the strict direction of a "director," a "*metteur en scene,*" and, as such, is radically distinct from a "revival" or "repetition" of Nazism in the dangerous shape of neo-Nazism.

I want to wind up by speculating on why it is that this trend of "playing" the Holocaust by means of toys, appears to characterize the art of this current second, third, and fourth generation of post-Holocaust survivors and bystanders. In the face of the overdose of information and educational documentary material, clearly there is a need to complete a process of working through not yet "done" effectively. In the face of that overdose, "ignorance" is needed—an ignorance not in terms of information about the events of the Holocaust, but of everything that stands in the way of a "felt knowledge" of the emotions these events entailed. In this perspective, the toys with their childish connotations that "fake" such ignorance clear away the "adult" overdose of information standing in the way of felt knowledge. "Mastery" is then no longer an epistemic mastery of what happened but a performative mastery of the emotions triggered by the happenings. Only by working through on the level where knowledge is not "out there" to be fed to passive consumers but "felt" anew every time, can the participants of a culture keep in touch with the Holocaust.

NOTES

A version of this essay appeared in *Mirroring Evil: Nazi Imagery/Recent Art* (exhibition catalog), ed. Norman L. Kleeblatt (New York: The Jewish Museum; New Brunswick: Rutgers University Press, 2001).

1. The series *Comic Sketches* consists of the following "short stories": "Le mariage des parents" (Parents' marriage), "La maladie du grand-père" (Grandfather's illness), "les souvenirs du grand-père" (Grandfather's memories), "La toilette du matin" (The morning toilette), "La mort du grand-père" (Grandfather's death), "La grosesse de la mère" (Mother's pregnancy), "Le baiser caché" (The secret kiss), "Le grand-père à la pêche" (Grandfather fishing), "Les bonnes notes" (Good grades), "L'horrible découverte"(The horrible discovery), "La toilette de la mère" (Mother getting dressed), "Le recit du père" (Father's story), "L'anniversaire" (The birthday), "La naissance de Christian" (Christian's birth), "Le baiser honteux" (The shameful kiss), "La tache d'encre" (The ink stain), "La dureté du père" (Father's harshness), "La première communion" (The first communion), "La visite du docteur" (The doctor's visit), "Le père à la chasse" (Father hunting), and "La grimace punie" (The punished grimace).
2. "An Interview with Christian Boltanski—Paul Bradley, Charles Esche, and Nicola White," in *Christian Boltanski: Lost* (Glasgow: CCA, 1994), 3–4.
3. The French expression *interprétation* means interpretation in the sense of explanation, but also "performance." The quote comes from Delphine Renard, "Entretien avec Christian Boltanski," in *Boltanski* (exhibition catalog) (Paris: Musée National d'Art Moderne, Centre Georges Pompidou, 1984), 85.
4. For the documentation of this controversy, see Katzir's catalog *Your Coloring Book: A Wandering Installation* (Amsterdam: Stedelijk Museum, 1998).
5. A transcript of this very emotional discussion can be found in *Bulletin Trimestriel de la Fondation Auschwitz*, special no. 60 (July–September 1998): 225–40.
6. For an elaboration of this argument, see my book *Caught by History: Holocaust Effects in Contemporary Art, Literature, and Theory* (Stanford: Stanford University Press, 1997).
7. Shoshana Felman, "Psychoanalysis and Education: Teaching Terminable and Interminable," *Yale French Studies* 63 (1982): 28.
8. Gary Schwartz, "Teach It to the Children," in Ram Katzir, *Your Coloring Book: A Wandering Installation* (Amsterdam: Stedelijk Museum, 1998), 40.
9. Zbigniew Libera, "Discussion," Bulletin Trimestriel de la Fondation Auschwitz, special no. 60 (July–September 1998): 225.
10. Van Alphen, "Caught by History: How This Book Came About," in *Caught by History*, 1–15.

11. Ibid., 41.

12. Ibid., 27.

13. Ibid., 27.

14. Ibid., 31.

15. *The Complete Psychological Works of Sigmund Freud*, translated from the German under the general editorship of James Stratchey (London: Hogarth Press and the Institute of Psychoanalysis), 22:149; quoted by Felman, "Psychoanalysis and Education," 23, italics Felman's.

16. Terrence Des Pres, "Holocaust Laughter," in *Writing and the Holocaust*, ed. Berel Lang (New York: Holmes and Meier, 1988), 217.

17. Andrew Boardman, "Zbigniew Libera" (Warsaw: Zamek Ujazdowski, 1998).

18. James Young, "David Levinthal's *Mein Kampf*: Memory, Toys, and the Play of History," in David Levinthal, *Mein Kampf* (Santa Fe, N.M.: Twin Palms Publishers, 1996), 72.

19. Janet, who was working at the beginning of this century, was an influence on the theories of Sigmund Freud. For a discussion of Janet's ideas, see Bessel A. van der Kolk and Onno van der Hart, "The Intrusive Past: The Flexibility of Memory and the Engraving of Trauma," in *Trauma: Explorations in Memory*, ed. Cathy Caruth (Baltimore: Johns Hopkins University Press, 1995), 158–82.

20. Ibid., 160.

21. Mieke Bal, "Introduction," in *Acts of Memory: Cultural Recall in the Present*, ed. Mieke Bal, Jonathan Crewe, and Leo Spitzer (Hanover, N.H.: University of New England Press, 1999), ix.

22. Eric Santner, "History beyond the Pleasure Principle: Some Thoughts on the Representation of Trauma," in *Probing the Limits of Representation: Nazism and the "Final Solution,"* ed. Saul Friedlander (Cambridge: Harvard University Press, 1992), 144.

23. Ibid., 146.

Chapter 8

The Nazi Occupation of the "White Cube": Piotr Uklański's The Nazis and Rudolf Herz's Zugzwang

Norman L. Kleeblatt

A 1998 Harvard conference entitled "Change the Joke and Slip the Yoke" focused on racist stereotypes that have been appearing in a vein of progressive visual art by African Americans. Writing for *Artforum*, Ron Jones discussed the problems of the generational divide that pitted the ironic postmodern methods of thirty- and forty-something artists and critics against the contrasting affirmative approaches of their African American predecessors. According to reports and reviews of this two-day meeting, contention was rife. Not only were questions asked about the meaning and function of racist clichés, but they also were raised about the insidious nature of the considerable white patronage for this work. Additionally debated were the moral problems such art posed for the current states of multiculturalism and of affirmative action. Inevitably Jones compared the debates to the complex and still contentious interpretations that accrue to Anselm Kiefer's art and, ultimately, to the absurdity of a reductivist reading that would equate Kiefer's work with a "celebration of Nazi mastery."[1]

These racist representations have spawned much contention and turmoil in the last few years. This followed on the heels of the explicit sexual imagery that preoccupied the debates of America's culture wars.[2] Without a doubt, the artistic representation of Nazis and the symbols associated with them caused similar controversy. Like the subject matter debated at the Harvard conference, the entry of Nazi representations into the pristine, supposedly aesthetic sanctum of

179

the modern gallery space was as taboo as the confrontational post-modern aesthetic strategies that the artists deployed. Indeed, beginning in the 1970s, ambiguous Nazi imagery emerged with greater frequency in both fiction and film. This phenomenon intensified in the early 1980s with works using ambiguous aesthetic strategies and representing more perplexing messages. Yet aside from the art of Anselm Kiefer and later of Art Spiegelman, not until the late 1980s did this type of ironic, sometimes paradoxical imagery appear on a consistent level.[3]

Saul Friedlander coined the term "new aesthetic discourse on Nazism" in the early 1980s to investigate fiction and film embedding Nazi imagery into postmodern systems. For example, he trained his lens on George Steiner's 1981 novel *The Portage to San Cristóbal of A.H.* and, of course, examined Hans-Jürgen Syberberg's highly nuanced, brilliant, and provocative 1982 film entitled *Hitler, a Film from Germany*. Although Friedlander alludes to Anselm Kiefer, he never examines the specifics of his or any other art. Using these examples of film and fiction, he lays out the quandaries posed at the juncture between the moral and the aesthetic. On the one hand, he is concerned that such transgressive images and ironic stances may simply revoke all meaning. On the other, he understands that the new postmodern ways of probing these "limits of representation" might ultimately provide a fuller grasp of the dilemmas intrinsic to this onerous subject. Friedlander realizes that "Nazism represents an obsession for the contemporary imagination." He ponders whether attention given to its imagery functions as "a gratuitous review, the attraction of the spectacle, exorcism" or whether it is "the result of a need to understand." And he worries that the seduction of Nazi imagery operates as both "an expression of profound fears . . . and mute yearnings as well."[4]

Self-conscious and morally ambiguous, photo-based work appropriating Nazi imagery has become an unmistakable presence, internationally, in contemporary art of the last decade. In fact, the January and February 2000 issues of the popular German monthly *Der Spiegel Reporter* included articles about art that images and imagines Nazis. The magazine for January 2000 highlighted the work of Tom Sachs, a Jewish artist living in New York. February's journal included the work of Piotr Uklański, a Polish-born, Christian-raised artist who divides his time between New York and Warsaw. Uklański's work will form one part of my discussion.

With its lens on the depiction of perpetrators and its appearance in the aesthetic domain of the art gallery, such photo-based appropriation differs considerably from the reverential art that Andreas Huyssen has called "an often facile Holocaust victimology."[5] This so-called "Holocaust art," which has become increasingly prevalent during the 1990s, tends to be shown in exhibitions and programs that seek to teach straightforward moral lessons, to help heal the wounds of the remaining survivors, and to fight against time to keep memory alive. Its victim-oriented imagery often functions in an illustrative mode; its references and the interpretations of them remain mostly historical, less artistic. Given their divergent concentrations on victim and perpetrator and their differing positions of moral rectitude and moral ambiguity, these contrasting approaches to making art about World War II and the Holocaust readily illustrate Holocaust historian Sidra Ezrahi's "fundamental distinction between a static and a dynamic appropriation of history and its moral and social legacies."[6]

As offspring of victims as well as perpetrators, artists from a variety of national, ethnic, and religious backgrounds have shown on an international circuit during the last decade of the twentieth century. Exhibitions in Dusseldorf, Amsterdam, Berlin, Munich, Essen, London, Jerusalem, and New York have hosted some of these controversial works. The two particular installations that I will discuss deal with issues of desire, commodification, and spectatorship in general, and specifically with taboo Nazi imagery. Piotr Uklański's installation *The Nazis* opened at London's Photographers' Gallery in August 1998.[7] Rudolf Herz's *Zugzwang*, initially conceived and created for the Kunstverein Ruhr, was presented in Essen in December 1995. *Zugzwang*, which means obsession or compulsion, was reinstalled at the end of 1999 at the Hamburger Bahnhof in Berlin in a major exhibition entitled *Das XX Jahrhundert: Kunst in Deutschland.* The simplicity of means and the complexity of readings afforded Herz's and Uklański's works run the gauntlet between Duchamp and Warhol and connects them, as do the highly contested reception histories that ensued for Uklański and predated Herz's piece. Both installations purposefully trap the viewer within the confines of a white cube

Piotr Uklański, *The Nazis. Top:* Installation shot from Photographers' Gallery, London, 1998. *Bottom:* Detail from the installation. C-prints, 14" x 10" each. Courtesy of the artist and Gavin Brown's Enterprise.

exhibition space that the artists transformed, through image and metaphor, into Nazi-occupied territory.

Prompted by an article in *Arena* magazine about best-dressed actors, and realizing that a number of them had been shown attired in Nazi paraphernalia, Piotr Uklański set himself to the task of tracking photos of movie stars dressed for roles in which they personify Nazi evil. His installation *The Nazis* included more than 120 images in a frieze that wrapped the gallery's perimeter. Using a metal ledgelike

Rudolf Herz, *Zugzwang* (detail), 1995. Courtesy of the artist. Photograph by Hans Döring, Munich.

frame, Uklański self-consciously used every linear foot of gallery space, a clear homage to and indeed an appropriation of Andy Warhol's installation of the Pop master's Campbell's Soup paintings at the Ferus Gallery in Los Angeles in 1962. Uklański's fixation with film and its visual strategies have become dominant features of his work. For this project, the artist expanded obsessively upon his interest. Aesthetics aside, personal issues governed the creation of the installation. The project was motivated, in part, by silence about the war period that ruled his family, even though he knew his grandfather had fought with the Germans.[8] Thus, as with many among Generation X, Uklański gathered much of his early education about the war and the Holocaust from popular films and television.

Included among Uklański's cast of actors are Helmut Schneider and Dirk Bogarde, an all-too-casual Clint Eastwood, a boyish, even vulnerable Frank Sinatra, as well as the elegant Max von Sydow and the dashing, somewhat androgynous Ralph Fiennes. His visual litany is exhaustive, perhaps purposefully exhausting. The ambiguity is further confounded as he strategically rejects Walter Benjamin's imperative for the necessity of texts to clarify photographic images.[9] Clearly his exhibit *The Nazis* is related to postmodern art practice that intellectually scrutinizes and visually reframes representations from mass culture. Uklański also mimes the aesthetic preoccupation in which artists engage in anthropological or archival modes of research to prove the paradox and futility of collecting, as well as the collector's role in maintaining established power structures.[10] Using the Duchampian prerogative to label any cultural property as the object of the artist's own genius, Uklański also refers to the deadpan Pop Art glorifications of Andy Warhol's celebrity pictures and the archival obsession of Marcel Broodthaers's fake museums. In this case Uklański's particular reference may be to Warhol's censored project for Phillip Johnson's New York State Pavilion in the 1963–64 New York World's Fair. In *Most Wanted Men* Warhol represented the images of hunted criminals from broadsides offering rewards for their apprehension. In selecting cinema celebrities performing criminal roles Uklański actually collapses these two seemingly disparate aspects of Warhol's portraiture.

In essence, Uklański presents a rogue's gallery as museum. Contradictorily, yet inextricably, he links Nazi banality and evil with Hollywood glamor and extravagance. If we participate in the artist's game, we are trapped in uncomfortable terrain, torn between desiring our favorite actors and the realization that the assembly of our beloved stars symbolizes how much the evil of the Third Reich has become banal in our everyday world.

As with Uklański's earlier exhibition at London's Institute of Contemporary Art, the popularity of his ventures attracted notice in many of the city's newspapers. The reception history of this work

Andy Warhol, *Thirteen Most Wanted Men,* 1964. Installed at the New York State Pavilion, New York World's Fair, 1964. Silkscreen on Masonite. 25 panels, each 48" x 48". © 2002 Andy Warhol Foundation for the Visual Arts. Courtesy of the Andy Warhol Foundation, Inc./Art Resource, N.Y. Photograph by Eric Pollitzer.

shows the remarkably contentious reactions such imagery can provoke, especially among audiences not conversant with contemporary art. The press was sent on a feeding frenzy by the negative responses of Lord Janner, chairman of the Holocaust Education Trust, and some members of the Jewish community who felt that the exhibition might become "a magnet for Neo-Nazi worship." The headline of the *Evening Standard* proclaimed "outrage as London gallery highlights 'glamour of Nazism.'" In deference to these concerns, it was suggested that the Photographers' Gallery add an educational component in the form of books about the Holocaust and photo blowups of Holocaust victims.[11] Yet Janner felt that nothing would temper the show's impact short of a corollary exhibition of photographs showing the misery that the Holocaust caused Jews and non-Jews.[12] In essence, Janner was asking for historical material to explain, validate, and even vindicate the art displayed. Although some funky youth magazines capitalized on the glamor and sartorial aspects of the display,[13] a serious group of critics were able to see through the situation's complexity and formulate a more judicious reading of Uklański's installation. Neal Ascherson of the *Observer* commented on the artist's "sinister, intelligent talent" in making the exhibition into "a pitfall out of which no one scrambles intact."[14] The *Sunday Times* reviewer Waldemar Januszczak took the matter most seriously. His article analyzed the project and the reasons for the ardent reactions it provoked. Januszczak sees Uklański's Polish origins as part of the predicament. Being of Polish birth himself, the critic empathizes with both artist and audience. He recognizes that the history of Polish anti-Semitism left wide mistrust in its wake. More important was Januszczak's understanding of the complicated reality concerning the British public's general lack of knowledge about and general mistrust of contemporary art. Januszczak also turns the blame back on the film industry for its "harmless," "picturesque" characterizations and merits Uklański's project for its scrutiny of such superficiality.[15]

In addition to the response of journalists and critics, there was one immediate artistic rejoinder to Uklański's *The Nazis.* The Austrian artist Elke Krystufek reappropriated some of Uklański's already appropriated imagery in her continuing series about male sexual exploitation. For Krystufek, Uklański's photo project served as proof positive of a male monopoly on art world hubris, and she simultaneously implicated the pornographic sexuality that Klaus Theweleit has shown as central to Nazi male fantasy.[16] In a 180-degree rotation of the "male gaze," Krystufek forced the viewer into complicity with the voyeuristic gazes of Uklański's now-infamous celebrity criminals. As viewers, we are made to stare at Krystufek's naked body at the same

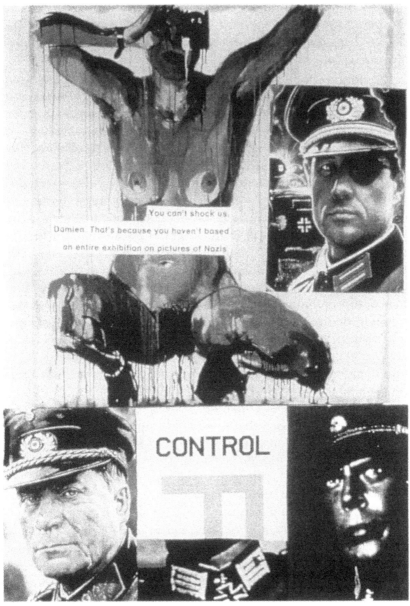

Elke Krystufek, *Economical Love (Pussy Control)*, 1998. Color photograph of collage with mixed media. 27½" x 19¾". Edition of three. Courtesy of the artist and Georg Kargl Gallery, Vienna.

time as we unwillingly pose for the female artist's camera. The viewer becomes both object *and* subject, as she exponentially raised the stakes of Uklański's already ethically compromising, socially interrogative enterprise.

As opposed to the contentious reception of Uklański's *The Nazis*, there was little controversial reaction to Rudolf Herz's installation *Zugzwang*.[17] Rather, it was the cancellation of the last two venues of a historical exhibition Herz had curated in his alternate occupation as photo historian that initiated the theme of his Essen installation. The 1994 exhibition in Munich's Stadtmuseum entitled *Hoffmann and Hitler* was Herz's scholarly investigation and thorough interpretation of the uses of photography to create and sustain the powerful and mythical image of the Führer. It was the culmination of years of intensive research. This project took Herz deep into the archives of Hitler's favored and sole photographer, Heinrich Hoffmann. The Munich showing was heralded by cultural critics and journalists, who saw it as an important step in understanding the mechanisms that shaped and promoted Hitler and the Third Reich. But its ensuing venues in Berlin and Saarbrücken canceled their planned participation. As with the discourse surrounding Uklański, fears that certain people could misinterpret the exhibition, that it may prove painful to others, and that it could become a meeting place for the Neo-Nazis were among the reasons cited for the cancellations.[18] The dialectical dilemma of silence versus openness continues to reappear with the display of similar imagery that some still consider taboo.

Originally installed in the Kunstverein Ruhr in Essen, Rudolf Herz's *Zugzwang* papered the gallery space from floor to ceiling with juxtaposed images of Adolf Hitler and Marcel Duchamp. He made strategic use of the paradoxical happenstance that both the "greatest terrorist of the twentieth century"[19] and the hero of the avant-garde each were photographed by the same cameraman—none other than Adolf Hitler's beloved photographer and public image manager, Heinrich Hoffmann. Hoffmann had a virtual cartel on staging and selling images of the Führer and of the Nazi movement. The photo of Duchamp was taken in Hoffmann's Munich studio in 1912; that of Hitler, exactly twenty years later.

Like Uklański's spare London installation, Herz's Essen project is physically simple, almost painfully so. Both deploy appropriated photographs with neither identification nor legend. Conceptually calculated, *Zugzwang* refracts both the historical and the art historical in a gallery installation that is at once physically empty and visually saturated. Its restrained form prompts a rapid-fire trajectory of references from Dada to Pop Art, Collage to Montage, Minimalism and Conceptualism to Installation Art. Simultaneously, and seemingly by pure coincidence, Herz pits two ideologically divergent players on the seemingly disconnected and highly fragmented chessboard of twentieth-century history and art. The Duchampian reference to chess is as important for the formal aspects of the work as it is for the installation's concept. Indeed, the work is organized physically as a chessboard, and intellectually as a chess match. In fact, its title (obsession or compulsion) is also a chess term that refers to the untenable position in which a player is limited to moves that will have a damaging effect on his position. As with the artist's other work, *Zugzwang* revolves around pictures of pictures, pictures of fragments, even defaced pictures. While the image of Hitler is instantly known as the arch villain of the twentieth century, Duchamp's face is not readily recognizable. One more easily recalls Duchamp's alter egos than the simple dark-suited man early in his career. How dare one combine the effigy of a mass murderer with the hero of the twentieth century's avant-garde? This question is crucial to the project, and ironic, considering that the Kunstverein occupies a historically loaded space on the ground floor of the now restored, former great synagogue of Essen. The upper level of the former synagogue houses a museum of Essen's Jewish history.

Herz permits the surface similarities and radical differences of this implausible marriage of *Zugzwang*'s two central characters to ricochet ad infinitum into an aesthetic, ideological, and physical stalemate. Coincidences abound, albeit superficial ones. Duchamp and Hitler were born only two years apart, the former in 1887, the latter in 1889. Both are dressed in similar bourgeois manner: dark suit, white shirt, and tie. Hitler is not shown in his standard uniform, nor is Duchamp in any of his assumed guises. Both men were artists. One is a boring traditionalist with neither sense of innovation nor talent. To call his work "academic" would be to dignify it. The other is the radical figure in this century's redefinition of the possibilities and meaning of art. Duchamp was a man who unlocked the traps of standard historical practice by looking outside art for alternatives to its suffocating traditions. In the process, he debunked the once holy domains of "aura" and "originality."

Zugzwang proposes yet another remarkably complex issue that is at stake in the intellectual battle between Hitler and Duchamp, Nazism and Dadaism. These are the diabolically contrasting notions of nihilism that pertain to each sitter's deeds. Nihilism was the paradoxical result of Hitler's totalitarian holism, the havoc his terrorism wreaked for history. Such a reading of the consequences of Hitler's rein of horror was in circulation as early as the 1930s and was reiterated, for example, in Hitler's early postwar biography by Alan Bullock.[20] On the other hand, Duchamp's self-imposed nihilism, his play with contradictory ideas and identities, opened infinite avenues for exploration that have proved to be virtually inexhaustible.

Deploying an arsenal of aesthetic tropes, *Zugzwang* communicates a virtual lexicon of ideas and moods associated with Duchamp. Aside from the previously mentioned references to use of the photograph as ready-made, and to chess in particular, there is doubling, mirroring, replication, multiplication, discontinuity in a *mise-en-abyme* that result in a dizzying experience for the viewer. David Joselit's recent observations about Duchamp's "relay between the 'elastic' body and a geometric system" and his "compulsive repetition of reproduction" are pertinent here. Herz has "stolen" these systems conceptually and reapplied them physically in his appropriation of retrograde photographs by Hoffmann onto practices liberated by Marcel Duchamp.[21] As Thomas Elsaesser observed in relation to Syberberg's film, Herz also has Hitler dissolve as a "subject."[22] He needn't dissolve Duchamp; the Dadaist already beat Herz to that punch.

One element that has gone unobserved until now in the considerable literature on *Zugzwang* is Herz's cagey contrast of Duchampian multiplication with the Nazis' very differently intended use of the same device. The Nazi employment of multiplication was central to its orderly and overwhelming massing of humans and machines. This was an essential element in its pageantry, and of ultimate importance in its consolidation of power.[23] Of course, Duchamp used replication precisely to dispel notions of power, originality, and genius.

Given the infinite and ambiguous meanings that accrue to *Zugzwang*, one might have thought that the display of Herz's piece would have engendered controversy. However, it received mainly positive notices and was mostly reviewed as art. It has come to be considered a signal work of German art in the 1990s. Even the rather historically oriented and aesthetically conservative director of the Jewish Museum in Essen approved of the artistry and ambiguity that is central to *Zugzwang*.[24]

These projects are but Herz's and Uklański's singular investigations into Hitler and the Third Reich. The work of each artist has evolved as natural extensions of other, earlier interests. Given the imagery they employ, I am not entirely sure how well they fit under the rubric of art about the Holocaust, but then sequestering art in artificial categories has always proved problematic. Dichotomies are especially evident in the area of so-called Holocaust art, where some artists have become pigeon-holed in the separate realms of art or history. Saul Friedlander has observed that art can become a pawn for politics, even within Jewish communities. And he is blatantly open about the remarkably minor position Holocaust representation holds within the "ideological and cultural" discourses of the last half-century.[25] But grandiose claims have been made to the effect that a Holocaust era may now be emerging for art, however unnerving such an idea may sound.[26] Artists must be allowed to play at the interstices between history and art, to twist and to manipulate formal and strategic elements with historical and moral meanings. The issues raised by the refracted aesthetic and cultural operations of Uklański's and Herz's works are manifold and dizzying. Essentially, Herz's installation reveals the muddiness of history: according to strictly political boundaries, it seems illogical for both a villain and a hero to have patronized the same photographer. Alternately, while art is not often granted such freedom, Uklański's work demonstrates how popular culture wields the power to break taboos.

From a purely art historical stance, Herz's and Uklański's images, created from photographic detritus, function at the intersection of political and popular culture. They leave the viewer within a state of moral strain and ambiguity. Their art avoids clear lessons, which, in itself, is highly significant. Such art turns away from recent morally coded and rhetorical work that has become known in connection with identity, multiculturalism, and marginalization. These three issues played seminal roles in the discourse on art during much of the

1990s. On the other hand, Herz's and Uklański's work seduces and repels. Naturally, it provokes questions about its meanings, the subjectivity of the artists, and possible exploitation, whether conscious or not. In her dialectical discussion, Sidra Ezrahi characterizes modes of Holocaust representation as either static or dynamic. She explains how today "[a] work of history or art is . . . performed at a distance" and emphatically demonstrates the fact that it is precisely "distance itself which is at stake."[27] Holding us within the fascinating machinations of their installation, Uklański and Herz trap us in a relay between past and present, truth and meaning, intentionally frustrating the very meaning of distance at all.

NOTES

This essay has been presented at Princeton University, Lehigh University, Drew University, the University of Pennsylvania, and the annual conference of the College Arts Association. Parts of this essay were published in *Mirroring Evil: Nazi Imagery/Recent Art* (exhibition catalog), ed. Norman L. Kleeblatt (New York: The Jewish Museum; New Brunswick: Rutgers University Press, 2001). A similar essay was published in Hebrew in the Israeli journal *Plasitka.*

1. Ron Jones, "Crimson Herring," *Artforum* 36, no. 10 (summer 1998): 17–18. See also Lorraine O'Grady, "Poison Ivy," *Artforum* 37, no. 2 (October 1998): 8. The full title of the conference was "Change the Joke and Slip the Yoke: A Series of Conversations on the Use of Black Stereotypes in Contemporary Visual Practice."
2. For an in-depth discussion, see Wendy Steiner, *The Scandal of Pleasure: Art in an Age of Fundamentalism* (Chicago: University of Chicago Press, 1995).
3. Cornelia Gockel, *Zeige deine Wunde: Faschismusrezeption in der deutschen Gegenwartskunst* (München: Verlag Silke Schreiber, 1998).
4. Saul Friedlander, *Reflections of Nazism: An Essay on Kitsch and Death*, trans. Thomas Weyr (Bloomington: Indiana University Press, 1984), 19 (also 11–22). See also Saul Friedlander, *Memory, History, and the Extermination of the Jews of Europe* (Bloomington: Indiana University Press, 1993), 49–52, as well as his *Probing the Limits of Representation: Nazism and the "Final Solution,"* ed. Saul Friedlander (Cambridge: Harvard University Press, 1992), 1–21.
5. Andreas Huyssen, *Twilight Memories: Marking Time in a Culture of Amnesia* (New York: Routledge, 1995), 13.

6. Sidra DeKoven Ezrahi, "Representing Auschwitz, " *History and Memory* 7, no. 2 (fall/winter 1995/6): 122.
7. This installation has recently been published as Piotr Uklański, *The Nazis* (Zurich: Edition Patrick Frey, 1999).
8. Alice Yaeger Kaplan discusses the problematic purveying of the history of World War II using the tale of her friend Margaret, who was told the stories by her grandmothers "on the sly." See Alice Yaeger Kaplan, "Theweleit and Spiegelman: Of Mice and Men," in *Remaking History*, ed. Barbara Kruger and Phil Mariani (Seattle: Bay Press, 1989), 167–68. This information about his family is included in a number of the articles about Uklański's exhibition. The artist also spoke about his familial reaction (or lack thereof) with reference to the Holocaust and World War II in an interview with the author on January 16, 1999.
9. In fact, the organizers of the exhibition found some viewers attempting to identify as many of the actors and roles as they could. Told to the author in a meeting on January 21, 2000, with Paul Wombell, director, and Jeremy Millar, curator, both of the Photographers' Gallery, London.
10. For other examples, see the catalog for the exhibition at P.S.1, Long Island City, New York. Ingrid Scaffner, *Deep Storage* (Munich: Prestel Verlag, 1998). For examples of Broodthaer's ironic collecting enterprises, see Marge Goldwater, "Introduction, " in *Marcel Broodthaers* (Minneapolis: Walker Art Center; New York: Rizzoli, 1989).
11. Meeting with Wombell and Millar, January 21, 2000
12. *Evening Standard*, July 29, 1998, 21.
13. For example, see Stuart Shave, "Nice Nazi, Nasty Nazi," in *I-D* (August 1998), or Peter Lyle, "The Reich Stuff," in *The Face* (June 1998).
14. Neal Ascherson, "It's Only David Niven Dressed Up: Why Do We Feel a Chill?" *Observer*, August 23, 1998, 9.
15. Such debates about the authenticity of difficult cutting-edge contemporary art have been particularly visible during the 1990s in London, especially since the by-now historic show *Frieze* organized by Damien Hirst. Ironically, its negative public debates have actually benefited a certain group of British artists and not least the market for their art. Waldemar Januszczak, "Dressed to Kill," *New York Times*, August 16, 1998, 10.
16. Barbara Ehrenreich, "Foreword," in *Male Fantasies*, by Klaus Theweleit, trans. Stephen Conway with Erica Carter and Chris Turner (Minneapolis: University of Minnesota Press, 1987), x.
17. See *Frankfurter Allgemeine Zeitung* for a glowing review of the installation.
18. *Suddeutsche Zeitung, Frankfurter Allgemeine,* and *Die Zeit* all were highly positive about the intentions of the organizers and importance of the show

to open a discussion and analyze the mechanisms that produced Nazism and helped it penetrate society.

19. Georg Bussman, "Kunstgeschichte als symbolierte Realgeschichte: oder Und wer ist der Andere?" in *Rudolf Herz* (exhibition catalog) (Essen: Kunstverein Ruhr, 1995), 5.

20. Ibid. Peter Friese, "Zugzwang," in *Rudolf Herz* (Essen: Kunstverein Ruhr, 1995), 13–39. With reference to nihilism, see Friedlander, *Reflections of Nazism*, 58.

21. David Joselit, *Infinite Regress: Marcel Duchamp 1910–1941* (Cambridge, Mass.: MIT Press, 1998), 53, 142.

22. Thomas Elsaesser, "Myth and the Phantasmagoria of History: H. J. Syberberg, Cinema, and Representation," *New German Critique* 24–25 (fall/winter 1981–82): 114.

23. Susan Sontag, "Fascinating Fascism," in *Under the Sign of Saturn*, ed. Susan Sontag (New York: Farrar, Straus & Giroux, 1980). Friedlander, *Reflections of Nazism*, 52.

24. Conversation with Peter Friese and Friederieke Wappler, October 17, 1999.

25. Friedlander, *Memory, History, and the Extermination of the Jews of Europe*, 46, 51–52.

26. Stephen Feinstein, ed., *Witness and Legacy: Contemporary Art about the Holocaust* (Minneapolis: Lerner Publications, 1995), 7.

27. Ezrahi, "Representing Auschwitz," 122.

Chapter 9

On Sanctifying the Holocaust: An Anti-Theological Treatise

Adi Ophir

Many years from now, decades, perhaps centuries, when the stories have become intertwined and interwoven through the distilling violence of forgetting, what form will the saga of the destruction of European Jewry take? How will storytellers then nourish their legends of terror—if there still remain storytellers, if a nuclear holocaust does not erase the signs of all the atrocities that preceded it? Will the survivors be gathered in an ark of the righteous people of their generation, will the destruction be seen as the Jewish flood? Or perhaps those of the ghetto revolt, the partisans, the few who took to arms, will be seen as the sons of light against the sons of darkness. Will their struggle be the first battle between Gog and Magog? Perhaps a new story of sacrifice will be told, that an entire people was brought as a sacrifice, without an angel and without a ram in the bushes?

Perhaps from that Holocaust altar, whose dimensions are the dimensions of an ancient continent, a mighty belief will spring forth, seven times greater for its absurdity than the belief of Abraham, the first Hebrew who, after all, continued in his innocence to believe—because his God refrained from telling him that his descendants, multiplied as the stars of the heavens, would be slaughtered in the death camps of Europe.

A religious consciousness built around the Holocaust may become the central aspect of a new religion, one that has at its core a story of revelation that goes something like this:

In the year five thousand seven hundred since the creation of the world according to the Jewish calendar, in central Europe, Absolute Evil was revealed. The Absolute—that is, the Divine—is Evil. Every act has a part, to a greater or lesser extent, in this Absolute Evil, every act is an expression of it. But until the emergence of the Absolute Evil no one believed that there was a hidden lawfulness controlling every appearance of evil in our world. Until then, no one had placed his or her trust in the absolute, transcendent, one and only Evil, which is the ground of our lives and deaths, the logic of our finitude and suffering, the rock of our destruction, and the promise of our annihilation. Indeed, time has passed before the meaning of this horrible event could be digested and understood completely, but how is it possible that an event of such dimensions of horror could have no meaning? From a secure distance of time the individual acts of extermination have been collected—particular pullings of the trigger, particular and repeated acts of the opening of gas-pipes, lighting of furnaces—and they have woven together to form the infinite face of the Absolute. The proper place of each atrocious act is in the infinity of Evil, those six years can already be seen as a single unique revelation of the Absolute.

The God described in this religion, revealed in the furnaces, will be seen as a vengeful God, visiting the iniquity of the fathers upon the children, unto the third and fourth generations. Their iniquity—that they did not reject their Jewishness while there was still time, that they did not bother to change their names, to hide their descent one hundred, one hundred and fifty years before the calamity. Vengefulness requires bookkeeping, listing, and documentation. Absolute Evil is a perfect bookkeeper, an all-documenting bureaucrat, supervisor, and detective; he is a beneficiary of Providence in the full sense of the word. Every Jew was accounted for; grandchildren and great-great-grandchildren were also accounted for. After which the accounts of loading and unloading were managed, dates were coordinated for the travel of the trains, the rate of expiration was discussed, the volume of the ashes was measured. The face of Absolute Evil was revealed, or at least this is how the myth will reconstruct it, as the face of a bureaucrat (the Absolute, even the embodiment of Evil, cannot be understood without a certain degree of personification). The Holocaust is God. In a way we are today already partners to this utterance. The ears of my readers are ringing, I know. But the new religion is already taking form today, and already there are few who would reject the popular interpretation of its revelation: the commandments that echo from within the thick cloud that arose from the earth of iron to the empty iron heaven of Europe (Deut. 28:23).

The four commandments of the new religion (Exod. 20:3): Thou shalt have no other holocaust before the Holocaust of the Jews of Europe; Thou shalt not make unto thee any graven image or any likeness; Thou shalt not take the name of the Holocaust in vain; Remember.

"Thou shalt have no other holocaust." There is no holocaust like the Holocaust of the Jews of Europe. To what lengths Jewish historians, educators, and politicians go to remind us over and over of the difference between the destruction of the Jews of Europe and all other types of disasters, misfortunes, and mass murders! Biafra was only hunger; Cambodia was only a civil war; the destruction of the Kurds was not systematic; death in the Gulag lacked national identification marks. Even those who are wary of a demonization of the Holocaust, even those who take care to present the slaughterers as human beings, soldiers, police officers, and common clerks, go on to claim: There was never before such an organized, comprehensive, and horrifying outburst of evil as in the Holocaust. The Holocaust is a collection of human acts that has turned into a transcendent event.

"Thou shalt not make unto thee any graven image or likeness." It is possible to draw another Guernica, to sing the songs of the Partisans, to present "Ghetto," but the Holocaust itself cannot be represented. No artistic or literary representation can succeed. Whoever tries to peek through the furnace of revelation and describe what he saw with his own eyes, or in his mind's eye, is destined to fail. The best of literature, drama, or cinema can only touch upon the margins of the atrocity, document it through fragments of memories of those still living —they do not dare be caught in the world of the slaughtered, and anyone who actually tries to describe the hell is punished severely by the critics. (Claude Lanzmann's *Shoah*, a movie that takes place in the present, is an exception.) What was then real is beyond the capabilities of poetry, art, and dramatic reconstruction. Exactly as it is impossible to understand the transcendental in the framework of a scientific theory, it is equally impossible to capture it in the realms of the imagination. The outcome of every such analytical or artistic attempt

is distortion rather than representation, camouflage rather than re-construction, forgetting rather than remembering. These are almost a priori rules of the critics, which are independent of the nature and quality of the specific artistic piece toward which they are directed.

"Thou shalt not take the name in vain." How many outbursts of rage did Menachem Begin earn when he dared to profane the name? How many warnings have been uttered since then by researchers of the Holocaust, politicians, and educators against that disreputable phe-nomenon, a transgression, no doubt, derogating the Holocaust by borrowing its name for calamities and disasters of a lesser order of atrocity, the earthly order?

"Remember the day of the Holocaust to keep it holy, in memory of the de-struction of the Jews of Europe." This is the most important command-ment. This is the burden whose shirking is the archetype of sin. Not only the organized drive to forget, but also the innocent forgetting, the result of assimilation or simple lack of interest in the remnants of the Jewish possessions that a person carries with him or herself, is an act of terrible renunciation. Those who cause forgetting, to say noth-ing of those who deny, cooperate with the enemy. Those who assimi-late complete the Nazis' work. Those who are faithful to themselves, and to their people, will repeat the tale until the end of time. Even if a thousand years pass and all the documents are lost, the revelation of Evil will be present in the midst of the nation through the count-less threads of its common memory.

Absolute Evil must be remembered in exquisite detail. And al-ready scattered throughout the land are institutions of immortaliza-tion and documentation, like God's altars in Canaan one generation after the settlement. Already a central altar has arisen that will grad-ually turn into our Temple, forms of pilgrimage are taking hold, and already a thin layer of Holocaust priests, keepers of the flame, is grow-ing and institutionalizing; only, instead of rituals of sacrifices, there are rituals of memorial, remembering, and repetition, since the sac-rifice is completed and now all that is left is to remember.

The mythologization and demonization of the Holocaust are inextri-cably tied to one another. They are part of the same process of "sanc-tification" that adds an important layer of religiosity to our lives, as freethinking and secular as we may be. It is quite possible that the more the secular self-awareness is developed, the deeper the distancing from what is required from the revelation at Sinai, the stronger is the tie to and the need for a modern revelation, the revelation of Absolute Evil. The commandments reside almost by definition beyond the political Left and Right, beyond the power struggles and ideological conflicts, beyond the opposing interests and worldviews. They establish the boundaries of Jewish legitimacy; they establish the Holocaust as a transcendent event that precedes and qualifies any attempt to fashion a modern Jewish identity. Who will dare deny them publicly? Who will dare deny the uniqueness of the Holocaust? Who will dare claim that he or she has comprehended it, in theory or in a work of art, as it actually was? Who will admit bearing its name in vain? Who will dare to let loose the reins of forgetting, to relieve the burden of the memory?

Why is our Holocaust myth so dangerous? Because it blurs the humanness of the Holocaust; because it erases degrees and continuums and puts in their place an infinite distance between one type of atrocity and all other types of human atrocities; because it encourages the memory as an excuse for one more nation-unifying ritual and not as a tool for historical understanding; because it makes it difficult to understand the Holocaust as a product of a human, material, and ideological system; because it directs us almost exclusively to the past, to the immortalization of that which is beyond change, instead of pointing primarily to the future, to the prevention of a holocaust—like the one that was, or another, more horrible—which is more possible today than ever before but is still in the realm of that which is crooked and can be made straight.

Is it possible to break away from the myth in a responsible way, without wicked cynicism and without pleasure for its own sake at the bursting of a myth? It seems to me to be possible. First of all, I must state explicitly: I am in no way trying to say that the Holocaust was anything less than Absolute Evil, that we may already forget, that we can use the name indiscriminately. But I do want to deny the commandments as they were formulated above and as they are present in public Jewish life and political discourse in Israel and abroad. And more than anything else I wish to deny the one assumption hidden behind the entire Holocaust myth, that the Holocaust is an exclusively

Jewish matter. I do not necessarily refer here to the destruction of the Gypsies, the slaughter of Russian captives, or the persecution of the communists and other opponents of the regime, even though these should be accounted for, and the exact differences should be considered carefully. I mean to say that the Jewishness of the Holocaust (like its Germanness) is only one aspect of the horror, the most crucial aspect from our point of view but by no means exclusive, and that the overlooking of other aspects, which are not necessarily related to the Jewish issue, is no less dangerous than the denial of the Holocaust by contemporary anti-Semites.

It is impossible to explain Nazism without explaining what gave birth to and maintained in Nazism that "cruel lust for total destruction" of the Jews. But to the same degree it is impossible to explain how that same lust could be filled, in such a systematic, exact, prolonged, and insane manner, without explaining those modes of discourse that expelled the Jews from the domain of humanity, the technologies of power activated to implement the ideological statements, and the erotica of power used to guarantee complete execution of the mission, until the last moment, until the final breath. The Jew was, of course, placed, from the first moment of the Nazi phenomenon to its last, in the focus of these modes of discourse, a final target of all the power technologies and a last release of its eroticism. One question is what were those things that made it possible to turn the Jew into the object of that "excluding" discourse, an insane discourse of power penetrated with eroticism but complete in its mechanisms? This is the "Jewish Question" of Holocaust research.

Another separate question (in theory, though in reality not completely separate) is the structure, the enabling conditions, and those factors that allowed those same modes of discourse and those same power arrangements, from which the Nazi phenomenon was composed, to emerge and to persist. This is the "Universal Question" of Holocaust research. It is a question that we too rarely ask.

A similar distinction can be made from another direction. What distinguishes Nazism, like what distinguishes the Holocaust, is the unique combination of a series of extreme factors, each one of which alone would not have been able to give birth to the terror. One question is what made possible the combination that turned Nazism and the destruction of the Jews of Europe into phenomena without compare in human history. And another question is what were those extreme factors, how do they appear in less extreme conditions, what encourages their radicalization, and what is likely to prevent it? The question of reconstructing the unique combination is the "Jewish Question," the question of deconstructing that combination into factors is the "Universal Question." The reconstructive question presents the Holocaust, whether consciously or unconsciously, as a transcendent event that lies beyond the limits of human reach, an event whose horrors we, as humans, will never be able to come close to repeating. The deconstructive question, on the other hand, returns to the horror of its humanness and points out the possibilities and their degrees and continuity. The Jewish Question turns the Holocaust into a holy source of reference to the past. The universal question presents the Holocaust as a permanently necessary background to interpretations of the present and intentions for the future. In the final account, the difference is a question of where we choose to place Absolute Evil: as a revelation whose place is in the past, or as a possibility whose place is in the present.

A possibility whose place is in the present. This can be understood only if we try to deconstruct into factors, only if we try to closely examine the humanness of the structures of discourse and power, only if we stubbornly insist upon seeing them as the realization of human possibilities, or in other words, as our own possibilities. First of all, the "excluding" and "another," reference to another that serves as the borderline, as the archetype of negation, as a focus for the definition of a reverse identity; a package of "excluding" oppositions wrapped in the same fundamental distinction and drawn after it: superior-inferior, authentic-unauthentic, holy-profaned, pure-impure, healthy-sick, living-dead; a systematic application of the conceptual borderline (Aryan–non-Aryan) over geographic space (and also over historical time: before and after the Jewish pollution, before and after the German revolution); the revealed and concealed mechanisms for encouraging, distributing, and imposing the "excluding" modes of discourse, its internal organization and principles of the hierarchy contained within it, the sterilizing of channels of debate, and blocking of the possibilities of disagreement and deviance.

Parallel to these, the development, organization, and nurturing of the technology of power: use of all existing power mechanisms while developing new tools of power; complete exploitation of the social potential for supervision, surveillance, policing, and exclusion, and a refinement of those mechanisms responsible for these functions; takeover of the educational system and establishment of cadres of the reliable and loyal; management of the individual among the masses, and of the masses for purposes determined in advance; rationalization and bureaucratization of the power mechanisms, independent of the irrationality of the goals; adaptation of the academic world and the takeover of the sources of applied knowledge; accelerated development of new technologies of destruction.

And finally, the tremendous eroticism invested in the organization of the power order: the training of the individual's body, along with the massive parade exercises; the emotional bond between the individual and the masses, between each individual and the leader, and between the leader and the masses; the development of obedience as the model of love relations; covert and overt opposition to objectivity, rationality, and modernity, and an emphasis on inner life, emotion, and mysticism; the transformation of "nation," "race," "people," and "fuhrer" into objects of love, loyalty, and sacrifice, with the necessarily adjacent concepts as objects of hate, disgust, and "lust for destruction."

This list is not meant to be exhaustive, the analysis is not meant to be radical (modes of discourse were never detached from mechanisms of power, and power has never been very separate from its erotic overtones), but these, or something close to these, are the factors that can be the basis for possible continuums. Of course, the distinction between the search for the unique combination, which is meant to protect the transcendence of the Holocaust, and its division into factors, which can specify the range of possibilities, is not unequivocal. These two questions are doubtless interconnected and interdependent. But the difference exists and is decisive. It is the difference of priorities in the directions of research, of emphasis in the rhetoric of mourning and remembrance, of directions in learning for the future. In short, the difference is essentially political: It is the difference in the use that the living make of the memory of the dead, the present of its history. This is the difference in whose light I propose to part with the myth and to rewrite the commandments of the Holocaust. To rewrite means that we ourselves interpret and write, while we strive for self-awareness in our attitudes to the Holocaust. To rewrite means not to listen silently to the voice carried to us directly from the destruction of Europe, from the sight of the revelation of Evil. To rewrite means to determine commandments whose hidden assumptions are open to the light of day and may stand over and over again the test of critical thought. To rewrite, something like this:

> *Thou shalt have no other holocaust.* In reality. One Holocaust was; another is possible; therefore do everything possible so that you will not have, so that they will not have, so that there will be none at all.
>
> *Thou shalt not make unto thee any graven image or likeness.* Do everything that you can to concretize the horror. Honor its intricate details. Present as much as possible of its creeping before the explosion, its day-to-day occurrences, its uncountable human, all too human, faces.
>
> *Remember.* First of all, try to understand. Remember in order to understand. To understand the technology of power and the modes of "excluding" discourse that made the Holocaust possible: the discourse that made it possible to exclude a group of people from within the borders of the human race, and the technology that made it possible to massively deport them to their deaths.

What is being discussed here is no simple problem of historiography. What hangs here in the balance is the process of the political institutionalization of a joint national memory, and essentially the borders of the self-awareness of the modern Jew, the self-identity of post-Holocaust Jewry. The Jew who, in relating to the Holocaust, accepts, whether explicitly or implicitly, the theological treatise that I described, is as a firebrand saved from the fire who counts his or her losses over and over again in ritual periodicity; one whose memory is always a nightmare and whose nightmares fashion dreams, whose mere live presence is a reminder of the destruction, who does not cease to blame, judge, and accuse others, to swear that s/he will never again be their sacrifice.

But perhaps it is already possible to make a breach in the theological treatise that requires such a stance—perhaps it is already impossible not to—to strive for a more delicate balance between the enslavement of the present to the burden of the past, and the interpretation of present reality in terms of the possibilities that this past presents to it as its own real possibilities? Perhaps it is already possible to restrain the laments, immortalizations, and blaming, to make a little room for the deconstructive effort, which is essential and urgent because it also means an effort of location and deterrence? Our lives are already penetrated with the presence of some of those very factors that should be deconstructed; the hour is urgent.

From that conflagration we must today carry a different message, a message at whose center lies the humanness of the atrocity, the fact that the atrocity is an existing human possibility—that is, our possibility. This is the proper basis for modern human solidarity. When the required modes of discourse exist, when the technologies of power are at hand, when love and hate are present in the proper dose and directed in the appropriate channels, then every person may be the sacrifice, and everyone may be a participant in the slaughter. And we must also take into account how much the technologies of destruction have advanced since then, and how much, as a result, the investment in obedience, loyalty, and lust, required to operate them, has been reduced.

The moral confrontation of a Jew today with the Holocaust entails the personalization of the acts of destruction and the universalization of its possibilities. The universalization of the Holocaust is today an essential component in the consciousness of the Jew, one generation after Auschwitz, and a necessary condition for our moral existence.

NOTES

This essay appeared in *Tikkun* 2, no. 1 (1987).

Part IV

CURATING MEMORY

Chapter 10

Holocaust Icons: The Media of Memory

Oren Baruch Stier

I want to submit that the positioning of both the writer and the audience in relation to this mountain or this defiled center [the image
of the Holocaust] functions much as does the positioning of the pil-
grim vis-à-vis the holy mountain or the sacred center; in what closely
approximates a theological quest at the postmodern end of our millennium, a new aesthetics and ethics of representation are being
forged with Auschwitz as the ultimate point of reference.
                    —Sidra DeKoven Ezrahi, "Representing Auschwitz"[1]

"Thou shalt not make unto thee any graven image or likeness." It is possible to draw another *Guernica,* to sing the songs of the Partisans, to
present "Ghetto," but the Holocaust itself cannot be represented.
No artistic or literary representation can succeed. Whoever tries to
peek through the furnace of revelation and describe what he saw
with his own eyes, or in his mind's eye, is destined to fail. . . . What
was then real is beyond the capabilities of poetry, art and dramatic
reconstruction. Exactly as it is impossible to understand the transcendental in the framework of a scientific theory, it is equally impossible to capture it in the realms of the imagination. The outcome
of every such analytical or artistic attempt is distortion rather than
representation, camouflage rather than reconstruction, forgetting
rather than remembering.
                    —Adi Ophir, "On Sanctifying the Holocaust"[2]

The assumption that the Holocaust is the ultimate reference point
for any contemporary discussion of ethics, violence, totalitarianism,
and the like—the "master moral paradigm" as one scholar has put

it[3]—is becoming increasingly commonplace. What is equally recognized is that the terrible truths that occupy that "defiled center" and point of reference are becoming increasingly "unknowable." This is not, as many argue, because the Holocaust itself is unrepresentable (it is not), but because, as representations proliferate, the real-life referents for those representations grow old, die, or otherwise become increasingly tangential to the representations themselves. What we are left with as our main access points to the Holocaust are these representations, all straining toward the truths to which they refer, truths that nonetheless continually evade our grasp.

The struggle to represent the Holocaust is, for the most part, a struggle for adequate and appropriate modes of representation. Sidra Ezrahi, concluding the introduction to her remarkable study *Booking Passage*, writes:

> The ultimate challenge to the Israeli writer is how to keep images from becoming icons, archaeology from becoming eschatology, "arrival" from becoming the terminus of a vengeful excess of memory, the eros of an unconsummated journey from being extinguished in the killing fields of exclusive visions—how to *reopen* the narrative so that narrative itself can continue and one can hear the suppressed, the silenced, the restless and unpatriated voices.[4]

Drawing upon and refining Ezrahi's dichotomy, I shall argue that, properly understood, the concept of an "icon" actually plays a significant role in "reopening" Holocaust narratives, allowing us to hear those forgotten voices. The icon, I argue, offers the best concept for achieving symbolic integration and repatriation. In my argument, the "idol" rather than the icon embodies the "eschatological" transformation of memory. In this reading, where Ezrahi speaks of icons, I would substitute idols.

The struggle of Holocaust representation, at least in the case of the display of objects I call iconic, is to overcome the victimization motif borne by the remnants themselves without overcompensating and fetishizing, which ultimately creates an idol in place of an icon.[5] This investigation is motivated by a concern for how the meanings of the Holocaust are determined, represented, and, especially, conveyed. Among the questions with which I am concerned are: How are specific representational distillations of such meanings created through the use and contextualization of Holocaust symbols? Where do our images and understandings of the Holocaust originate, how are they produced and reproduced, and toward what do they ultimately point? What is it that is used to stand in for or otherwise symbolize the Holocaust, and what does it tell us about how we remember?

In the representation of the Holocaust, there is, of course, a great deal of discomfort with the use and reuse of imagery and with appropriation, voyeurism, commodification, pornography, and kitsch.[6] These are valid concerns. However, these can best be met not by the regulation of such imagery but rather by the careful examination of strategies of representation.

One could begin to classify these strategies of representation through two general categories: metaphoric and metonymic. While metaphorical language maintains its important place in Holocaust representation ("the Holocaust is now among the most scrutinized— and contested—subjects of metaphor in American public culture"),[7] metonymic modes of engagement are claiming an ever greater share of the representational pie. In these variegated metonymic cases, the Holocaust is represented by way of symbolic, often visual pointers that are themselves directly derived from the events to which they refer. As parts of the whole, these pointers act as mediators for Holocaust awareness and memory, in that they refer metonymically to the events of which they somehow once took and still take part and present in condensed form images of what is deemed most essential to the process of remembrance.

We know by now that redemption, especially in the case of the Holocaust, is impossible, an ever-deferred wish. But in this hyper-mediated, post-Holocaust age, it isn't simply that the medium is the message (and messenger as well) but that it is the totality of our experience of the Holocaust past. The symbolic media of Holocaust memory are, in many cases, all we have to work with. Consequently, to avoid the idolatrous temptation toward redemption, we must engage in a critique of those media of representation and transmission. Only through attention to effects and contexts can those icons and the people who memorialize with them resist the seductive pull of idolatry.

As a way of initiating a discussion of the role such images play in Holocaust representation and memory, I will call certain uses of these metonymic images "icons." My usage of the term "icon" is meant to convey the sense of an image being put to a religious use, thereby conveying meaning in a symbolic context. Icons act as cultural reminders, vehicles (literally) for the construction of memory and the public sense of the past. As I shall argue below, as in the case of the use of Holocaust-era railway cars in museums and memorials, certain images and artifacts, when utilized iconically, are transformed into bearers of memory aimed at transporting those who engage with their symbolic presentations to a deeper understanding of the Holocaust. The term "icon" immediately raises the issues of the propriety of such religious applications of metonymic imagery.

The *Oxford English Dictionary* defines "icon" (from the Greek: likeness, image, portrait, semblance, similitude, simile) as "an image, figure, or representation; a portrait; a picture, 'cut,' or illustration in a book" and "an image in the solid; a monumental figure; a statue." Of course, it also notes the religious meaning of the term: "*Eastern Church.* A representation of some sacred personage, in painting, bas-relief, or mosaic, itself regarded as sacred, and honored with a relative worship or adoration." In the contemporary literature on Holocaust representation, the term is used frequently, sometimes carelessly, sometimes more critically, but in all cases as a common linguistic indication of the representative, even paradigmatic, status of a particular object, image, or personality. Generally, such icons are deemed capable of standing in for the events of the Holocaust and conveying their enormity in some way, while nonetheless reminding viewers and readers that what is being symbolized remains more complex than the icon itself.

While the term icon invokes a certain degree of discomfort, particularly in the Jewish context, it also evokes powerful notions of sacralization that are at once attractive from a theoretical standpoint and apropos of the "theological" styles of reference and representation alluded to in the epigraphs to this chapter. Indeed, the notion of sanctity in Holocaust symbolization, whether derived from the presumed sanctity of the Holocaust itself or from its "sacred" artifacts and narratives, is a key subtext to this entire discussion. In this sense Holocaust icons and Holocaust idols are competing versions of sanctification and sacralization.

W. J. T. Mitchell's typology of images in *Iconology* is helpful in this regard because Mitchell outlines a view of the iconic mode of representation that, while respecting its religious orientations, also broadens the meaning of the term in a way that invites such an interdisciplinary perspective. Here the author identifies a "family tree" of different types of imagery, ranging from the graphic (on the left side of his schema), to the optical, the perceptual, the mental, and finally (on the right side) the verbal categories of images, each with its own disciplinary discourse. Over all these is the parent concept (the patriarch?), the image "as such," whose institutional discourses, incidentally, are philosophy and theology.[8] Mitchell's typology opens up the concept of the icon as an image *of something* while naturalizing the term, so to speak, so as not to engage the charge of the impropriety of such imagery (the idol, presumably, remains the term for the "improper" image or representation).

What attracts me to Mitchell's schema, besides the seductiveness of the "logos" of the icon he develops, is the important correction he offers for any theoretical consideration of visual imagery. Mitchell broadens the range of imagery one may rightfully consider iconic even as he restores the "icon" to its place as the image as such. His typology accepts as iconic those classes of images on the right side of his spectrum—perceptual, mental, and verbal images—against the idea that such icons are "improper," thereby engaging the debate over the propriety of images. Thus he rightly suggests that the "icon," in and of itself, is nothing to be feared. Lest anyone set graphic and visual icons apart from mental and verbal ones, Mitchell maintains that there is nothing more or less proper about any class of imagery. This is not just because of the fallacy of such charges of impropriety regarding the perceptual, mental, and verbal classes of images, but also because, according to Mitchell, the very root of the idea of the image —the notion of "likeness" in the Bible—is resolutely nonpictorial, immaterial, spiritual. This "spiritualization" of the concept of the icon allows it to continue to resonate aesthetically and religiously while further distinguishing it from idolatry. Moreover, in calling the "parent concept" of the image the "icon," Mitchell suggests a concept of imagery that is at once broadly inclusive and deeply engaging. Representation of any sort, then, relies on some form of imagery, and in calling the pivotal type of Holocaust imagery "iconic" I wish to reflect this argument and counter any misguided charges of impropriety. As

I have suggested already, it is more constructive to debate the effectiveness and form of different types of images than it is to legislate which images may not be permissible.

Thus, because of its religious connotations the term "icon" enables us to address the issue of the presumed sanctity of Holocaust symbols and, especially, artifacts. Indeed, as I shall attempt to demonstrate, when physical remnants are put on display—items that are actual artifacts from the time of the Holocaust such as shoes or railway cars—the iconic mode of presentation is at its most visible. All these present themselves as unmediated effects of the Shoah, material witnesses, though mute, to the events that produced them. Attention to the contexts of their presentation—to the fact that they have been placed, arranged, naturalized, domesticated—makes clear that mediation is nonetheless present.[9] When they are displayed in memorial-museological environments, they carry, as vehicles of and for memory, an abundance of signification. Icons like these enact the past and offer a physical reminder of its weight and enormity.

The concept of the icon also enables us to highlight a major problem of Holocaust representation; for if we pay close attention to the nature of these remnants on display, we notice a disturbing characteristic: their abundance of signification speaks a language of victimization and loss. Their sanctity is the product of two forces of objectification: that of the Nazis, who (sometimes) unwittingly but nonetheless disturbingly memorialized their victims by collecting their belongings in massive quantities, and that of museum curators, who memorialize those same victims by *re*-collecting (hence, *recollecting*) their belongings in display cases. "[T]hese remnants rise in a macabre dance of memorial ghosts. Armless sleeves, eyeless lenses, headless caps, footless shoes: victims are known only by their absence, by the moment of their destruction. In great loose piles, these remnants remind us not of the lives that once animated them, so much as the brokenness of lives."[10] The struggle of the Holocaust icon, then, is the struggle to transform this ghostliness and loss into life and presence, without violating the truth to which it refers in the service of the memory those employing it wish to create.[11]

Thus, I use the word "icon" to evoke the power and mystery attributed to Holocaust symbols and remnants, to suggest the religious aura that is taken to surround them, and to call to mind the memorial roles they play in specific contexts. When the propriety of Holocaust symbols is invoked—specifically, the concern for protecting the sacred core of the Holocaust from abuse, as expressed by survivor-commentators like Elie Wiesel—the Holocaust becomes a sacred mystery held "over there" behind a carefully circumscribed fence that, presumably, protects it from abuse at the hands of all who would violate its memory and its symbols. But the fact is that those symbols are not so easily controlled. They have a life of their own. It is that life to which I point in using the term "icon."

In the case of images that I call Holocaust icons, those that are built out of authentic artifacts from World War II are especially potent as conveyors of perceptions. We rely on such artifacts to communicate some aspect of the enormity of the events in which they somehow participated. They often speak in their multiplicity to the reality of devastating loss. Such discourse was already operative in the first journalistic accounts of liberation. Note, for example, this report in 1944 from *Time-Life* correspondent Richard Lauterbach on visiting a "shoe warehouse" at Majdanek:

> I stepped up and went inside. It was full of shoes. A sea of shoes. I walked across them unsteadily. They were piled, like pieces of coal in a bin, halfway up the walls. Not only shoes. Boots. Rubbers. Leggings. Slippers. Children's shoes, soldier's shoes, old shoes, new shoes. They were red and grey and black. Some had once been white.[12]

Such images of atrocity indicate, however indirectly, the destruction of which the shoes are, presumably, the only remnants. As metonyms of the Holocaust, they are already iconic because, in their roles as artifacts, physical representations of the destruction that produced them, they come to be regarded with a certain degree of veneration. Their roles as icons are further reinforced by their later incorporation into visual and oral narratives that are often dramatically reenacted. This can be seen in the following account of a witness in the Eichmann trial who also spoke of finding many shoes during a visit to Treblinka after liberation.

> As he spoke these words, he carefully unwrapped a tiny pair of shoes and held them up for the whole courthouse to see. . . . This dramatic testimony . . . provided a potent image of the "Holocaust," later to be incorporated into the Historical Museum at Yad Vashem where a

lone child's shoe is displayed on a plinth bearing the number of child victims of the Holocaust.[13]

The dramatic reproduction of these material icons raises their potency for standing in metonymically for the entirety of the Holocaust.

We rely a great deal on these types of representation for our "sacred" engagement with the Holocaust and its meanings. However, such reliance on hypersymbolic representation entails a number of risks, all of which revolve around how remembrance is performed and what is remembered with and through these icons. At the extreme, we, as visitors to contemporary constructed memorial environments, risk "forgetting" the events referred to, the things we are asked to try to remember, and "remembering" only the representations of those events. In these cases the icons cease to mediate memory and cease to facilitate the referentiality that is central to the memorialization process. I associate this potential forgetfulness, this cessation of mediation, with the notion of idolatry. Such idolatrous representation is problematic because it erases the voice of the past in favor of the more audible noise of the present and the increasingly vicarious memories of contemporaneous visitor-voyeurs fashioning their memories at the altar of these Holocaust idols.

The *Oxford English Dictionary* defines "idol," from the Latin for "image, form, spectre, apparition" in several ways. In the Jewish and Christian context, it is an "image or similitude of a deity or divinity, used as an object of worship" and "*fig.* Any thing or person that is the object of excessive or supreme devotion, or that usurps the place of God in human affection." In classical Greek (and Latin) use, it is an "image, effigy, or figure of a person or thing; esp. a statue," "a counterpart, likeness, imitation" and a "mental fiction; a phantasy or fancy," among other meanings.

In the case of Holocaust representation, idols offend not so much because they cross some line of propriety (though they often do) but because they demand allegiance more to the image itself and its own mode of presentation than to what it purports to represent. The idol is meant to serve as the supreme object of such worship.

In contrast to such idols, what I refer to as an icon is a successful appropriation of a memorial artifact that does not elide the past in establishing a relationship to it. In embodying memory, icons act as mediators for memory's enactment, while idols serve as false gods in the quest for memorial embodiment. Icons, seen in this way, are representations which, though complex and inspiring a certain level of discomfort, nonetheless communicate something of the meaning of the past without overly distorting it.

The term for idolatry in the Jewish rabbinic tradition, *avodah zarah*, literally means "strange worship." This can be read in two ways: as the improper form of worship or a reference to the improper god being worshiped ("the strangeness of the ritual or the strangeness of the object of the ritual").[14] Jewish thought rejects the latter. The former definition, which is more ambiguous, allows for acceptable and effective iconization. Thus, a Jewish icon, as a memorial representation, would act as a reminder—of G-d, of catastrophe, of past redemptions and their long-awaited but ever-deferred future recurrence. Icons thus call attention to the gap between then and now, there and here, as well as to the necessary vicariousness of (re)presentational strategies. Idols, encouraging the forgetting of this distinction, offer too much closure.[15] Whenever an object's memorial trajectory is turned in a different direction—inward, or toward some contemporary, immediate form of redemption—idolatry rears its ugly head. Whereas icons are dynamic, idols are static. Whereas a religious icon is a medium for worship, an idol is the object of worship itself.

Holocaust icons operate according to the same structure. When the image points beyond itself as a mediator of memorial experience and as a model of sacred engagement and embodiment, then it is an effective icon. Icons become idols only when a mistake of interpretation is made: when the voyeur mistakes the part for the whole, the artifact for the events that generated it, or when the object is allowed to conceal the discourse that produced it. In this way the object becomes instrumentalized, idolized, made into a false god. Idol making shows a misplaced (or displaced) impatience for redemption.

This notion of the Holocaust icon, in all its complexity and multiplicity, may be situated in the middle of a continuum of possible representational styles. At one extreme lies the Holocaust idol, the problematically embodied distortion of memory; at the other end lies the more disengaged Holocaust symbol. Symbols crop up everywhere and are not regulated or controlled in any way, whereas icons, as I define them, are always presented in a performative and visual context, often in memorial-museological environments. They are thus embodied, invested with a surfeit of signification. In this way, one could say that Holocaust symbols (the Jewish star, for example, or the swastika) constitute the *grammar* of Holocaust representation, while Holocaust icons, especially when taken in their museological or memorial contexts, participate in establishing the *narratives* of representation. To make this distinction clear, I would like to turn to the ways in which Holocaust-era railway cars are incorporated into broader memorial narratives as a visual reminder of the deportation of Jews.

In the United States, memorial presentations of authentic railway cars tend to be housed *inside* museums and treated as artifacts. The first one ever displayed in the United States is at the Dallas Holocaust Memorial Center, which opened in 1984. The best known boxcar in the United States is most likely the one housed at the United States Holocaust Memorial Museum (USHMM) in Washington, D.C. The USHMM specimen fits within the overall narrative and collection philosophy of the Washington museum's organizers, who sought to ground the validity of their project, as well as the reality of the Holocaust and its narration, in an impressive array of genuine artifacts. The railway car in the USHMM is thrust in the path of the museumgoer. Here, the visitor is encouraged to go through the boxcar to get to the next section of the exhibit; those wishing to avoid this experience may discover the clear but less-than-obvious way around the railcar. In Dallas, the car forms the entrance to the exhibit space; a secret panel installed to the side of the boxcar provides a way around for survivors wishing to avoid passing through the icon of their own suffering.

In another example, the Florida Holocaust Museum in St. Petersburg also features an authentic fifteen-ton freight car ("Auschwitz boxcar #113 0695-5," according to the museum's web site), which, like many of these artifacts, actually dates back to World War I. Here, the railcar stands as the focal point of the main exhibit area in the central atrium of the museum: it can be touched but not entered. A narrative supplement to the boxcar's presentation is provided by museum founder Walter Loebenberg: while cleaning the car after its arrival in Florida, workers discovered a child's ring that had evidently been knocked loose by the force of the water hoses. After having it ex-

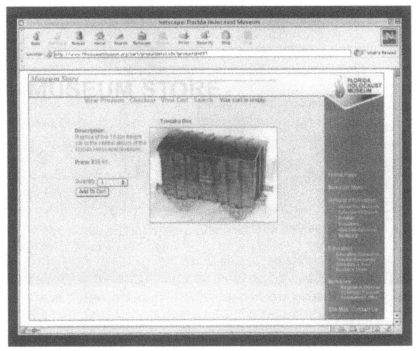

Web page, Florida Holocaust Museum online store, featuring a *Tzedaka* box for sale. © 2001 Florida Holocaust Museum. Reproduced with permission of the Florida Holocaust Museum.

amined, museum officials confirmed that the ring dated to the Holocaust era and speculated that it was hidden in the floorboards by a girl en route to a camp[16] (or perhaps trampled into the wooden floor by the press of the crowd inside). The ring is prominently displayed like a religious relic next to the railway car. The museum also advertises for sale an "artist's interpretation" of the boxcar, as described in the web site's virtual gift shop, as a "*tzedaka*," or charity box, for $39.95, plus $4.95 shipping and handling.[17] As disturbing as this miniaturization may seem, it nonetheless makes of the Holocaust-era railway car a powerful and provocative memorial symbol. The *tzedaka* box(car), through its curious mix of consumer kitsch and Jewish memorialism, offers a redemptive slant on the commemoration of deportation.[18]

Moshe Safdie, *Memorial to the Deportees*, 1995. Yad Vashem, Jerusalem, Israel.

In contrast to the domesticization of Holocaust-era railway cars housed inside U.S. museums and centers, the example found outdoors in Jerusalem is strikingly monumental. Walking around the sprawling memorial sculpture park that rings Yad Vashem, Israel's "Holocaust Martyrs' and Heroes' Remembrance Authority," a visitor discovers one as the central element of Moshe Safdie's *Memorial to the Deportees.*[19] Situated on a hillside overlooking one of the many pine-filled valleys that ring Israel's memorial mountain,[20] the *Memorial to the Deportees* (1995) is visually arresting. It features an authentic Deutsche Reichsbahn railway car (donated by Polish authorities) perched precariously on an iron rail line jutting out from the steep slope. The viewing platform restrains the visitor from approaching the boxcar, which appears to have stopped abruptly, moments before it would have tumbled off the edge of the track into the valley below. The broken track is described on Safdie's web site as the "replicated remains of a bridge after an explosion."[21] Together, railway car and track mark out an impossible journey, frozen and suspended in time and space over the steep hill. This line ends, as it did for so many deportees, violently, a moment symbolized by the twisting and shearing of the rails. As a symbol of the Holocaust turned into a memorial icon, the *Memorial to the Deportees* literally stops us in our tracks.

Of the four examples cited, the *Memorial to the Deportees* at Yad Vashem is the most self-consciously iconic. The context of its presentation reinforces this view. The Safdie memorial presents the railcar on its track extending from a viewing platform inscribed with the famous short poem by Dan Pagis, "Written in Pencil in the Sealed Railway Car": "here in this carload / i am eve / with abel my son / if you see my elder son / cain son of man / tell him that i."[22] One of the most widely anthologized poems of the Holocaust (and one of the "most highly crafted . . . in modern Hebrew,"[23] "Written in Pencil" has achieved "canonical status" through its inscription here, so that it has become "embalmed in official Israeli memory."[24] This brief but searing distillation of biblical myth and primal fratricide/genocide offers itself as an artifact of the Shoah, as if it were actually written, and abruptly cut off, inside one of those infamous railway cars. By itself the poem is a literary icon, a fictitious remnant, invoking the presence of its speaker through its form and mythic resonances. It symbolically enlarges the narrative of Nazi deportations through the retelling of the "family drama" of the West's religious origins (recall that when Cain killed Abel, he murdered one-fourth of the current human population), even as it compresses the scope of genocidal history into a scant six lines.

As a *fictional* artifact, we can read the poem more as an example of Holocaust presentation than representation, suggesting itself as a direct and unmediated link to the past. "Death is not *represented* in this truncated poem but *enacted.*"[25] In breaking off so abruptly and evocatively, the poem becomes an urgent and direct message to us as readers to complete the transmission—finish the sentence, deliver the message, carry on the story.[26] We are thus implicated in Pagis's (re)writing of myth and history: we participate in it, we are drawn into the memorialization process. In the context of the *Memorial to the Deportees*, the presentation is intensified: the railcar becomes the physical marker of the poem's possible embodiment so that the visitor imagines it is *this* car that produced or contained *this* written message. Together, poem and artifact appear to etch into the Israeli landscape an iconic presentation of memory with a voice that speaks directly to the visitor. In juxtaposing verbal and visual imagery in this way, Safdie reenacts the scene of deportation by cattle-car, bringing it out of the distant and disengaged past into the engaged present of memorialization.[27] The visitor is encouraged to imagine the deportation scenario even as it is transplanted and arrested in monumental form over a Judean valley. This transformation of memory presents a multilayered image of the railcar; we regard it as it may have been "then" and as it appears now simultaneously.

This embodiment of memory presents both a challenge for interpretation and a model for Holocaust representation. How do we read these symbolic vehicles of Holocaust memorialization? How can we contextualize their strategies for embodying and thus transmitting memory? The other presentations of railway cars offer their own, somewhat different strategies for embodiment and transmission. In Dallas and Washington, for example, the visitor becomes part of the (imagined) unfolding narrative of deportation and, indeed, must supplement through imagination any literary or linguistic icon—any text—of the sort that Pagis has (unwittingly) provided for the Israeli memorial. This makes the narrativization of the icon more personal and individual, which is accentuated, if the visitor is particularly lucky, by the story of deportation told by a local survivor-docent. The work of reenactment through artistic presentation and juxtaposition performed by Safdie at Yad Vashem is done in Washington and Dallas by way of emplacement and emplotment. If in Jerusalem I would need to use Pagis's poem as a vehicle for imagining the space of deportation, in Washington and Dallas I can stand in that space myself. The story here is literally more engaging.

The embodiment of memory in Florida works more indirectly. As in Israel, the car is closed to visitors, though its proximity to the voyeur can give rise to a more pronounced engagement with the car through imagination and touch: though closed, the railcar in St. Petersburg is accessible and may be tactilely explored. But the memory is best embodied here through the story of the child's ring and through the *tzedaka* box, both offering redemptive narratives that counterbalance the mute presentation of the boxcar itself. Each of these supplementary narratives, based on additional artifacts (authentic or not) provides an access point for the otherwise mysterious railway car.

Nonetheless, the overtly artistic and self-consciously iconic presentation of the boxcar at Yad Vashem will serve as the primary reference point for my discussion here. I will argue that it offers a provocative and ultimately problematic example of a Holocaust icon: presenting a blend of representation, presentation, and embodiment, it challenges expectations concerning the proper use of artifacts and goes far beyond the largely symbolic and more disengaged modes of Holocaust representation. Because its narrative context is less personal and literally set in stone, because it is more public and monumental, the Safdie memorial raises issues concerning the memorial and ideological appropriation of Holocaust symbols and artifacts, their roles in referring to the "defiled center" that is the Shoah, and the potential for the co-option of those roles. As a monumental incorporation of the railway car, Safdie's memorial stands out as a powerful Holocaust icon and, possibly, an idol.

To further clarify the representational problems under discussion, I turn to the issue of the display of women's hair. Arguably one of the most viscerally moving and ethically complex displays is that of women's hair shorn from camp inmates. Once again we must pay attention to the complexities encompassed by the strategies of display and resist the urge to see the icon as self-evident (and self-presenting), as unmediated reenactment. Consider, for example, that at the Auschwitz museum nearly two tons of hair are displayed inside an enormous glass case—pure physical presence, unmediated "evidence of evil." The USHMM, in its quest to locate and display authentic artifacts as part of its museum narrative, had intended to display twenty pounds of the hair on loan from the Auschwitz museum. Though this amount would not have had the "weight" of the display at Auschwitz, it nonetheless would, one presumes, have created the desired effect. But several women survivors on the content committee objected to the presentation. "For all I know, my mother's hair might be in there," one said. "I don't want my mother's hair on display."[28]

Clearly, there was something about hair, as a literally (formerly) embodied remnant, that disturbed survivors. Because of its connection to human life, its display was considered by some to be sacrilegious, a desecration of that life. So the museum decided to install a wall-length *photograph* of the nearly two tons of human hair exhibited in Auschwitz, instead of the "real thing." But twenty pounds of that hair remain in a storage facility in Maryland, perhaps awaiting a time when no objections will be raised to its display. Had the hair been displayed, as it is at Auschwitz, the USHMM would have had to contend with the risk of fetishizing the hair and commemorating the perpetrators' acts of destruction. It also would have had to deal with claims of impropriety from survivors, of going too far in exhibiting victimization. But, in not displaying it, the Washington museum has chosen representation over presentation. It has reduced the icon to a disengaged symbol, one that may not have the authenticity and directness to adequately carry the burden of memory.

Holocaust icons, in their broadest sense, are thus "living," embodied distillations of Holocaust images, of the "Holocaust" itself. Better yet, they are enlivened embodiments of the Holocaust, whose life comes from a blend of their own inherent qualities and their emplacement in museological contexts and memorial narratives. They have a degree of presence (or present-ness) that cannot be ignored. This quality marks them as different from other symbolic representations. Ernst van Alphen's conceptualization of the Holocaust effect, though it differs from mine in one important respect, helps to further clarify the concept of icon as I use it: "When I use the term *Holocaust effect*, therefore, I do so to emphasize a contrast with the term *Holocaust representation*. A representation is by definition mediated. It is an objectified account. The Holocaust is made present in the representation of it by means of *reference* to it. When I call something a Holocaust effect, I mean to say that we are not confronted with a representation of the Holocaust, but that we, as viewers or readers, experience directly a certain aspect of the Holocaust or of Nazism, of that which led to the Holocaust. In such moments the Holocaust is not re-presented, but rather presented or reenacted."[29] This sense of reenactment informs my notion of the enlivened quality of the Holocaust icon. I therefore find van Alphen's distinction supremely important and useful.

I differ with his argument with respect to the issue of mediation: for van Alphen, Holocaust "effects" are *un*mediated; whereas for me, Holocaust icons remain mediators of the memorial process. While the term "effects" strikes me as emphasizing the outcomes of memorial and representational processes, "icon" preserves the dual import of an object as at once an artifact of that time and place and a present-day image standing in metonymically for the whole to which it refers. Direct experience of an aspect of the Holocaust is *never* completely unmediated, and mediation is in fact crucial to the experience of Holocaust effects *and* Holocaust icons. One might distinguish between *external* mediation, what van Alphen calls Holocaust representation, because of its objectivized and referential qualities, and *internal* mediation, which is what occurs in any "reenactment" of an aspect of the Holocaust. In the latter case, the presence of the Holocaust is still invoked through the mediation of the reenactment, but because of the economy of presentation and its proximity to the subject, much of the work of mediation is transferred to that subject. As a result, she "experiences" the Holocaust "directly," but mediation is still central to her experience, even if it is masked as subjectivity. I think van Alphen may ultimately agree with this assessment: "We are there; history is present—but not quite," he argues, we respond to the objects of his study directly, but "in a different way."[30] That difference, I argue, is the all-important trace of mediation at the heart of what I call the Holocaust icon. Without it, we are lost; we become an indistinguishable part of the effect so that, in the case of Holocaust reenactments, the distinction between then and now, there and here, disappears.

The "re" of "reenactment" is therefore important, for no experience of a Holocaust representation or of a Holocaust effect is original.[31] Equally important is the enactment itself, as it is the performative quality of the manner in which an aspect of the Holocaust is contextualized that gives it its vibrancy and lends the illusion of immediacy. This performative aspect is better captured by the term "icon" in my estimation, especially in its religious connotations—ritual and ideological qualities that also highlight its simultaneous embodiment of past and present. As results of representational strategies, Holocaust icons share one key quality with Holocaust effects: both are necessarily "after the fact," and their study is to be seen in the context of the work of several scholars engaged with these issues.[32] Despite their differences, what many have in common is that they turn their attentions to those who relate to and identify with the Holocaust through its memorialization: those who seek to articulate a *relationship* to the Shoah, in spite of the historical-temporal distance from the events being remembered. Holocaust icons as reenactments *"post-histoire"* engender the kinds of relationships these scholars find compelling.

What finally distinguishes Holocaust icons from Holocaust symbols is their rich discursive context: these particular symbols are over-determined because they are formed by and through the discourses that have sprung up around them, which enhance their significance and provide narrative contexts for their memorial applications and social engagements. Such a discursive framework has made an icon of "Auschwitz" itself: the verbal image that partakes of the mystery of the whole, stands for it, represents it, and even presents it for memorial consumption. It is precisely this phenomenon Sidra Ezrahi points to in the epigraph to this chapter. Ezrahi situates her discussion against the background of sacred mystery and the language used in approaching it, which brings us back to our starting point.[33] To summarize: Holocaust icons are intensified forms of Holocaust symbols because they embody memory, model sacred engagement, mediate experience, and establish re-membered (re-memoried?) relationships to the past. Following Mitchell, they are complex images that challenge assumed proprieties of representation. Moreover, the most provocative icons are complex hybrids, intersections of two or more classes of imagery. These icons, like the *Memorial to the Deportees*, are what interest me the most.

But the very idea of a Holocaust icon—especially as sacred embodiment—may be viewed as problematic, particularly from the Jewish perspective. This speaks to the issue, alluded to above, of discomfort with iconic representation. In the Jewish context there is a long history of religious and political debate over icons, largely because of the presumption that icons are idols. This requires a brief digression. It is a common assumption that Jewish thought is opposed to visual representation. This originates with the biblical prohibition against "graven images," generally taken to refer to the pictorial representation of the divine; such representation is understood to be problematic in the traditional view because it runs the risk of setting up alternative gods. But "why are linguistic representations of G-d apparently permitted while visual representations are forbidden? If it is permitted to describe G-d as possessing a hand, why is it forbidden to draw it?" ask Moshe Halbertal and Avishai Margalit.[34] Why indeed? It might seem that, based on the fallacy that linguistic images are not really images, Jewish thought has found a way to circumvent its own prohibitions against representation in order to imagine the divine linguistically, while maintaining that such imagination is not at all representative of the divine. This circumvention has the added advantage of maintaining an illusion of unmediated relation: the idea that through a linguistic mode of imagery a divine-human relation is engendered that is unsullied by graphic images (understood as illegal mediators).

It would seem, therefore, that Judaism has long preferred the safety of seemingly aniconic verbal, rather than pictorial, language. Thus the apparently long-standing privileging of word over (traditionally conceived) image; similar status is purportedly accorded to sound over sight, the ear over the eye. All these may be viewed as political dichotomies, in that they preserve structures of power and preference for certain styles of communication and representation. In this light, is it any wonder that the Holocaust narrative still has primacy in discussions about appropriate memorial representations? It appears to offer a more politically and religiously acceptable strategy for approaching that "sacred mystery" without invoking the potential wrath of the memory police and their presumed charge of improper iconic representation.

But we need not accept the supposedly traditional dichotomy—not only because we learn from Mitchell that such hierarchies are essentially political at heart, but also because the opposition within Jewish thought to graphic representation is itself neither long-standing nor particularly rigid (with the exception of the prohibition against representing G-d, which I uphold right here in this sentence). Kalman Bland, in his ground-breaking recent study, argues successfully that Jewish aniconism is an "unmistakably modern idea," dependent more on the "construction of modern Jewish identities" than on an actual history of aniconism.[35] Bland's observations suggest that resistance to the concept of the iconic within Jewish thought says more about Jewish struggles with modernity than it says about aesthetics. One could conclude from this that Holocaust icons, therefore, are properly Jewish icons; at the very least they are not, by nature, improper. Holocaust icons therefore play a crucial, necessary, and appropriate role in the construction of Holocaust memorial consciousness. Distinguishing them from their inappropriate relations, Holocaust idols, is a project that clarifies the contemporary production of that consciousness and its other possible outcomes.

Holocaust icons, as vehicles of Holocaust memory, have much to teach us about mediation and representation. As modes through which we approach the "sacred mystery" of the Holocaust, these icons are excellent models for memorial engagement. "Graven images" are both possible and appropriate for apprehending the "transcendental" experience Adi Ophir cynically calls the Holocaust in the second epigraph to this chapter. Representation of course must be endorsed, and Ophir's parody of a second Holocaust "commandment" is actually part of a larger argument *against* such a commandment and against the kind of "theological" representation that creates idols. Rather, Ophir is in favor of more engaged and embodied presentations that veer away from theological mystifications that make of the Holocaust and its effects false (though unrepresentable) gods. If there is anything "sacred" about the Holocaust it must be contained within the icons that serve as its mediators, its transmitters, if it is to be communicated to those who would appropriate its memory.

This brings us back to the issue of mediation, so crucial to the effectiveness of the icon and to its distinction from the idol. If Holocaust icons are to embody and re-member memory, they must nonetheless perform this task in a sufficiently self-conscious manner so as not to efface the very representational strategies that make them iconic. In other words, we as visitor-voyeurs must be able to trace a path *through* the icon *to* memory in order to discover our relationships to the past. This is what the best of the Holocaust icons should strive for.

Let me flesh this mediation process out through the discussion of another provocative example, Emily Prager's novel *Eve's Tattoo*, which frames in interesting ways an essential element of the symbolic vocabulary of Nazism as it is specifically inscribed on victims' bodies: tattooing. The literal embodiment of Nazi ideology in the tattooed identification number itself reflects the notion of the icon as a form of memorial embodiment. When that potent remnant of Nazism's assault on European Jewry is itself appropriated in Prager's novel and made both the subject and, within the book, the object of fictional narrative, the literal embodiment becomes a literary embodiment.

The novel thus brings together the literary and the visual, the real and the fictional, within a narrative that engages issues of propriety and sanctity. The ways Prager's novel adapts what has up until now been viewed only as a largely static, museological-memorial model of iconic presentation, transforming it into a fictional version of performance art and filling out its narrative potential, shows how an icon like the image of the tattoo can become a medium for Holocaust memory. But let me first frame this discussion with reference to an image borrowed from the United States Holocaust Memorial Museum.[36]

Here in one memorable room there is a wall almost entirely covered with photographs of camp inmates' forearms—seventy-two of them, roughly life-sized—with the tattooed numbers clearly visible. In the center of the display is a posed photo of four men from Salonika, all heads and tattooed arms, taken at a survivors' reunion, showing that their bodily inscriptions have hardly faded with the passage of time. All this is set below a quotation from Primo Levi's remarkable memoir *Survival in Auschwitz*: "My number is 174517; we have been baptized, we will carry the tattoo on our left arm until we die."[37] The image is arresting, and it speaks to the multiple and mass experiences of the Nazi language of domination as it is literally inscribed into human flesh. Yet the image is complicated by Levi's (borrowed) inscription, which speaks in a decidedly Christian idiom. Moreover, the disembodied arms make it more difficult to see any gender differences in these individuals, presenting instead the perspective of a unified Nazi "master" narrative that sought to strip gender away from its victims. As if to respond to this issue, it is not coincidental that, on the opposite side of the same room at the USHMM, separated by a partition, is the glass case containing the photograph of women's hair discussed above: against the multiplicity of individual arms and their gender indeterminacy the massive photo of the hair speaks specifically to women's experiences. Both images, incidentally, flesh out the narrative more indirectly represented by the boxcar in a previous room: these photographs show, we presume, what became of the people we imaginatively place in the railway car. These images thereby highlight issues concerning memorial embodiment, engagement, and narrativization explored more fully in Prager's novel.

Eve's Tattoo tells a fairly straightforward story whose narrative

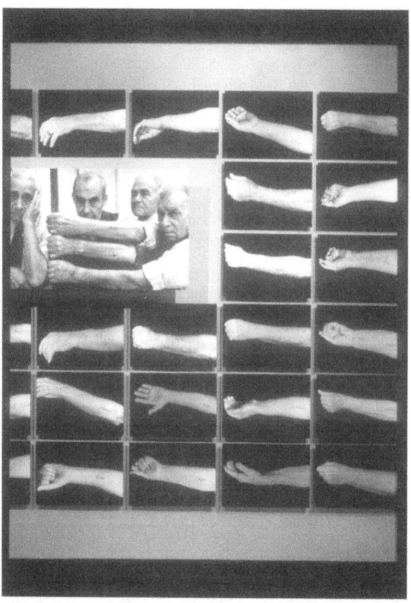

Detail of a mural comprised of photographs taken by Frédéric Brenner, located at the United States Holocaust Memorial Museum, Washington, D.C. In the upper left are four Holocaust survivors from Salonika. Photograph by Edward Owen. Courtesy of the USHMM Photo Archives.

context tells us much about the Holocaust's iconic representation. The narrative begins with protagonist Eve Flick's trip to Big Dan's Tattoo Parlor ("a monument to male violence"[38] and Nazi fetishism) to get herself a fortieth birthday present. Her gift? A tattooed ID number copied precisely from a photograph of an anonymous female death camp victim who bears an uncanny resemblance to Eve (who is not Jewish): blond and blue-eyed, the "perfect Aryan specimen." Eve's goal is clear: "'I want to remember her. I want to keep her alive. I'm wearing the tattoo like an MIA bracelet'" (11).[39] Eve's project is nothing less than the memorialization of all women who lived and died during the Holocaust, the reinscription of women's stories into the flesh of the historical record and memorial discourse that have largely excluded them. It is also the quest for the expiation of a personal sense of guilt: "'[The tattoo is] about the hearts and souls of women. About me. I'm of German ancestry. I'm a Christian. I'm a woman and I have to know—do I have mass murder in my blood or what?'" (51).

Thus, Eve's project is one of re-membering women through her act of bodily inscription, an in-corporation of women in history through memory. Within the novel, Eve's representations of "Eva" (the name she gives to the woman in the photograph) serve to refigure and recast as multiple individuals the generic woman of Holocaust discourse, commonly thought of (*if* she is thought of) as a nameless, faceless victim. Eve's embodiment of Holocaust memory through her tattoo en-genders seven stories about seven different "Evas," returning gender to a discourse which has largely excluded it and also giving women multiple voices over an oppressive monologue. There is thus a double reinscription and rememorialization going on here, the reinscription of gender into the master narrative of the Holocaust and the reinscription of individuality.[40] But as Eve's women reenter history and memory under the tattooist's gun, the reinscription and re-membering occur via a problematic reappropriation of the image of tattooing. Can that image be rehabilitated?

Eve's project of reinscription depends on her sense of the urgency of remembrance:

> "Well, in a very few years . . . the people who lived through the Third
> Reich will all be dead. And when the people who experienced an

event are no longer walking the planet, it's as if that event never existed at all. There'll be books and museums and monuments, but things move so fast now, the only difference between fantasy and history is living people. I'm going to keep Eva alive. She'll go on living, here, with me." (11)

But Eve is blind to her own confusion of fantasy and history: the fictional project of historical revision Eve attempts, conceived as an alternative to the museal mode of memorialization, depends on the fantasies she creates about her different Evas. Eve's mission of (re)memory turns not only on the disturbing symbolic appropriation and embodiment of a copied tattoo, something many might call improper for a variety of reasons. Eve's memorial (re)inscription also loses something "in translation." Consider, for example, her summary of Nazism: "a psychotic obsession with glory, a murderous mania for purity, and a visceral hatred of women" (28). Where are the Jews in this description?

Prager credits Claudia Koonz's noteworthy *Mothers in the Fatherland* [41] as a key source for her novel. Without it, she notes, "Eva's tales could not have been imagined." Unlike the historian Koonz, who keeps the parallel discourses of Nazism distinct (Nazis versus women and Nazis versus Jews), the fictional character Eve seems to sacrifice the nature of the Jewish experience of the Shoah for that of women in her memorial tapestry. Thus only two of the seven tales Eve tells are about self-identified Jewish women: the first, for example, is about "Eva Klein," a Jewish yuppie "U-boat" hiding "underground" in Berlin for most of the war, posing as an Aryan. [42] If Prager, as the author, is reclaiming gender as a forgotten category for apprehending and representing the Holocaust, her protagonist may be accused of violating the propriety of Jewish memory in her own parallel project. Indeed, it is this aspect of the novel that makes it both provocative and problematic as a Holocaust "tale." The construction of an icon of remembrance here appears to involve some degree of forgetfulness in the interplay of representational agendas.

Or it may simply rest on a shaky foundation. In attempting to personalize the Holocaust in her fourth tale, told to her gay uncle Jim who is dying of AIDS, Eve begins to slip. This story tells of "Eva Marks," a Red Cross nurse assigned to dole out water to troop transports at the Berlin *Bahnhof.* One day she sees a different sort of train pull in, made of cattle-cars and guarded by SS men. As she tries to give water to those inside, she is shoved in and trapped by one of those guards. Eva Marks was "gassed by mistake at Auschwitz six months later" (92). Was it a mistake? Is there a difference between her death by gas and that of all the others?

Eve's fifth tale marks a further deterioration in the protagonist's qualities of discernment and the concomitant dangers of memorial embodiment. From the moment she got her tattoo, Eve's lover, Charles César, refused to have sex with her and eventually left her. "Now that Charles César was gone, Eve had begun to talk to Eva in her mind, their relationship had progressed from remembrance to cohabitation, from the past to the present. People, Eve thought, would think her mad if they knew. But they'd be wrong. It was keeping her sane" (93). Eve's Holocaust fantasies have become her reality; she has fully appropriated them, and they have taken up residence in her mind. When Eve picks up a young man at a club and takes him home for a one-night stand, he asks about her tattoo:

> "Oh," he said, examining it, "were you in a camp?"
> "What?" she asked.
> "Were you in a Nazi camp?" he asked again.
> Eve looked at him sharply. She had told him she was thirty-five.
> He was looking back at her, concerned, empathetic, sincere. Could it be that he didn't know that World War II ended in 1945?
> "Yes," she ventured. "Yes. I was at Auschwitz."
> He saw no contradiction there. He just felt rotten about it. (98)

Ignoring the implied critique of Americans' lack of historical awareness, in the context of the progression of the novel Eve's tattoo has become more than a vehicle of and for memory. It has become the embodiment and object of fantasy—new rather than mediated experience.

Eve proceeds to tell the young man about herself as the Jewish "Eva Flick" (Eve's "real" last name), who was arrested by the Gestapo during a roundup of Jews with police records—"Eva" once received a speeding ticket. But this revelation serves only to arouse the young man. Has Eve's memorial representation veered off into kitsch eroticism and away from its purported goal? In this fictional episode, the young man's fascination with Eve's tattoo highlights its symbolic potency as a vehicle for a variety of performative and representational agendas. At the same time, this episode makes a powerful statement regarding gender representation and women's sexuality, working against both male objectifying representations and radical feminist ones that make a victim of any woman who seeks out heterosexual relations.[43]

Issues of sexuality, gender representation, and propriety come to a head when Eve faints at a film screening and an old man, Jacob Schlaren, helps her. Schlaren, who bears an authentic tattooed number (and the authentic "memory of offense," to use Primo Levi's phrase),[44] tells Eve his "real" Holocaust story. He recounts how he, like her, looked "the perfect Aryan specimen" (150). And he tells how he survived for a while by posing as an Aryan girl, "becoming" a boy again only in the railway car on the way to the death camp, assuming the identity of a dead passenger and thus "qualifying" for work rather than gassing. Noting that "his sexuality was indeterminate" (147), Eve soon learns that Schlaren is in fact a renowned Yiddish transvestite. We would think that Schlaren's tale, which in the context of the novel is not "fantasy," would expose Eve's appropriations as improper, but he does not condemn Eve for her memorial activity and, therefore, neither does the reader. His "true" tale reflects both the story of gender indeterminacy of Holocaust victims—shaved heads, unisex uniforms, tattooed numbers instead of names, and starvation all served not only to dehumanize but also to strip away gender distinction—and the suggestion, made by several commentators, that women possessed certain skills (despite greater responsibilities) that better equipped them for survival.[45]

Right after this episode, Eve sets out to discover the "real identity" of the woman whose tattoo she wears. On the way she gets into an accident that serves as a convenient plot device: run over by a van, Eve's arm is shattered, the bone protruding right at the tattoo. After the arm is operated on, Eve wakes to realize that "the tattoo was gone— in its stead, a neat row of suturing staples. Eva's lifeline to earth had been severed, her memory imprisoned by a newfangled barbed-wire fence" (176). "Eva's" memory is once again made inaccessible, because its adopted icon has disappeared. As a result, however, she and her lover are able to reconcile, and they immediately have sex in the hospital bed.

What can we make of this disturbing resolution? Sara Horowitz writes, "Pushed to its extreme, the idea of seeing the Holocaust solely in terms of eros and sexual violation (as in Emily Praeger's [*sic*] novel, *Eve's Tattoo*) domesticates the Holocaust, diminishing its horror to something more ordinary and sparing the reader a more disturbing confrontation."[46] Isn't the erasure or cover-up of Eve's tattoo[47] much too easy a way out for the protagonist? How many victims and survivors have tattoos and memories that are indelibly inscribed (represented by the wall of photographs at the USHMM)? How do we assess this attempt at iconic presentation and embodiment?

In the denouement of the novel, Eve learns "Eva's" "real" story, and this too is disturbing: "Eva" was Leni Essen, a good Nazi mother who took great pride in her twin sons, enrolling them in the Hitler Youth. But as the war progressed, Leni's sons rebelled and joined an anti-Nazi gang. Beside herself with worry, anger, and shame, there was nothing Leni could do until one day she learned they were being hanged for their activities; Leni ran with a butcher knife, screaming, and stabbed the first Nazi she saw. She was arrested, sent to Auschwitz, and "murdered by a capo a week before liberation" (193). Again, such a tale threatens to de-Judaize the story of the Holocaust (it does not help that Eve says Leni was "tattooed by mistake" [193]), and confounds our expectations about Nazi tattooing. But it also makes a profound statement about the nature of the Nazi assault on women, illustrating the effect of the internal separation of the "folk organism" that Eve might call (in another context) a "self-disembowelment."[48] The layered, fictional narrative of one woman's appropriation of Holocaust memory through its reinscription in her own flesh and its exposure to various improprieties thus ends with a complex and provocative image. As a (fictional) vehicle for memory, the iconic tattoo has served as a medium for storytelling, but some of these stories complicate our expectations concerning what the Holocaust means.

Roz Kaveny, in a review of the novel, notes that "it is difficult for a non-jew [*sic*] to find a voice in which to talk about the Holocaust without being accused of insulting the memory of the dead."[49] Do we accuse Eve of this as well? If, in Prager's attempt to turn an icon

at the very core of Nazism's literal and symbolic vocabulary of violence around to serve the project of memorialization, she pushes
the bounds of propriety, shouldn't she nevertheless be commended?
Clearly, there is a difference between Eve, the storytelling protagonist
with a shaky grip on history and propriety, and Prager, who has after
all created Eve as a fictional character. Prager is in the position of
making Eve whoever she wants her to be, while Eve is constrained by
her creator's wishes. But because Eve is herself an author of stories, a
certain parallel structure and movement is initiated. Prager is to Eve
what Eve is to Eva: creator and thus mistress of iconic construction
and memorial presentation. Thus, if we momentarily forget the differences between them, we see how Eve mirrors Prager's memorial
acts and, moreover, surpasses them through her willing embodiment
of the mark of memory's inscription and enactment. In this way, *Eve's
Tattoo* resonates with re-membrance, enacting through narration the
process of internal mediation posited above.

Furthermore, by making Eve (and Eva's "real" embodiment in
Leni Essen) such a "perfect Aryan specimen," who nonetheless is
moved to embody Holocaust memory through her own, albeit adopted, tattooed icon of remembrance, the author challenges those who
would claim ownership of the Shoah and its symbols, challenging as
well the religious exclusivity that would make idols of icons. Against
such notions of a "memory offended," Eve appropriates the fictional
Leni's tattoo in order to en-gender a historical revision, reinscription,
and re-membering. Eve's physical embodiment of Holocaust memory
in her tattoo initiates a quest for the lost presence of this memory.
The narrative image thus created is one of Holocaust iconization and
presentation merged, at least within Prager's narrative framework, to
peak effect.

Thus, Eve's particular confrontation of the past confronts as
well the challenges faced by those whose distance—whether by gender, generation, or faith—from the Holocaust and its memorial discourses is pronounced.[50] It is this distance that is increasingly commonplace and yet, at the same time, creates the "theological quest"
Ezrahi refers to in the first epigraph to this chapter. Indeed, it is this
distance that also creates the need for Holocaust icons. Prager as the
author attempts to preserve both the universal and the particular aspects of the Holocaust and its memory as she attempts to make it rel-

evant for the contemporary era: despite their apparent impropriety, their unsuitability, Eve's seven tales are actually tailor-made, ideally suited for their audiences. As such, they jolt their listeners and readers to a certain historical awareness, even as they reclaim some of that history, in its fragmented multiplicity, for women. In this way, they accentuate the iconic potential, at least in fictional form, of the (appropriated) Holocaust tattoo, where a mark of suffering can be transformed into a vehicle of remembrance. And so, perhaps the reader should follow Schlaren, the Yiddish transvestite, who, as an "authentic" survivor, is *allowed* to allow Eve access to Holocaust symbols as she struggles to re-member women, and find a place for herself, in Holocaust memory.

Or perhaps we should follow James Young, who argues that "[t]o remove the Holocaust from the realm of the imagination . . . to sanctify it and place it off-limits, is to risk excluding it altogether from public consciousness. And this seems to be too high a price to pay for saving it from those who would abuse its memory in inequitable metaphor. Better abused memory in this case, which might then be critically qualified, than no memory at all."[51] To the question of memorial propriety, then, Prager responds, in her novel, by arguing that any symbolic ownership must be shared by men and women, Jews and non-Jews; Holocaust icons are the proper possessions of no one and, in a way, that is part of what makes them iconic.

This discussion posits a model, albeit fictional, for iconic engagement with and transformation of a Holocaust symbol that, however "improper," nonetheless displays the mediative potential of such an appropriation. Such an icon, generative of so many meanings, allows the process of Holocaust signification to remain open and flexible, resistant to the closure of meaning generated by the idol. In these cases, when the literalism of the icon is overpowering, or when it simply lacks the internal reflexivity that prevents a literal reading, the icon is overdetermined and veers into idolatrous territory. If the icon is bounded on one end of its spectrum by the disembodied symbol, its other extreme is the idol. While this version of idolatry is less of a risk in the case of verbal and graphic imagery, it is a greater concern in the case of artifactual presentation. Peter Novick is struck by how "'un-Jewish'—how *Christian*" Holocaust commemoration has become, as in the "fetishized objects on display like so many fragments

of the True Cross or shin bones of saints. . . . Perhaps most signifi-
cantly, there is the way that suffering is sacralized and portrayed as the
path to wisdom—the cult of the survivor as the secular saint. These
are themes that have some minor and peripheral precedent in Jewish
tradition, but they resonate more powerfully with major themes in
Christianity."[52] Clearly the transposition of such objects to the American context has in many cases required a translation of their presentation and reception into the local religiocultural idiom. Such
a process participates in the broader debate between universalistic
and particularistic interpretations of the Holocaust's legacy, which
extends beyond the boundaries of this discussion. Nevertheless, in
terms of this analysis, idolatrous representations of the Holocaust
would appear as transformations of Holocaust icons, redemptive clo-
sures to the complex, multivocal narratives icons initiate, intensified
sacralizations of the images out of which they are constructed. As a
way of engaging this distinction, let me return to the use of railway
cars in memorial contexts. This will also serve as a conclusion to this
discussion.

How is the risk of idolatry played out in the case of the boxcars
under consideration here? For the *Memorial to the Deportees*, the stability of the icon as a nonidolatrous symbol is threatened by its inacces-
sibility and inflexible narrative voice. But as long as the visitor understands this icon as only a *possibility* of reenactment and presentation,
as long as we do not believe that it was *this* car that yielded this poem,
as long as this memorial remains a vehicle for reminding visitors of
the history that lies behind it, then the icon remains an icon, open in
its memorial possibilities. But when the memorial is put in the service
of a different historical-memorial narrative, when the overall image
the icon presents is given closure in pointing toward a redemptive
narrative that points away from the Holocaust, the problem of idolatry arises. Precisely this kind of narrativization is expressed in Yad
Vashem's web site describing the *Memorial*: "Although symbolizing
the journey towards annihilation and oblivion, facing as it does the
hills of Jerusalem the memorial also conveys the hope and the gift of
life of the State of Israel and Jerusalem, eternal capital of the Jewish
people."[53]

This alternative narrative voice calls our attention to the way
in which this memorial is positioned ideologically, for it is a staple

of contemporary Holocaust memorialization that the birth of the State of Israel be configured as coming out of the ashes of Jewish Europe. Even in the standard structure of commemoration, "Holocaust" is coupled with heroism, destruction with rebirth in the Promised Land, understood as the symbol of national redemption.[54] In the memorial strategy of dis- and replacement, Safdie's railcar has been transplanted from its original environment, brought "home" to perch precariously over a Judean valley. In this context the icon has been made into an idol of the state.

Idolatry is also a possibility in the implicit fetishization of the railcar instigated by the Florida Holocaust museum's *tzedaka* box miniaturization, which makes the vehicle of memory and historic suffering, through the artist's interpretation, into a vessel for charitable giving and, perhaps, religious reflection. One would hope that those purchasing and using the *tzedaka* box(car) find ways to remember something of the Holocaust in the course of their charitable reflections, rather than merely remembering their visit to the museum in St. Petersburg through their kitsch souvenir. Perhaps a good balance between fetishization and idolatry, on the one hand, and disengaged, disembodied symbolization, on the other, occurs at the USHMM. Here, as visitors walk through the railway car, memory is embodied and personalized without becoming commodified and/or theologized. Because they walk through and also emerge from the car, visitors can take away both a sense of victimization and loss blended with the awareness of life and continuity in the present. Perhaps this is the mix of memory and forgetfulness that is the hallmark of the effective Holocaust icon.

The concept of the icon, I argue, is a useful tool that makes it possible for us to distinguish between appropriate and inappropriate visual and material representation of the Shoah. While some would deny the validity of any visual representation of the Holocaust, I argue for the necessity of the iconic mode of representation in providing a link to the past being put on display and for the necessity of an analysis of this mode in order to better apprehend its memorial role. Situated at the center of the spectrum ranging from the nearly disengaged symbol to the overengaged idol, these icons (along with their strategies for emplacement and emplotment) model techniques for effective memorialization. Attention to the mechanics of

symbolization, iconization, and idolization therefore sharpens our
ability to assess those techniques critically.

Holocaust icons are the media of Holocaust memory in the
twenty-first century. Though they are often given homes in museums
and memorials far from their birthplaces or inscribed and adopted as
appropriated images, they retain their connections to the events that
spewed them out and convey the multiple meanings of those events
through their roles as vehicles of and for memory. These meanings,
embodied by the icons, are endlessly renewed and renewable, because the icons that convey them do not close off the routes to memory that continue to sustain and enliven their significatory roles. Were
they to do so, memory would calcify, icons would become idols, and,
in the extreme, the Holocaust itself would be forgotten. In the face of
so much suffering, that would be the ultimate memorial impropriety.

NOTES

An excerpt of an earlier version of this chapter appears in *Religion, Art,
and Visual Culture: A Cross-Cultural Reader,* ed. S. Brent Plate (New York: Pal-
grave, 2002), 216–23. This chapter itself is adapted from a longer version included in *Committed to Memory: Cultural Mediations of the Holocaust,* by Oren
Baruch Stier (Amherst: University of Massachusetts Press, 2003). I would like
to thank the editors of this volume for their endless patience and continual
feedback, and I am especially grateful to the anonymous editor for helpful
criticisms and interventions that were invaluable in preparing the final version of this chapter.

1. Sidra DeKoven Ezrahi, "Representing Auschwitz," *History and Memory* 7,
   no. 2 (fall/winter 1996): 121.
2. Adi Ophir, "On Sanctifying the Holocaust: An Anti-Theological Treatise," *Tikkun* 2, no. 1 (1987): 62. Italics in original. Reprinted as chapter
   9 in this volume. Quote appears on p. 197.
3. Jeffrey Shandler, *While America Watches: Televising the Holocaust* (New York:
   Oxford University Press, 1999), xii.
4. Sidra DeKoven Ezrahi, *Booking Passage: Exile and Homecoming in the Modern Jewish Imagination* (Berkeley: University of California Press, 2000), 23.
   Italics in original.
5. For an extended discussion of the USHMM's debates concerning the

display of hair, see Edward T. Linenthal, *Preserving Memory: The Struggle to Create America's Holocaust Museum* (New York: Viking, 1995), 210–16.

6. For the seminal discussion of this issue, see Saul Friedlander, *Reflections of Nazism: An Essay on Kitsch and Death*, trans. Thomas Weyr (New York: Harper and Row, 1984).

7. Shandler, *While America Watches*, 212.

8. W. J. T. Mitchell, *Iconology: Image, Text, Ideology* (Chicago and London: University of Chicago Press, 1986), 10–11.

9. See James E. Young, *The Texture of Memory: Holocaust Memorials and Meaning* (New Haven: Yale University Press, 1993), 127–28.

10. Ibid., 132.

11. For a more extensive discussion of the Holocaust museum's representational strategies and ideologies, see my article, "Virtual Memories: Mediating the Holocaust at the Simon Wiesenthal Center's Beit Hashoah-Museum of Tolerance," *Journal of the American Academy of Religion* 64, no. 4 (winter 1996): 831–51.

12. Richard Lauterbach, "Murder, Inc.," *Time*, September 11, 1944, 36; cited in Barbie Zelizer, *Remembering to Forget: Holocaust Memory through the Camera's Eye* (Chicago: University of Chicago Press, 1998), 55.

13. Tim Cole, *Selling the Holocaust: From Auschwitz to Schindler: How History Is Bought, Packaged, and Sold* (New York: Routledge, 1999), 61–62. Cole cites M. Pearlman, *The Capture and Trial of Adolf Eichmann* (London: Weidenfeld and Nicolson, 1963), 304, as evidence for the Eichmann trial testimony.

14. Moshe Halbertal and Avishai Margalit, *Idolatry*, trans. Naomi Goldblum (Cambridge: Harvard University Press, 1992), 3.

15. See James E. Young, *At Memory's Edge: After-Images of the Holocaust in Contemporary Art and Architecture* (New Haven: Yale University Press, 2000), 2.

16. See the videotape by Walter Loebenberg, "The Story of the Boxcar" (St. Petersburg: Florida Holocaust Museum, n.d.).

17. See http://www.flholocaustmuseum.org/fhmcontent.cfm?page_name=store.

18. For another discussion of these uses of Holocaust-era boxcars, see Cole, *Selling the Holocaust*, 160–61 and 164–65.

19. See http://www.yad-vashem.org.il/visiting/sites/deportees.html. Safdie (b. 1938), an Israeli architect, is perhaps best known for his "Habitat" housing complex, built for the Montreal exposition in 1967 and made of stacked modular prefabricated "boxes." He has also designed the late Yitzhak Rabin's tomb and Yad Vashem's children's memorial (itself a model of iconic reflection in its seemingly infinite visual repetition of a single candle flame), and he is currently working on the renovations

for Yad Vashem's historical museum. See http://cac.mcgill.ca/safdie/Biography/biopage.asp.

20. Yad Vashem, on Jerusalem's *har ha-zikkaron* (literally the "mountain of memory"), sits on the backside of *har Herzl* ("mount Herzl"), named for the founder of the modern Zionist movement and known as the burial site for Zionism's and Israel's most notable dead, including Hannah Senesh and Yitzhak Rabin.

21. http://cac.mcgill.ca/safdie/Biography/biopage.asp.

22. Dan Pagis, "Written in Pencil in the Sealed Railway Car," in *The Selected Poetry of Dan Pagis*, trans. Stephen Mitchell (Berkeley: University of California Press, 1996; reprint of *Variable Directions*; San Francisco: North Point Press, 1989), 29, reprinted by permission of the publisher; for the Hebrew, see "Katuv be-'iparon ba-karon he-hatum," from *Gilgul*, in *Kol ha-shirim; 'Abba' (pirkei proza)* [Collected Poems and "Father" (prose passages)], ed. Hannan Hever and T. Carmi (Jerusalem: Ha-kibbutz ha-me'uhad and Bialik Institute, 1991), 135. I have substituted the more literal "elder son" for Mitchell's "other son" in the translation.

23. Sidra DeKoven Ezrahi, "Dan Pagis—Out of Line: A Poetics of Decomposition," *Prooftexts* 10, no. 2 (1990): 343-45.

24. Ezrahi, *Booking Passage*, 161.

25. Ibid. Italics in original.

26. It is also possible to read the poem in a circular, cyclical fashion: "tell him that i / [am] here in this carload. . . ." This circular reading works a bit better in the original Hebrew: "tagidu lo she-ani / caan bamishloach ha-zeh. . . ." This reading is one encouraged by educators (see Ezrahi, *Booking Passage*, 162 n. 12).

27. It is worthwhile to remember that the railway car was not always symbolic of Jewish suffering. Ezrahi writes, in a consideration of Sholem Aleichem's "Railroad Stories," "Trains shuttled Jews back and forth in the Pale of Settlement and provided the locus for their stories and jokes for several decades before becoming the metonymy of their collective doom." See Ezrahi, *Booking Passage*, 109.

28. Timothy Ryback, "Evidence of Evil," *New Yorker* 69, no. 38 (November 15, 1993): 68.

29. Ernst van Alphen, *Caught by History: Holocaust Effects in Contemporary Art, Literature, and Theory* (Stanford: Stanford University Press, 1997), 10.

30. Ibid., 11.

31. The original experience of the Holocaust is left only to those who were there. And for them, curiously, the experience can be original more than once: because of the structure of traumatic memory, survivors who

give testimony of their experiences, for example, are often creating knowledge that they do not yet possess. This knowledge emerges only in the telling of their story to the one listening to it, who authorizes it and mediates its birth. See Dori Laub, "Bearing Witness or the Vicissitudes of Listening," in *Testimony: Crises of Witnessing in Literature, Psychoanalysis, and History*, by Shoshana Felman and Dori Laub (New York: Routledge, 1992), 57–74.

32. James Young, for example, who in his latest book discusses the "after-images of the Holocaust in contemporary art and architecture," sees his subjects as engaged in creating a "vicarious past" for themselves. Marianne Hirsch discusses the phenomenon of "postmemory," and, perhaps most apt, Michelle Friedman, following Toni Morrison in *Beloved*, analyzes "rememory." See, respectively, Young, *At Memory's Edge*, 1–11; Marianne Hirsch, "Family Pictures: *Maus,* Mourning, and Post-Memory," *Discourse* 15, no. 2 (1992–93): 3–29; Marianne Hirsch, *Family Frames: Photography, Narrative and Postmemory* (Cambridge: Harvard University Press, 1997); and Michelle Friedman's essay, chapter 2 in this volume.

33. On the issue of discursive frameworks and religiosity in the post-Holocaust environment, see also Zachary Braiterman, *(God) After Auschwitz: Tradition and Change in Post-Holocaust Jewish Thought* (Princeton: Princeton University Press, 1998), especially his conclusion, "Discourse, Sign, Diptych: Remarks on Jewish Thought after Auschwitz," 161–78.

34. Halbertal and Margalit, *Idolatry*, 2. See also Lionel Kochan, *Beyond the Graven Image: A Jewish View* (New York: New York University Press, 1997).

35. Kalman P. Bland, *The Artless Jew: Medieval and Modern Affirmations and Denials of the Visual* (Princeton: Princeton University Press, 2000), 8.

36. Jeshajahu Weinberg and Rina Elieli, *The Holocaust Museum in Washington* (New York: Rizzoli, 1995), 122.

37. Primo Levi, *Survival in Auschwitz*, trans. Stuart Woolf (New York: Macmillan, 1961), 23.

38. Emily Prager, *Eve's Tattoo* (New York: Vintage Books, 1992), 24. All further references to the novel will be noted in the body of the text by page number only.

39. This act reminds me of the climax of David Roskies's Holocaust midrash *Nightwords*, which is read, incidentally, in public performance annually as part of the University of California, Santa Barbara *Yom ha-Shoah veha-Gevurah* (literally, the Day of Holocaust and Heroism) commemorations. In Roskies's text the participants pass a ballpoint pen around the reading circle, writing consecutive numbers on neighbors' forearms while simultaneously intoning the digits solemnly. But of course those

tattoos wash off. See David Roskies, *Nightwords: A Midrash on the Holocaust* (Washington, D.C.: B'nai B'rith Hillel Foundation, 1971).

40. Think, for example, of our paradigm for the woman's experience of the Holocaust, our only female icon: Anne Frank. Yet we do not think of Frank as a woman, with women's concerns and thoughts, but rather as a young girl, as the title of the popular version of her "diary" suggests. Indeed, the popular rendition of her journal had most of the parts referring to her sexual awareness and womanhood excised, and it is only in the critical edition of the *Diary* that the entire text is restored. Compare *Anne Frank: The Diary of a Young Girl* (New York: Simon and Schuster, 1953) with *The Diary of Anne Frank: The Critical Edition*, ed. David Barnouw and Gerrold Van Der Stroom, trans. Arnold Pomerans and B. M. Mooyaart-Doubleday (New York: Doubleday, 1986). For a discussion of Anne Frank as cultural icon, see Cole, *Selling the Holocaust.*

41. Claudia Koonz, *Mothers in the Fatherland: Women, the Family, and Nazi Politics* (New York: St. Martin's, 1987).

42. The second tale, about "Eva Hoffler," a loyal Protestant supporter of Hitler's policies, is interesting in terms of the question of racial identity. This Eva's fate turns when it is discovered she is of "Jewish ancestry"—orphaned of Jewish parents but raised all her life as a Lutheran—but up to her death at Auschwitz she could not comprehend her own "Jewish blood" (43–47).

43. According to Jane Flax, this latter view argues that, "If [the woman] thinks she enjoys genital heterosexuality, she is only motivated by and is displaying a profoundly disturbed false consciousness." Though Eve may indeed display such a disturbed false consciousness on a different level, in her sexuality she is giving expression to the "autonomous female, internally motivated sexuality" repressed in the radical feminist discourses about which Flax writes. See Jane Flax, "Re-Membering the Selves: Is the Repressed Gendered?" Special issue: *Women and Memory*, ed. Margaret Lourie, Domna Stanton, and Martha Vicinius, *Michigan Quarterly Review* 26, no. 1 (winter 1987): 101.

44. See Primo Levi, "The Memory of Offense," in *Bitburg in Moral and Political Perspective*, ed. Geoffrey Hartman (Bloomington: Indiana University Press, 1986), 130–37.

45. Koonz argues: "Memoirs of male survivors suggest that they underwent a certain 'feminization' similar to soldiers' experiences on the front in wartime. They learned to share, trust, and comfort one another, admit their fears, and to hope together. But most men had to learn behaviors women already knew." See Koonz, *Mothers in the Fatherland*, 380–81.

46. Sara R. Horowitz, "Mengele the Gynecologist and Other Stories of

Women's Survival," in *Judaism since Gender,* ed. Miriam Peskowitz and Laura Levitt (New York: Routledge, 1997), 210.

47. The scar is "like a thick stroke of White-Out where the tattoo has been" (179).

48. The context here is actually the Nazi Euthanasia program; the entire citation reads: "No matter what the Nazis claimed, Eve thought . . . the killing of 'worthless Aryan life' was not about killing another race. It was a self-disembowelment."

    "The killing of 'other' was a tradition in human history. The killing of 'self' was new. Surely this first killing of 'worthless self' was intricately connected to the mass killing of 'other' in Nazi Germany. Surely in understanding why mass murder of other, one had to understand this self-murder first." (126)

49. Roz Kaveny, "Suffering in Style," *Times Literary Supplement,* January 24, 1991, 21. My thanks to Rachel Bargiel for providing me with this reference.

50. I am thinking of Carol Rittner and John K. Roth here, who ask: "[H]ow does one confront the past? How should one remember and memorialize, recognizing that our identities and needs are both those of a shared humanity and of a varied particularity—cultural, ethnic, national, religious—without which humanity is lost? As each generation grows further and further from Auschwitz and what led to it, people find it more and more difficult to remember together, particularly when they already remember differently." See Carol Rittner and John K. Roth, "Introduction," in *Memory Offended: The Auschwitz Convent Controversy,* ed. Carol Rittner and John K. Roth (New York: Praeger, 1991), 7.

51. James E. Young, *Writing and Rewriting the Holocaust: Narrative and the Consequences of Interpretation* (Bloomington: Indiana University Press, 1988), 133. This is in fact the conclusion to Young's discussion of Sylvia Plath's poetry, but it is surely applicable here. Earlier in the same chapter Young writes: "For the most part, the critics of Plath's Holocaust figures object primarily to the want of apparent empirical connections between Plath's life and the death camps, as well as to the 'impropriety' of her borrowing from what they consider the emotional 'reserves' of the Holocaust." Ibid., 129.

52. Peter Novick, *The Holocaust in American Life* (Boston: Houghton Mifflin, 1999), 11. For a fascinating discussion of Holocaust survivor-icon Elie Wiesel's own self-translation into and for a Christian milieu, see Naomi Seidman, "Elie Wiesel and the Scandal of Jewish Rage," *Jewish Social Studies* 3, no. 1 (fall 1996): 1–19.

53. See http://www.yad-vashem.org.il/yadvashem/visit/deportees.html.

54. See Saul Friedlander in collaboration with Adam Seligman, "Memory of the Shoah in Israel: Symbols, Rituals, and Ideological Polarization," in *The Art of Memory: Holocaust Memorials in History*, ed. James E. Young (New York: Jewish Museum; Munich: Prestel-Verlag, 1994), 149–57.

Chapter 11

Sense and/or Sensation: The Role of the Body in Holocaust Pedagogy

Susan Derwin

"The very first demand on education is that there not be another Auschwitz."[1] Thirty-five years after Adorno first spoke these words in a radio address broadcast from Frankfurt, the urgency of this imperative remains strong. The Simon Wiesenthal Center's Beit Hashoah— Museum of Tolerance in Los Angeles is committed to teaching young people about the history of the Nazi genocide of the Jews and others as one step in the larger process of genocide prevention. The main assumption guiding the museum's educational program is that the most effective way to reach groups of young people today is to create opportunities for them as a collective to feel their way into the experience of the victims—in other words, to identify with them. This approach founders, I will argue, because it conflicts with another, unspoken set of assumptions operating in the museum that concerns the way it conceives of its target audience. Both the individual exhibits and the overall configuration of the museum suggest the presence of an anxiety, if not a fundamental skepticism, about whether the museum's audience has the capacity to develop a sense of political and social responsibility. This lack of trust in its audience, built as it is into the museum's presentation, sends a message that is at odds with the museum's educational purpose.

The museum aims to foster tolerance and personal accountability through its presentation of the Holocaust, which comprises the second of the two sections into which the museum is divided, and through its smaller but preparatory first section, which addresses intolerance and genocide in a more general framework. Much has been made of the museum's sophisticated and expensive design features—its multimedia approach, its elaborate sets and settings into which its visitors enter and at times participate in hypothetical scenarios, and its emphasis on entertainment technology. Critiques have been leveled at its technological approach as well.

Nicola A. Lisus and Richard V. Ericson have given an excellent analysis of how the museum creates simulacra that negate reality by standing in for it. The power of these simulacra, they argue, depends upon the way the museum manipulates its visitor through an innovative use of media. They claim that the museum "transmodifies" a crucial feature of media:

> A masterfully planned underlying dynamic exists within the walls of the Museum of Tolerance . . . the "power of the remote" is displaced from the viewer's hand to the hand of the Museum. Moreover, the free flicker becomes a controlled flicker. . . . the museum has managed to tap into and mimic the emotive power of the television format but at the same time has managed to transmodify it. . . . [T]hrough its design, the Museum has refined the notion of "captive audience." The visitor is entertained into submission. The aesthetics of emotion become the aesthetics of control.
>
> The tension between entertainment and control permeates all aspects of the exhibitry. Upon approaching the building, one is struck by the imposing presence of the structure. Despite the warm, pink granite from which the structure is built, the symmetrical windowless towers exert an imposing presence. . . . The warm sunlit, pastel atmosphere of the atrium of the Museum is undercut by the control format that the docents themselves orchestrate. The timed tours, accurate to the minute, the absence of amenities including even washrooms on the exhibit level, and the docent who makes sure we see and choose in the correct way, provide undiluted entertainment in its most controlling form.[2]

Lisus and Ericson offer a convincing analysis of the way the museum manipulates its visitors. However, one point concerning the museum's reasons for using entertainment technology gets lost in their argument. The museum's goal is not to provide "undiluted entertainment" but to educate. Indeed, Lisus and Ericson are aware of this, and even quote a museum official who states, "The Museum's sole interest is in raising educational levels."[3] To this end, the Museum also provides one- and two-day seminars for professionals on "diversity, tolerance, and cooperation in the workplace and in the community. School districts, police departments, corporations and government agencies statewide participate."[4] But Lisus and Ericson focus upon the similarity between the museum's approach and entertainment. They write, "In reducing the horror of the Holocaust to the same level as Hollywood, the pirate experience and Disney World, the baseball experience at Toronto's Skydome, or the McDonald's experience in no particular place, they end up trivializing both the Holocaust and their audience."[5]

Considered in the context of the museum's educational intent, the trivialization to which Lisus and Ericson refer runs an even greater risk than they indicate. For while it is true that the museum shares with these popular cultural experiences a common way of conceiving of its visitors, namely, as children, there are differences in their attitudes toward them. Whereas these "trivializing" entertainment experiences present spectacles for consumption that appeal to the fantasies and appetites of children, and of the child in the adult, the museum's approach works in a different way. It, too, takes into account what it imagines to be the appetites of its audience, not with an aim toward satisfying them, but toward subduing them. In the course of educating its audience, the museum sets up an opposition between gratification, particularly of a physical kind, and identification with the suffering of others. To become empathic, the individual is first subtly coaxed into making certain renunciations. The suggestion seems to be that this is what is required if one is to feel for others.

Notwithstanding the diverse audience the museum now has, its exhibitions were designed with a particular visitor in mind—the average teenager. As such, the ways in which the museum attempts to influence its visitors reflect its assumptions about the identities of these young people. Gerald Margolis, the museum director, explains why this typical teenage visitor responds best to a multimedia format: "Look, young people today don't read. We can pretend that they do and that they'll learn about the Holocaust in their classrooms. But they won't. So you have to give them information about this period and its moral lessons in a form that they are used to receiving it—the tube."[6] The perceptions of Rabbi Hier, founder of the Beit

Hashoah—Museum of Tolerance, echo those of Margolis: "Where are your kids now? . . . They're at the computer, and after that they're going to watch television. That's the kids of America. This Museum wants to speak to that generation. We have to use the medium of the age."[7]

Underlying Margolis and Hier's assumption that reading is opposed to watching television or using a computer, is another one, namely, that visual media stimulates emotion more than reading does. The museum therefore aims "to tap into and mimic the emotive power of the television format."[8] David Altshuler, director of the Museum of Jewish Heritage in New York, sees the emotional experience a museum offers as a form of information as valuable as facts: "For learning factual information . . . books and courses in school can be more effective. But some kinds of information—some kinds of feelings, emotions—can be unlocked with a billboard, with an advertisement, with a museum that no college course will ever unlock. I taught college for 15 years. I rarely, only occasionally, saw anybody cry in class."[9] Even if, for the sake of argument, we accept their distinction between viewing and reading, as the difference between "emotion and image" on the one hand versus "contemplation, thought, and analysis" on the other, it would still be impossible to say what the content is of the emotional experiences the museum ends up precipitating in its students.[10] No doubt people experience many different emotions for a variety of reasons. My interest is in the signals the museum transmits about its perception of its audience, in the image it constructs of its imagined viewers.

Of the designers' decision not to have its students see any historical artifacts until the end of the standard two-and-a-half-hour tour, one consultant explained, "Instead of saying: 'We've got a collection to show,' they've started from: 'We've got people to change.'"[11] In place of "historical," that is, human artifacts, the museum's two main sections are punctuated by a series of installations that use media to expose its students to a variety of situations of brutal victimization. As we shall see, in some of these installations there are human figures that I read as doubles of the museum visitors. These figures serve as reflections of the way the museum envisions its (ideal) visitors as reacting to the installations. In other installations, the position assigned the visitor is not represented by any single figure, but is implicit in the task given the visitor. Taken in sequence these installations reveal the museum planners' preconceptions about their audience and also the direction in which the museum hopes to work its changes.[12]

The first of the two main sections of the museum is called the Tolerancenter. Outside its entrance we meet the first of our model visitors, the Manipulator, which is the name given to a bank of television screens arranged in the shape of a larger than life human torso. On the screens plays a film in which a man—another Manipulator—addresses the visitors. He calls out, "Hey, there! You look like average people. I mean, you've gotta be above average or you wouldn't be in a museum in the first place, right?" After soliciting the visitors in this way, the Manipulator proceeds to make statements laden with sexist, racist, and antisemitic innuendo, saying to the visitor, "But I can tell you're not like them." This first installation, which the visitors see before beginning the formal tour, identifies them as in need of reform. The visitors' initial reaction to the human manipulator is in all likelihood to want to dismiss him because he is so obnoxious. But to do this is to risk joining him in his self-ignorance. The installation seems to be suggesting that the visitors' recognition of their prejudice is the one thing that distinguishes them from the Manipulator.

Notwithstanding the difference between the Manipulator and the visitors viewing him, the arrangement of the screens in the form of a human torso sends another message. The human form points to the common content of the Manipulator and the visitors from the point of view of the museum planners (recall Margolis and Hier's assumptions): the visitors appear to consist of nothing but the media images they mindlessly internalize. This may account in part for the museum's desire to provide its visitors with an emotional experience. It is another way of saying that they need to be made more human, less machinelike.

This perception of the visitors is predicated upon another assumption evident in the installation that comes directly after the Manipulator. The visitors are asked to walk through one of two entrances into the Tolerancenter. The first is marked "prejudiced"; the second, "unprejudiced." This is a setup, however, because the door marked "unprejudiced" is locked. Everyone must pass through the first door, and the docent reinforces the message being conveyed by telling the visitors that, whether or not they know it, they are all prejudiced. This installation is no less than a declaration to the visitors: "you are all prejudiced." Regardless of the truth or falsehood of the statement, it is the form of the pronouncement that interests me. The installation recognizes the visitors' capacity for self-reflection only within a structure of authority that assigns the power of judgment to the museum. The museum tells the visitors what they are, and if they are to go on with the tour, they must accept that judgment, or at least act as if they do; literally and figuratively, that is the only door that remains open to them. In categorizing its audience thus, the museum implies that its audience shares the Manipulator's prejudices.

In this opening installation, the museum also introduces a practice it will come to rely upon throughout the exhibit: it propounds its message physically. The museum does not only label its visitors "prejudiced"; it reinforces its determination by requiring the visitors to walk through the door of the museum's choice. At this early stage of the tour, this physical manipulation amounts to little. Nevertheless, it is a first indication of tendencies that will become more pronounced as the visitors proceed further.

Now labeled, the visitors are launched into the journey of self-reform through a series of encounters with situations of victimization. The first of these takes place in the Point of View Diner. The area is a realistic simulation of a diner, with red vinyl seats and stools and gleaming chrome counters and tables. Behind the counters, in full view, are coffee cups, soda glasses, and the like. On the counter before each seat stands a machine that looks like a jukebox but which houses touch screen computers and telephone earpieces. After entering this installation, students are shown a film on a large screen on the wall that sets up a situation of violence—a drunk driver is killed in an accident in which a young girl also dies; a racist comment escalates into a fight in which someone gets shot. The visitors are then asked to decide who is to blame for the outcome. Their answers are tabulated statistically and the results flashed on the big screen. Next the visitors are given the chance to "interview" the participants in the scenario by choosing questions that flash on their individual computers. Finally, the visitors watch a series of images on the main television of various victims: war victims in Bosnia, Nazi prisoners, victims of racism, homeless men and women, child laborers. The narrator concludes, "If we all assume responsibility when we witness evil, we can change the world." The docent reinforces this lesson at the end of a question-and-answer session he or she leads. On both my tours, the lesson was the same: the individual must take responsibility for injustice around the world and do something about it.

Even though the Point of View Diner is interactive in its approach, the visitors' participation is restricted. They choose from predetermined questions and preselected answers. Nevertheless, the "progress" the visitors have supposedly made by this point in the tour is indicated by their assigned role as judges. Whereas initially they were deemed incapable of exercising good judgment—hence their need for the museum's guidance—here they are asked to identify with the judging agency. The idea is that the visitors have the capacity to internalize the museum's authority as they sit in judgment of people who hurt other people.

It is worth considering the museum's decision to conduct this part of the exhibition in a gleaming diner. The setting could just as easily have been stadium bleachers, a park, a schoolyard, a bus stop, a convenience store—wherever young people gather. But a diner is a place where adolescents go expressly to satisfy their appetites, both hunger and the libidinal pleasures of social exchange, and the museum was painstaking in its efforts to re-create this environment in realistic detail. The Point of View Diner suggestively stimulates appetite and then serves up lessons to digest in place of the gratifications evoked by the setting. This kind of tease, reminiscent of the trick of the entrance doors, establishes an implicit relation between learning tolerance and renouncing sensuous pleasures. While such manipulation is certainly part of the museum's "aesthetics of control," the duping of sensuality also says something about the museum's assumptions about its visitors. It suggests that the very adolescents who need to feel more of a certain emotion, such as empathy, are the same people who are perceived as too feeling in other, perhaps bodily, ways. The Point of View Diner creates a questionable equivalence between learning to tolerate others and becoming indifferent to aspects of oneself.

The third and final installation in the Tolerancenter that works through identification is an eight-and-a-half-minute film, projected in a small theater, about violence in the postwar world. Its message is that mass annihilation did not end with the defeat of Germany.

Viewers are subjected to a montage of images capturing genocide around the world, including scenes from Bosnia, Rwanda, the United States, Russia, Germany, and Israel. As Marcuse remarks, "Viewers are unlikely to forget the images of bloody corpses on Yugoslavian streets or desiccated corpses in the African sun."[13] What makes these images memorable is the gruesome physicality of their content and the fact that a preponderance of them are of children or adolescents. But since these stripped bodies are also stripped of their historical specificity—the film does not discuss the precise conditions under which these massacres occurred—the value of their educational content is questionable. It seems as if the visitors are meant to identify with the victims (or with victimization as a whole, since none of the victims is presented as an individual) on the basis of their common youthfulness.

At the same time, the sheer accumulation of images is not without function. One might see these bodies as bodies without desire, for the images are drained of life and thus of appetite. As such, it could be suggested that these filmic images are now offered to the visitors as a kind of perverse compensation for the renunciation of pleasure advocated earlier. In this respect, the images form a counterpoint to the very marked attempt to suppress the visitors' physical appetites in the Point of View Diner.

After the onslaught of gruesome scenes of victimization in foreign countries, the visitor is brought back home through a final scene in which a teenage girl blows out the candles of a birthday cake (is it a sweet sixteen?). The party is also a celebration of the girl's induction into the Ku Klux Klan. This image is meant to show that fighting intolerance begins at home. Still, having a teenage girl represent the domestic enemy is a peculiar choice. As we will see, this is the first of two instances in the museum in which femininity is portrayed as a disruptive force. It is also noteworthy that this enemy is shown enjoying a cake, whereas the visitors to the Point of View Diner were asked to relinquish such pleasures in the name of tolerance. Femininity, then, in particular, seems to be represented here as disruptive because it is a consuming force.

This film marks the end of the Tolerancenter part of the museum. The visitors are then taken into a waiting area before entering the Beit Hashoah. Now reformed, they move through a series of stations in which the intention of having them identify with victims of the Holocaust is borne out in both explicit and subtle ways. Like the Manipulator, the first installation of the Beit Hashoah greets the visitors before they enter this section of the museum: the docent gives each person an identity card bearing the name and photograph of a Holocaust victim. This person's history is told in a few paragraphs that are made available on computer screens in the course of the tour. The visitors carry their newly assigned identities around now that they have left behind their own.

If the museum planners attempted to disarm the visitors of their more unruly attributes and appetites in the Tolerancenter, in the Beit Hashoah they rehabilitate the visitors, literally in their own image. The visitors enter the Beit Hashoah only to encounter a series of dioramas in which three mannequins identified as a historian, a researcher, and a set designer discuss how the museum should be organized. The figures are uniformly made from white plaster, and in their relative blankness, they are like spaces into which the visitors can project themselves. It is worth noting that upon leaving the Beit Hashoah, the visitors watch a film in which an American G.I. refers to the camp inmates he discovered as looking like plaster of Paris. It seems likely that this contributed to the museum's decision to use this material to make the figures.

While all three of them have the same sticklike body and bobbed hairstyle, the two males—the designer and the scholar—have prominent noses. It is difficult not to notice their physiognomies: in one diorama, the male figures suggestively stand together beside a Nazi poster labeled "Juden" that depicts a stereotypical Jewish profile. Taken together, the attributes the figures share suggest their resemblance to Jewish concentration camp prisoners. However, there is one distinction between them in their dress. The two men are wearing jackets, but the female researcher stands in shirt sleeves, a variation that accentuates her necktie. By insuring that her masculine clothing is conspicuous, the museum establishes a contrast between the feminine Ku Klux Klan inductee or enemy, just seen in the final installation of the Tolerancenter, and the masculine nature of responsibility. For insofar as these plaster figures are exemplary, their appearance suggests that to occupy oneself with this historical material (as first they, and now the visitors, will do) is a significant (read: masculine) undertaking. Only from this subject position, the logic goes, can the visitors take into themselves the experiences of the victims of the Nazi genocide. One could even suggest that in order to be receptive to the victims, sexuality—which the museum understands as synonymous with femininity—must become neutralized or whitewashed like the mannequins themselves.

In the museum's exhibition of the Wannsee Conference, visitors encounter images of the victims more directly, unmediated by the presence of the plaster of Paris figures. As the visitors peer through a glass window into a miniature meeting room, they listen to a scripted "re-creation" of the meeting of January 20, 1942. They "eavesdrop" on this conference, overhearing the Nazis discuss in a matter-of-fact tone how to get rid of the Jews. No one actually sits in the seats around the table. Meanwhile, projected on invisible screens are scenes of mass executions that seem to hang in the air above the empty conference chairs and the table. The contrast between the horrific images of the human hunt and the bureaucrats' dispassionate tone in planning wholesale murder heightens the impact of the images, encouraging the visitors to feel for the victims.

Harold Marcuse notes that the pathos of the installation is created at the expense of historical accuracy: "Aiming at maximum effect the narration contends that the genocide of the Jews was 'launched' at the conference. Actually, SS division chief Heydrich called the meeting merely to inform the various government ministries that he was now in charge of the genocide, which had begun months earlier."[14] Tweaking history to create effect, and thereby affirming a common stereotype—the cold German bureaucrat—serves another purpose as well. It emphasizes anew the museum's valorization of emotion above all else. Whereas earlier the Manipulator, a kind of fetishist of technology, personified a lack of empathy, here that lack is embodied in the Nazi bureaucrat.

The photographs of the victims stand out because of their realism. At the same time, there is something uncanny about the placement of the images. It is as if the physicality of the horror, already softened to a degree by the reproductive form of the photographic image, is rendered even more remote by having the bodies hover above the miniature conference world like disembodied spirits. Ironically, this way of manipulating the images makes it difficult to connect with the humanity of their subjects.

If the Wannsee installation renders the victims ghostlike, the final opportunity for the visitors to identify with the victims takes place in a space where there are no images of victims at all. Instead, the visitors enter into a physical space designed to evoke the camps. With their own bodies, the visitors create a living tableau of victimization. The museum encourages this dynamic by decorating the ensuing rooms through which visitors walk so that they resemble the wartime environment of the Holocaust victims. Rough concrete floors replace the carpeting; the walls look like bombed-out buildings. After viewing a small model of a concentration camp gate and another of Auschwitz-Birkenau, the visitors enter one of two tunnels marked "Children and Others," or "Able-Bodied." It is as if the model of the camp has grown to life-size and the visitors now stand in the place it represents. This reality effect continues as the visitors proceed through arched brick doorways, reminiscent of the ovens in which the victims' bodies were burned, to a room called the Hall of Witness.

As Marcuse observes, "no physical Holocaust installation ever looked like this."[15] The "gas chamber" marks the tour's culmination, the point to which the earlier sections have been leading. It is here that visitors and victims merge, as the former inhabit, through the imagination, the re-created physical and, by implication, emotional space of the latter. Also, for the first time during the tour, real victims address the visitors, who sit on benches before video monitors mounted high on the walls. The monitors play testimonies of individuals who relate stories first of unimaginable torture and then of incredible endurance. While the words testify to the victims' personal survival, given that victims and visitors have merged, the words simultaneously certify that the visitors have survived their transformation into victims.

But this moment of peak authenticity is in fact one of peak simulation. Although the visitors are not told this, they are watching actors play survivors.[16] The real victims have been further subjected to the displacement that began in the Wannsee installation. Whereas there, the horror of their physical suffering was to a certain extent neutralized by the placement of the images, here the victims who perished are replaced entirely. Survivors who were never in the chambers speak in place of the murdered victims, actors speak for the survivors, and the visitors lend their bodies to the actors' voices. What was impossible for the gassed victims, surviving their own murder and burning, becomes a living drama acted by the visitors.

As Omer Bartov characterizes it, "a simulated Holocaust converts the event into a mere image in a museum which can be 'experienced' and discarded at will. By trying to make the audience 'feel' the event, the museum extracts it from its historical context, negating its past reality altogether. By faking the event, even if with the intention of telling the truth, the museum creates an imaginary lie."[17] Attempting to make the audience feel accounts for the most obvious distortion of historical fact in the Hall of Witness. Although the Nazis burned the victims' bodies after gassing them, the museum reverses these two steps in its dramatic re-creation: visitors first walk into the oven (through the brick archway) and then into the simulated gas chamber. This creates the odd impression that one could walk out of the ovens alive. It turns the finality of the real victims' burning into one dramatic moment superseded by others. Of course, the reality of the victims' deaths is negated yet again when the visitors walk out of the gas chamber; but this distortion is slightly different, because, due to the substitutions on the videotapes, the visitors have already traded in their identities as dead victims for that of the living survivors.

Though history seems to evaporate in the Hall of Witness, it does not disappear entirely. After the visitors exit the Beit Hashoah, they are taken to view the small collection of artifacts housed two floors above. Before viewing the artifacts, though, they are allowed to use the restroom facilities. For all intents and purposes, the stop at the bathrooms marks the end of the tour, as the museum now acknowledges and responds to the embodied nature of their visitors, apart from the visitors' earlier delegated roles as provisional bodies of the victims.

In the small room housing the collection of artifacts stands a wooden bunk bed from Maidanek and an American flag sewn by concentration camp prisoners for their liberators. Some of the objects in the room are mysteriously unexplained. There is, for example, a display of musical instruments made from Torah scrolls. This collection, which offers a glimpse into the calculated cruelties of the Nazis, bears no indication of the conditions under which the instruments were made, or who made them, or what they were used for. It points to a larger absence in the museum regarding the representation of the perpetrators. It is true that one film in the Beit Hashoah is devoted to emphasizing that the men who committed the mass executions were ordinary people.[18] But immediately following it is the Wannsee Conference installation, which undercuts the message of the preceding exhibit by presenting the bureaucrats as unfeeling automatons. This makes them seem to be anything but ordinary. Significant, too, is the absence of physical representations of these bureaucrats in the Wannsee installation. The fear seems to be that concrete images of the perpetrators would tempt the visitors to identify with the wrong models.

Beginning when its visitors are instructed about what they are—prejudiced, incapable of critical reflection, immoderate of appetite—the museum's approach seems to suggest their belief that education about the Holocaust does not entail the raising of critical consciousness, the development of critical self-reflection, or the promotion of autonomy; instead it requires the remolding of their visitors through discipline and obedience. The manipulation of the bodies of the visitors sends the message that whatever conscious awareness the museum will raise depends upon the visitors' submission to the museum's authority. Particularly from the Wannsee Conference installation on, when the bodies of the visitors are called upon more and more to stand in for the victims' bodies, the museum's preoccupation with achieving maximum emotional effect prevents them from doing justice to the material itself. Precision is compromised to pathos.

The manipulation of the visitors' bodies may itself be a piece of repressed history pointing, perhaps, to certain unexamined conflicts on the part of the museum planners regarding issues of witness, testimony, commemoration, and the transmission of knowledge. The Point of View Diner is interesting in this respect because it embodies fantasies that do not seem to be expressions of today's teenagers. It is a nostalgic re-creation from the fifties that seems like a piece of the museum planners' history, as does one of the videos playing in the Tolerancenter that depicts a cocktail party in which people of all races utter epithets.

The cynicism about their audience that one can detect in the educational approach of the museum planners may itself be the effect of an unreflective identification with the victims of the Nazi genocide. For the museum's lack of faith in its young visitors' minds is reminiscent of Jean Améry's analysis of how survivors of Nazi brutality lose their faith in humanity. In an essay on the long-term effects of torture upon the victim, Améry, a survivor of Auschwitz, writes, "Whoever has succumbed to torture can no longer feel at home in the world. . . . That one's fellow man was experienced as the antiman remains in the tortured person as accumulated horror. It blocks the view into a world in which the principle of hope rules."[19] In view of the existential and psychological wounds of the survivor, as Améry characterizes them, the question arises whether, given its pedagogical agenda, it is in the best interest of the Beit Hashoah—Museum of Tolerance to try to foster a relation of identification between its visitors and the victims of Nazi brutality through the bodies of its visitors. For if the visitors absorb the most profound effects of victimization through this physical relation, the change that comes upon them might well be in the direction of greater hopelessness rather than tolerance. The inadvertent exercise of punitive pedagogy suggests that those who planned the museum may have followed a psychological tendency common in our culture, that of loss of trust, which, regrettably, has influenced their preconception of the trusting students who enter through the museum's doors.[20]

NOTES

1. Theodor W. Adorno, "Education after Auschwitz," trans. Edwina Lawler, in *Never Again! The Holocaust's Challenge for Educators*, ed. Helmut Schreier and Matthias Heyl (Hamburg: Krämer, 1997), 11.
2. Nicola A. Lisus and Richard V. Ericson, "Misplacing Memory: The Effects of Television Format on Holocaust Remembrance," *British Journal of Sociology* 46, no. 1 (March 1995): 8.
3. Lisus and Ericson, "Misplacing Memory," 11, originally quoted in B. Higgins, "A Gala for a Museum to Remember," *Los Angeles Times*, February 9, 1993.
4. Museum of Tolerance flyer, "Tools for Tolerance for Educators."
5. Lisus and Ericson, "Misplacing Memory," 17.
6. Harold Marcuse, "Experiencing the Jewish Holocaust in Los Angeles: The Beit Hashoah—Museum of Tolerance," in *Other Voices: The (e)Jour-*

nal of Cultural Criticism 2, no. 1: February 2000, 10 (www.english.upenn .edu/~ov/2.1/marcuse/tolerance.html).

7. Lisus and Ericson, "Misplacing Memory," 5. Quoted from T. Tigend, "Spielberg 'Blown Away' by Tolerance Museum," *Heritage Southwest Jewish Press*, March 5, 1993.

8. Lisus and Ericson, "Misplacing Memory," 6.

9. Julie Salamon, "Walls that Echo of the Unspeakable," *New York Times*, September 7, 1997.

10. Omer Bartov, *Murder in Our Midst: The Holocaust, Industrial Killing, and Representation* (New York: Oxford University Press, 1996), 184.

11. Marcuse, "Experiencing the Jewish Holocaust," 11, quoted from *Los Angeles Times*, January 3, 1993, A1.

12. My analysis of the museum is not meant to be exhaustive. I do not discuss all the installations, only the ones that feature these doubles of the visitor.

13. Marcuse, "Experiencing the Jewish Holocaust," 6.

14. Ibid., 8.

15. Ibid., 9.

16. The museum planners decided to have actors read scripted monologues rather than showing survivors speak, "so that the accents of the survivors do not distract the visitors" (Marcuse, "Experiencing the Jewish Holocaust," 9). There was another option, using real survivors and subtitling their words, but presumably it was decided that reading would make the experience less immediate for the visitor. We must also not forget that this audience, according to the planners, does not read.

17. Bartov, *Murder in Our Midst*, 186.

18. Marcuse notes that the presentation "amalgamates widely-debated interpretations put forth by Holocaust scholars Christopher Browning in 1992 and Daniel Goldhagen in 1996." "Experiencing the Jewish Holocaust," 8.

19. Jean Améry, *At the Mind's Limits: Contemplations by a Survivor on Auschwitz and Its Realities*, trans. Sidney Rosenfeld and Stella P. Rosenfeld (Bloomington: Indiana University Press, 1980), 40.

20. For a discussion of the intergenerational transmission of unresolved conflicts through pedagogy, see Alice Miller, *For Your Own Good: Hidden Cruelty in Child-Rearing and the Roots of Violence,* trans. Hildegarde and Hunter Hannum (New York: Farrar, Straus, & Giroux, 1990).

Artists' Works

A selection of works by artists Alice Lok Cahana, Judy Chicago, Debbie Teicholz, and Mindy Weisel, who participated in the Berman Center's conference, "Representing the Holocaust: Practices, Products, Projections."

ALICE LOK CAHANA

Plate 1. Alice Lok Cahana, *Terezin: Children's Poem, I Still Believe*, 1976. Mixed media on paper, 26" x 2". Photograph by Charlotte Goldberg.

Plate 2. Alice Lok Cahana, *Arrival to Auschwitz: No Names,* 1992. Acrylic on canvas, 85" x 46". Photograph by Charlotte Goldberg.

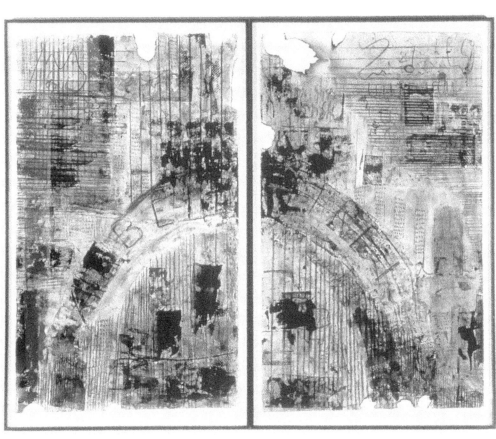

Plate 3. Alice Lok Cahana, *Arbeit Macht Frei: Concert in Auschwitz*, 1993. Mixed media on paper (diptych), 80" x 96". Photograph by Charlotte Goldberg.

Plate 4. Alice Lok Cahana, *Where Are Our Brothers, the Strong Free Men? Silence Was the Answer of the Free Men* (from the poem "The Shadows at Night," by Alice Lok Cahana), 1995. Mixed media on canvas, 80" x 84". Photograph by Charlotte Goldberg.

Plate 5. Alice Lok Cahana, *Waiting for the Magic Bird,* 1995. Mixed media on canvas, 80" x 84". Photograph by Charlotte Goldberg.

JUDY CHICAGO

Plate 6. Judy Chicago with Donald Woodman, *Arbeit Macht Frei/Work Makes Who Free?* from the *Ho̶caust Project*, © Judy Chicago 1992. Sprayed acrylic, oil, welded metal, wood, and photography photolinen and canvas. Collection of the artists and Through the Flower Corporation. Photogra̶© Donald Woodman.

Plate 7. Judy Chicago with Donald Woodman, *Banality of Evil/Struthof,* from the *Holocaust Project* Judy Chicago 1989. Sprayed acrylic, oil, and photography on photolinen, 30¼" x 43¼". Collecti̶ of the artists and Through the Flower Corporation. Photograph © Donald Woodman.

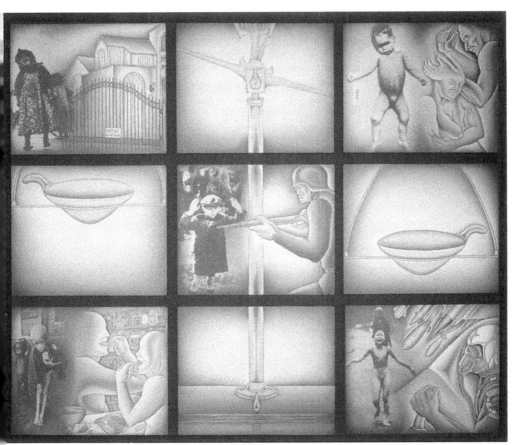

Plate 8. Judy Chicago with Donald Woodman, *Im/Balance of Power*, from the *Holocaust Project*, © Judy Chicago 1989. Sprayed acrylic, oil, and photography on photolinen, 6'5¼" x 7'11¼". Collection of the artists and Through the Flower Corporation. Photograph © Donald Woodman.

Plate 9. Judy Chicago, *Rainbow Shabbat*—Center Panel, from the *Holocaust Project*, © Judy Chicago 1992, stained glass. Fabricated by Bob Gomez, hand-painted by Dorothy Maddy from Judy Chicago's cartoon. Collection of the artists and Through the Flower Corporation. Photograph © Donald Woodman.

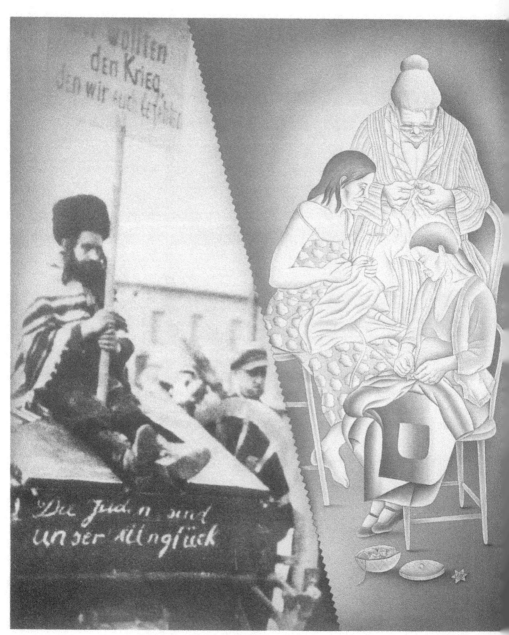

Plate 10. Judy Chicago with Donald Woodman, *Double Jeopardy*—Panel 1, from the *Holocaust Proje* © Judy Chicago 1990. Sprayed acrylic, oil, and photography on photolinen, silk screen, and em broidery on linen. Collection of the artists and Through the Flower Corporation. Photograph Donald Woodman.

DEBBIE TEICHOLZ

Plate 11. Debbie Teicholz, from the series *Prayer by the Wall*, 1991. Black and white triptych photograph printed on color paper, 35" x 64". Train tracks photographed in Hungary, earth in Israel.

Plate 12. Debbie Teicholz, from the series *Prayer by the Wall*, 1991. Black and white triptych photograph printed on color paper, 35" x 64". All three images photographed in Israel: Hand at the Western Wall, numbers on a branded cow, earth in field near Netanya.

Plate 13. Debbie Teicholz, *A Child's Holocaust*, 1995. Installation of thirty individually framed original photographs printed on acetate film, hung in burned boxes with individual night lights.

ate 14. Debbie Teicholz, *A Child's Holocaust,* 1995. Detail of the last box from the installation, which
s no photograph, only a light, 7" x 5".

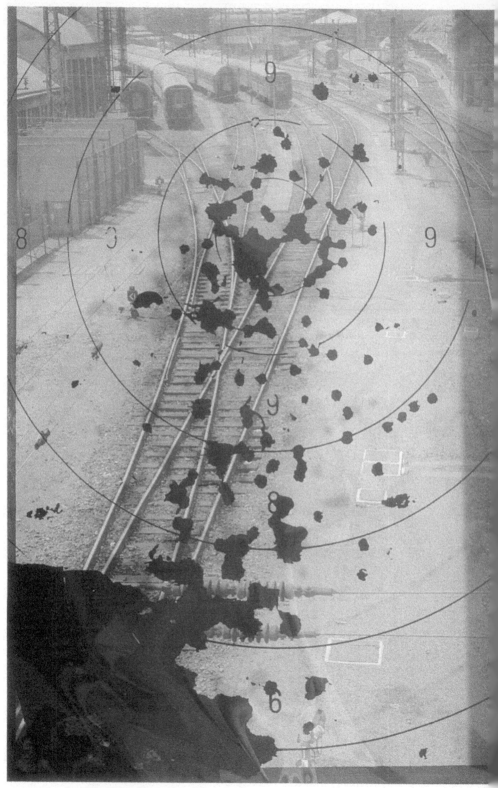

Plate 15. Debbie Teicholz, from the series *Never Again*, 1994. Photorelief, 30" x 20". Burned masonite box with photograph of Hungarian trains in the background and target from a rifle range in Israel glued to the front of the box.

MINDY WEISEL

Plate 16. Mindy Weisel, *Once Elegant*, 1980. Oil on paper, 22" x 30". Photograph by Gregg Staley.

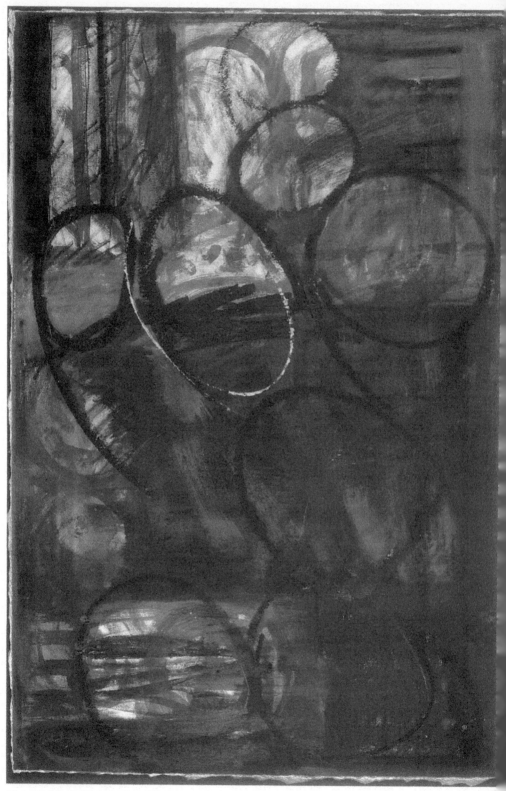

Plate 17. Mindy Weisel, *Out of Darkness*, 1998–99. Watercolor and oil pastel, 46" x 36". Photograph by Gregg Staley.

Plate 18. Mindy Weisel, *Furies,* 1989. Watercolor and acrylic, 40" x 60". Photograph by Gregg Staley.

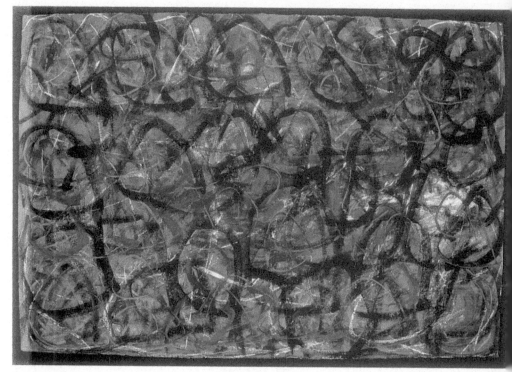

Plate 19. Mindy Weisel, *In the Presence of Absence,* 1999. Watercolor and acrylic, 40" x 60". Photograph by Gregg Staley.

Plate 20. Mindy Weisel, *Presence,* 1999. Watercolor and acrylic, 40" x 60". Photograph by Gregg Stale

About the Artists

ALICE LOK CAHANA, one of the few who survived Auschwitz and Bergen-Belsen, says that her art and her writing are her Kaddish for those who died: "All of us who survived took a silent oath, made a promise, to tell a glimpse of the story. My goal as an artist and Holocaust survivor is to affirm life, to build bridges between peoples, and to make others aware of the great danger of prejudice and hate."

Since 1959, Alice Cahana has made her home in Houston, Texas, where she studied art at the University of Houston and Rice University. In 1978 she returned to her hometown in Hungary, where she found no memorial to or remembrance of those Jews who had perished in the death camps. After the trip, her art went through a dramatic change. Abandoning her pure abstract painting style, she developed a visual language that could more directly express her memorial to the dead.

Cahana's solo exhibition *From Ashes to the Rainbow—A Tribute to Raoul Wallenberg* appeared at six major museums in the United States. Her solo retrospective *Remembering Not to Forget* was exhibited at the opening of the Houston Holocaust Museum. Her paintings are part of its permanent collection, and the collections of Yad Vashem and the U.S. Holocaust Memorial Museum. In 1988 she had a solo exhibition of her work in the U.S. House of Representatives Rotunda. Two of her paintings were reproduced in the 2002 *Encyclopaedia Britannica* under the title, "The Holocaust." Cahana was featured in the Steven Spielberg documentary, *The Last Days*.

JUDY CHICAGO is an artist, author, feminist, educator, and intellectual whose work and philosophy have had a worldwide impact on both the art community and the larger culture. Her best-known work,

The Dinner Party, is a monumental multimedia project symbolic of the history of women in Western civilization. During its fifteen exhibitions, it was seen by more than one million viewers. Her other major works are *Womanhouse, Birth Project, The Holocaust Project,* and *Resolutions: A Stitch in Time.*

Chicago is the author of seven books, including *Through the Flower: My Struggle as a Woman Artist, The Dinner Party: A Symbol of Our Heritage, The Birth Project,* and *Holocaust Project: From Darkness into Light.* In 1999, she presented the prestigious Robb Lecture Series at the University of Auckland in New Zealand and taught at Indiana University, where she received a Presidential Appointment in Art and Gender Studies. In 2000 she was an inter-institutional artist-in-residence at Duke University and the University of North Carolina, Chapel Hill.

For nearly four decades, Chicago has remained steadfast in her commitment to the power of art as a vehicle for intellectual transformation and social change. She is known and respected as an artist and humanist whose work and life are models for an enlarged definition of art and an expanded role for the artist. Her contribution to our culture was acknowledged by both Smith College and Lehigh University, where she was awarded honorary degrees.

DEBBIE TEICHOLZ, the daughter of Holocaust survivors, uses her own photographs of everyday places and objects to explore the memory of the Holocaust. By juxtaposing contemporary images of Eastern Europe and Israel, she transforms them into a "state of mind." She chose to photograph in Eastern Europe because her family memories were lost there along with the members of her family. She also photographed in Israel because she believes the collective memory of the Holocaust depends on the resilience of the State of Israel.

Teicholz's work is included in the collections of the Skirball Museum, the Tampa Bay Holocaust Museum, and the Yad Vashem Museum. She has exhibited throughout the United States at such places as the AIR Gallery in New York, the New Jersey State Museum, the Frye Museum in Seattle, the Tucson Art Museum, the Huntsville Museum of Art, the DeCordova Museum in Lincoln, Mass., and the United States Holocaust Memorial Museum. From 1995 to 2001, her large-scale triptychs were included in the traveling exhibit *Witness and Legacy: Contemporary Art about the Holocaust.* In 2001, her photographs were part of a traveling exhibit, *Here Is New York*, produced in response to the World Trade Center tragedy.

MINDY WEISEL, whose parents were survivors of Auschwitz, was born in the Bergen-Belsen displaced persons camp after World War II. In the beginning of her life as a painter, her art was a reaction to her personal history. In 1979, she completed a series of abstract, dark paintings, on which she wrote her father's concentration camp number, "A3146." After years of working with this dark palette, passionate and intense colors pushed through the black "as if having their own say." This *Black Gifts* series was followed by her series *Lili in Blue*, which exploded with the cobalt blues her mother, Lili, loved so much. In the years that followed, Weisel's work continued to pay homage to her past while also responding to the world outside herself. After her mother's death in 1994, she created her most colorful series to date, *Lili Let's Dance*, which celebrated her mother's life. "My paintings," she says, "express the desire to find light out of darkness and to hold onto a moment, a memory, an experience."

Weisel has twenty-one solo and thirty-one group exhibitions to her credit. Her paintings are in the permanent collections of the Hirshorn Museum, the Smithsonian, the National Museum of American Art, the Israel Museum, and the Yad Vashem Holocaust Memorial Museum, among others. They also appear on the covers of several volumes, including *The Reawakening* (1995) and *The Survival of Auschwitz* (1995), both by Primo Levi. She received a NASA "Celebrating Women in Space" Commission Award, and her work is part of the United States Art in Embassies program. In 2001 she was inducted into the "Archives of American Artists" at the Smithsonian Institution. Weisel is the author of *Touching Quiet: Reflections in Solitude* (2000) and editor of *Daughters of Absence* (2001).

About the Editors

SHELLEY HORNSTEIN, associate professor of art and architectural history at York University, Toronto, specializes in examining concepts of place and spatial politics in architectural and urban sites. She co-edited *Capital Culture: A Reader on Modernist Legacies, State Institutions, and the Values of Art and Image* (2000) and *Remembrance: Representation and the Holocaust* (2002). Currently, she is preparing a manuscript about how architecture captures memory, entitled *Losing Site: The Power of Architecture, Memory, and Place.* She is cocreator of the first on-line Jewish museum, "Project Mosaica," which is in its research phase. She has served as associate dean, codirector of the Centre for Feminist Research, and chair of the Department of Fine Arts, all at York University.

LAURA LEVITT is director of the Jewish Studies program at Temple University, where she teaches in the Religion Department and in Women's Studies. She is the author of *Jews and Feminism: The Ambivalent Search for Home* and, with Miriam Peskowitz, the editor of *Judaism since Gender.* She recently edited a special issue of *Intellectual Action: A Journal of Feminist Theories and Women's Movements*, "Changing Focus: American Jews and Family Photography." Her current book project, *Ordinary Jews,* is a book about twentieth-century American Jewish life.

LAURENCE J. SILBERSTEIN is Philip and Muriel Berman Professor of Jewish Studies at Lehigh University, where he directs the Philip and Muriel Berman Center for Jewish Studies. He is the author of *Martin Buber's Social and Religious Thought: Alienation and the Question for Mean-ing* (1989) and *The Postzionism Debates: Knowledge and Power in Israeli Culture* (1999). He is the editor of *New Perspectives on Israeli*

History, Jewish Fundamentalism in Comparative Perspective, and *Mapping Jewish Identities,* and coeditor, with Robert Cohn, of *The Other in Jewish Thought and History.* His current interests concern the application of cultural and poststructuralist theory to issues of contemporary Jewish thought and culture.

About the Contributors

ARIELLA AZOULAY teaches visual culture and contemporary French philosophy at the Program for Culture and Interpretation at Bar Ilan University and at the Camera Obscura School of Arts. She is the author of *Death's Showcase* (2001) and *Training for Art* (2001, in Hebrew) and is the director of the documentary films *A Sign from Heaven* (1999) and *The Angel of History* (2000).

JULIAN BONDER is an award-winning architect and teacher. An important part of his research and design work has been devoted to investigating the relationships between architecture and memory, with an emphasis on Holocaust memory and memorials. His design of the Center for Holocaust Studies at Clark University received the New England Excellence in Design Award from the American Institute of Architects and the Young Architects Award from the Boston Society of Architects. His other memorial projects include a memorial for Martin Luther King in Washington, D.C.; a project for the Asociacion Mutual Israelita Argentina, bombed in 1994; and the Buenos Aires Holocaust Museum.

SUSAN DERWIN is associate professor of German and chair of the comparative literature program at the University of California, Santa Barbara. Her fields of teaching and research are Holocaust studies, critical theory, the memoir, and the nineteenth- and twentieth-century European and American novel. She is the author of *The Ambivalence of Form: Lukács, Freud, and the Novel* and is currently preparing a book-length manuscript about Holocaust testimonies entitled *Living On*.

269

SIDRA DEKOVEN EZRAHI, professor of comparative Jewish literature at the Hebrew University of Jerusalem, is the author of *Booking Passage: Exile and Homecoming in the Modern Jewish Imagination* (2000). She has written about and been involved in conversations around the issues of representation and the Holocaust for over two decades. Recently, she explored the literary expressions of the reimagination of exile and homecoming in our time. She is a member of the editorial boards of *History and Memory* and *Tikkun* and academic advisor to the project "Words and Images," creating a video archive of Jewish writers worldwide.

MICHELLE A. FRIEDMAN, who has taught at Bryn Mawr College, Haverford College, and Lehigh University, recently completed her dissertation entitled *Reckoning with Ghosts: Second-Generation Holocaust Literature and the Labor of Remembrance*. Her essay "The Labor of Remembrance" appeared in an earlier Berman Center volume, *Mapping Jewish Identities*.

TAMI KATZ-FREIMAN, an independent curator and art historian based in Tel Aviv, has curated exhibitions in Israel's most prominent museums, as well as in the United States. She is cocurator of the traveling U.S. exhibition *Desert Cliché: Israel Now—Local Images* and recently curated *LandEscapes*, a multisite project of contemporary Israeli art in Philadelphia. In addition to contributing many essays to art catalogs, she writes for *Studio Art Magazine*, *Art Papers*, and *Art News* and teaches at Camera Obscura School of Photography and Filmmaking in Tel Aviv.

NORMAN L. KLEEBLATT is Susan and Elihu Rose Curator of Fine Arts at the Jewish Museum. His exhibitions include *Mirroring Evil: Nazi Imagery/Recent Art; The Dreyfus Affair: Art, Truth, and Justice; Painting a Place in America: Jewish Artists in New York, 1900–1945;* and *Too Jewish? Challenging Traditional Identities*. His 1998 exhibition, *An Expressionist in Paris: The Paintings of Chaim Soutine*, cocurated with Kenneth E. Silver, received second place for the best exhibition at a New York City museum from the International Association of Art Critics (AICA). He recently published "Report from Paris: Emigrés and Others" in *Art in America*.

ADI OPHIR is an associate professor in the Institute for the History and Philosophy of Science at Tel Aviv University and a fellow at the Shalom Hartman Institute for Advanced Studies. He is founding editor of *Theory and Criticism,* an interdisciplinary Hebrew journal for Israeli cultural studies and critical theory. He is the author of *The Order of Evils: Toward an Ontology of Morals* (Hebrew; English edition forthcoming), *Working for the Present* (Hebrew), and essays in Hebrew, English, and French journals and books.

OREN BARUCH STIER is an assistant professor of religious studies at Florida International University and associate director for Judaic studies in its Institute for Judaic and Near Eastern Studies. He is the author of "Holocaust: American Style" in *Prooftexts* and the recently published book *Committed to Memory: Cultural Mediations of the Holocaust.*

ERNST VAN ALPHEN is Queen Beatrix Professor of Dutch Studies at the University of California, Berkeley, and professor of literary studies at Leiden University. He is the author of *Francis Bacon and the Loss of Self* (1993); *Caught by History: Holocaust Effects in Contemporary Art, Literature, and Theory* (1997); and *Armando: Shaping Memory* (2001).

Index

Numbers in italics indicate pages with illustrations.

of, 95, 135, 136; return of the re-
pressed in, 94–95; ten stations of,
89, 91; title as an imperative, 91;
the viewer as transformed into Eva
Braun, 91–92; visual and textual
series of, 88–91
Loebenberg, Walter, 216
Loos, Adolf, 58–59
Lower East Side (New York City), 40
Lucie-Smith, Edward, 8n. 1
Lyotard, Jean-François, 115n. 25,
119

Ma'ayan, David, 148
Maor, Haim: artistic approach to the
Holocaust of, 130; *The Face of the
Race and Memory*, 138; *Light Num-
ber, 138,* 139; *Message from
Auschwitz- Birkenau to Tel Hai,*
137–38; qualified acceptance of
works of, 137–39
Marcel Marcel (Arad), 102–3, *102,*
115n. 23
Marcuse, Harold, 252, 254, 255,
259n. 18
Margalit, Avishai, 224
Margolis, Gerald, 247, 248
Marx, Gerry, 153n. 28
Maus (Spiegelman), 4, 147
Mein Kampf (Hitler), 105, 106, 112n.
1
Mein Kampf (Levinthal), 158, *159,*
170, 173
Memorial to the Deportees (Safdie),
218–21, *218,* 236–37
memory: alternative sites for, 121; architecture and, 55, 57–58, 78n. 17;
architecture of the heart, 15–16;
and commemoration, 53–55; contemporary culture as obsessed
with, 76n. 5; deep memory, 120; as

excuse for nation-unifying ritual,
199; Holocaust monuments as embodiments of, 60; Holocaust remembrance as a duty, 198;
Holocaust Remembrance Day, 97,
132, 152n. 14; hypersymbolic representations risking remembering
only the thing, 214; icons embodying, 214–15, 222, 224, 226,
237–38; modern memory as
archival, 15; Morrison on the past
continuing to be present, 32–34;
narrative versus traumatic, 174–75,
240n. 31; in order to understand,
199, 203; as partial and constructed, 4; postmemory, 241n. 32;
questioning in enacting, 16; toys
and Holocaust remembrance, 158,
161
*Message from Auschwitz-Birkenau to Tel
Hai* (Maor), 137–38
Mirroring Evil (Jewish Museum exhibit), 5, 9nn. 4, 5
Mitchell, W. J. T., 28n. 4, 210–11,
224, 225
Model Images (Boltanski), 157, 158
monuments, 58–60
Monuments (Boltanski), 157
Morrison, Toni, 32–34, 41
Mothers in the Fatherland (Koonz),
230, 242n. 45
mourning, 175
"Mourning and Mania" (Rothman),
113n. 10

narrative fetishism, 175
Nazi Germany and the Jews (Friedlander), 123
Nazis: as absent in Israeli Holocaust
representations, 125; collecting
the belongings of their victims,

Lightning Source UK Ltd.
Milton Keynes UK
UKHW012056050121
376480UK00003B/821